AESCHYLUS

The Oresteia

Translated by
ALAN SHAPIRO
and
PETER BURIAN

OXFORD
UNIVERSITY PRESS

OXFORD
UNIVERSITY PRESS

Oxford   New York
Auckland   Bangkok   Buenos Aires   Cape Town   Chennai
Dar es Salaam   Delhi   Hong Kong   Istanbul   Karachi   Kolkata
Kuala Lumpur   Madrid   Melbourne   Mexico City   Mumbai
Nairobi   São Paulo   Shanghai   Taipei   Tokyo   Toronto

First published by Oxford University Press, Inc., 2003
198 Madison Avenue, New York, New York 10016

www.oup.com

First issued as an Oxford University Press paperback, 2004
ISBN -13 978-0-19-513592-3 (pbk.)
ISBN 0-19-513592-x (pbk.)
Oxford is a registered trademark of Oxford University Press

Library of Congress Cataloging-in-Publication Data
Aeschylus.
[Oresteia. English]
The Oresteia / Aeschylus ; translated by Alan Shapiro and Peter Burian.
p.   cm. — (The Greek tragedy in new translations)
Includes bibliographical references.
ISBN -13 978-0-19-515487-0 (cloth)
ISBN 0-19-515487-8 (cloth)
1. Aeschylus—Translations into English   2. Agamemnon (Greek mythology)—Drama.
3. Orestes (Greek mythology)—Drama.   4. Electra (Greek mythology)—Drama.
I. Shapiro, Alan, 1952–   II. Burian, Peter, 1943–   III. Title.   IV. Series.
PA3827.A7 S53   2003
882'.01—dc21   2002066272

9 8 7 6 5 4 3 2
Printed in the United States of America

EDITORS' FOREWORD

"*The Greek Tragedy in New Translations* is based on the conviction that the poets like Aeschylus, Sophocles, and Euripides can only be properly rendered by translators who are themselves poets. Scholars may, it is true, produce useful and perceptive versions. But our most urgent present need is for a *re-creation* of these plays—as though they had been written, freshly and greatly, by masters fully at home in the English of our own times."

With these words, the late William Arrowsmith announced the purpose of this series, and we intend to honor that purpose. As was true of most of the volumes that began to appear in the 1970s—first under Arrowsmith's editorship, later in association with Herbert Golder—those for which we bear editorial responsibility are products of close collaboration between poets and scholars. We believe (as Arrowsmith did) that the skills of both are required for the difficult and delicate task of transplanting these magnificent specimens of another culture into the soil of our own place and time, to do justice both to their deep differences from our patterns of thought and expression and to their palpable closeness to our most intimate concerns. Above all, we are eager to offer contemporary readers dramatic poems that convey as vividly and directly as possible the splendor of language, the complexity of image and idea, and the intensity of emotion of the originals. This entails, among much else, the recognition that the tragedies were meant for performance—as scripts for actors—to be sung and danced as well as spoken. It demands writing of inventiveness, clarity, musicality, and dramatic power. By such standards we ask that these translations be judged.

This series is also distinguished by its recognition of the need of nonspecialist readers for a critical introduction informed by the best recent scholarship, but written clearly and without condescension.

Each play is followed by notes designed not only to elucidate obscure references but also to mediate the conventions of the Athenian stage as well as those features of the Greek text that might otherwise go unnoticed. The notes are supplemented by a glossary of mythical and geographical terms that should make it possible to read the play without turning elsewhere for basic information. Stage directions are sufficiently ample to aid readers in imagining the action as they read. Our fondest hope, of course, is that these versions will be staged not only in the minds of their readers but also in the theaters to which, after so many centuries, they still belong.

A NOTE ON THE SERIES FORMAT

A series such as this requires a consistent format. Different translators, with individual voices and approaches to the material in hand, cannot be expected to develop a single coherent style for each of the three tragedians, much less make clear to modern readers that, despite the differences among the tragedians themselves, the plays share many conventions and a generic, or period, style. But they can at least share a common format and provide similar forms of guidance to the reader.

1. *Spelling of Greek names*

Orthography is one area of difference among the translations that requires a brief explanation. Historically, it has been common practice to use Latinized forms of Greek names when bringing them into English. Thus, for example, Oedipus (not Oidipous) and Clytemnestra (not Klutaimestra) are customary in English. Recently, however, many translators have moved toward more precise transliteration, which has the advantage of presenting the names as both Greek and new, instead of Roman and neoclassical importations into English. In the case of so familiar a name as Oedipus, however, transliteration risks the appearance of pedantry or affectation. And in any case, perfect consistency cannot be expected in such matters. Reader will feel the same discomfort with "Athenai" as the chief city of Greece as they would with "Platon" as the author of the *Republic*.

The earlier volumes in this series adopted as a rule a "mixed" orthography in accordance with the considerations outlined above. The most familiar names retain their Latinate forms, the rest are transliterated; –os rather than Latin –us is adopted for the termination of masculine names, and Greek diphthongs (such as Iphigen*ei*a for Latin Iphigenia) are retained. Some of the later volumes continue this practice, but where translators have preferred to use a more consistent practice of transliteration or Latinization, we have honored their wishes.

2. Stage directions

The ancient manuscripts of the Greek plays do not supply stage directions (though the ancient commentators often provide information relevant to staging, delivery, "blocking," etc.). Hence stage directions must be inferred from words and situations and our knowledge of Greek theatrical conventions. At best this is a ticklish and uncertain procedure. But it is surely preferable that good stage directions should be provided by the translator than that readers should be left to their own devices in visualizing action, gesture, and spectacle. Ancient tragedy was austere and "distanced" by means of masks, which means that the reader must not expect the detailed intimacy ("He shrugs and turns wearily away," "She speaks with deliberate slowness, as though to emphasize the point," etc.) that characterizes stage directions in modern naturalistic drama.

3. Numbering of lines

For the convenience of the reader who may wish to check the translation against the original, or vice versa, the lines have been numbered according to both the Greek and English texts. The lines of the translation have been numbered in multiples of ten, and those numbers have been set in the right-hand margin. The (inclusive) Greek numeration will be found bracketed at the top of the page. The Notes that follow the text have been keyed to both numerations, the line numbers of the translation in **bold**, followed by the Greek line numbers in regular type, and the same convention is used for all references to specific passages (of the translated plays only) in both the Notes and the Introduction.

Readers will doubtless note that in many plays the English lines outnumber the Greek, but they should not therefore conclude that the translator has been unduly prolix. In some cases the reason is simply that the translator has adopted the free-flowing norms of modern Anglo-American prosody, with its brief-breath-and emphasis-determined lines, and its habit of indicating cadence and caesuras by line length and setting rather than by conventional punctuation. Even where translators have preferred to cast dialogue in more regular five-beat or six-beat lines, the greater compactness of Greek diction is likely to result in a substantial disparity in Greek and English numerations.

4. This volume

In this volume, the General Editors of the series offer their new translation of the only complete Greek tragic trilogy to survive the ravages of time. The plays constitute a continuous drama in three parts, a gripping enactment of the cycle of violent conflict in the House of Atreus finally brought to an end by the deeply hopeful transformation of a regime of vengeance into a rule of law. The *Oresteia* is at once a great defining monument of classical Greek civilization and one of the most admired and influential classics in all of European dramatic literature.

Durham, N.C.   PETER BURIAN
Chapel Hill, N.C.   ALAN SHAPIRO
2002

CONTENTS

Introduction,   3
On the Translation,   39
Agamemnon,   43
Libation Bearers,   105
Eumenides,   147
Notes on the Text,   189
  Agamemnon,   189
  Libation Bearers,   213
  Eumenides,   234
Glossary,   269
Selected Bibliography,   281

THE ORESTEIA

INTRODUCTION

THE NATURAL HISTORY OF JUSTICE

Aeschylus' *Oresteia*, first performed in Athens in 458 B.C.E., is the sole surviving Greek tragic trilogy, and one of those peaks (like Dante's *Comedy*, Michelangelo's frescoes for the Sistine Chapel, or Bach's *St. Matthew Passion*) that loom above the other mountains of Western culture as defining expressions of their age. The presentation by each tragic poet of three tragedies performed in a row was ordained by the rules of the competition at the Great Dionysia in Athens, but there was no requirement to offer three tragedies connected by subject. We know that Sophocles and Euripides did not usually do so. Indeed, Aeschylus may have been the only tragic playwright to use the trilogy on a regular basis as, in effect, a gigantic single drama in three parts. By a happy accident, the one Greek tragic trilogy that has survived the ravages of time nearly intact is exemplary in its structure: three plays, each a whole in its own right but each needing the others to complete the form and meaning of a far greater whole.[1] And to judge from such

---

1. It should be noted, however, that the trilogy was actually performed as part of a tetralogy. At least until sometime after the middle of the fourth century B.C.E., the three tragedies were followed by a satyr play written by the same author for the same occasion. Pithily defined by the philosopher Demetrius of Phalerum as "tragedy at play," satyr drama remains a somewhat enigmatic genre. Only one complete example, Euripides' *Cyclops*, survives, along with a large part of Sophocles' *Trackers* and many smaller fragments. Allied to tragedy in language and scenic resources, satyr drama presented a more lighthearted, rambunctious treatment of myth. Its chorus was made up of satyrs, men with physical traits of animals (e.g., goat ears and horse tails), and with emotional and moral traits to match. Satyrs are not creatures of the polis; they represent a world in which culture itself is still coming into being, they precede (and thus transcend) the division of tragic and comic, and they bridge the gap between gods and mortals. Their perspective presumably helped restore a sense of wholeness and offered a comforting closeness to Dionysus in his most benevolent and joyful aspects. One would give a great deal to know how Aeschylus (who was recognized in antiquity as the greatest writer of satyr plays) capped his tragic trilogy, but here our

evidence as the references to the *Oresteia* in the comedies of Aristophanes and the reflection of at least two of its plays in vase painting, the Greeks themselves regarded this trilogy as among Aeschylus' greatest achievements.

The myth that Aeschylus chose to dramatize in the *Oresteia* was already familiar to his audience in basic outline, and many would have known a range of earlier poetic versions. None of the Greek poets simply versify a given story; all rethink it with their own changes and additions, and in this sense they are themselves mythmakers. The tale of Agamemnon's death and its aftermath told in Homer's *Odyssey*, the earliest and best known version before Aeschylus, is surprisingly different from that in the *Oresteia*. In the *Odyssey*, Agamemnon's disastrous homecoming serves as a contrast to Odysseus' difficult but successful return and reunion with his faithful wife—and a warning along the way. Clytemnestra's betrayal of her husband with his cousin Aegisthus, left at home to be her guardian, makes for the strongest possible contrast with Penelope, Odysseus' faithful wife. Orestes, risking all to avenge his father's death, becomes a model of courage and duty for Telemachus, Odysseus' inexperienced and indecisive son, to follow. Aegisthus, not Clytemnestra, does the actual killing of Agamemnon, no moral question is raised about Orestes' matricide, and no furies pursue Orestes to exact revenge. To judge from the surviving fragments of other retellings, it was the sixth-century Sicilian lyric poet Stesichorus who offered the most important precedents for Aeschylus' treatment of the story. In Stesichorus, for example, Clytemnestra dreamed about a serpent as she does in *Libation Bearers*, although apparently the serpent in Stesichorus represented Agamemnon, not Orestes as in Aeschylus; and Apollo offered Orestes protection from his mother's Erinyes as he does in *Eumenides*, but only by giving him a bow to ward off his attackers. We can only speculate how much of Aeschylus' version is original to him, although given the greatness of the dramatic poetry, the question of originality in plot hardly seems relevant (as with Shakespeare's use of his many sources). There is every reason to believe, however, as we shall see, that Aeschylus' daring solution to the problem

---

luck lets us down, since we know little more than the title of the lost satyr play, *Proteus*. The title does, however, offer at least one clue. In the *Odyssey* (4. 384–570), Proteus is the Old Man of the Sea, a minor deity who has the power to change his shape, but if held until he resumes his own form will answer questions and foretell the future. Agammnon's brother Menelaus, driven off course on his return from Troy, lands in Egypt and learns from Proteus about his brother's fate and how to achieve his own homecoming. We can deduce that Aeschylus showed Menelaus surrounded by a band of satyrs on Proteus' island in the Nile, and contrasted his eventual return home with the terrible homecoming of Agamemnon.

of Orestes' guilt—trial and acquittal of the crime of matricide by an Athenian court—is entirely new.

Aeschylus' story of a court founded in Athens to try cases of homicide suggests the direction in which his version of the myth is headed. He will use the structure of the trilogy to offer a sustained dramatic and poetic argument on a theme of universal interest: the evolution of justice in human society from blood vengeance to the rule of law. As one might expect, however, the terms in which the argument unfolds are highly specific to their historical context, and this cultural "otherness" makes it important to establish the idea of justice firmly in its Greek setting. *Dikê*, the Greek word usually translated "justice," has a broad spectrum of meanings from quite abstract (designating what is right, proper, or fitting) to specifically legal (denoting trial or punishment), but it may equally well refer not to a human institution or custom at all, but to a broader conception of order and balance. At its furthest extension, for example in the usage of the Presocratic philosophers, *dikê* indicates nothing less than a cosmic ordering principle. Plutarch cites Heraclitus of Ephesus, the "dark philosopher" who was an older contemporary of Aeschylus, as declaring: "Sun will not overstep his measures, but if he does, the Erinyes, ministers of *Dikê*, will find him out."[2] (The Erinyes, or Furies, will appear in more than one form as agents of justice in the *Oresteia*.) This is evidently an illustration of the principle of order in nature, in which *Dikê* is the personifiction of balance, the guarantor of a necessary regularity in the movements of the heavens. The same point had already been made in reverse, as it were, in a fragment of the sixth-century thinker Anaximander of Miletus, about nothing less than the existence of the physical world itself. This fragment asserts that all things that come into being and perish do so "according to necessity, for they pay the penalty (*dikê*) and retribution to each other for their injustice (*a-dikia*) according to the disposition of time."[3] It is usually said that Anaximander is using a legal metaphor here, but it is also important to notice that this fragment, like that of Heraclitus, suggests a notion of *dikê* as something more than a customary legal standard. *Dikê* in both fragments expresses a fundamental, natural principle, enforced by necessity, on the grandest possible scale. The principle is balance, and its enforcement takes the form of retribution to redress imbalance. Retribution comes by what

2. Plutarch, "On Exile," 11, 604a; fragment 226 in Kirk, Raven, and Schofield, *Presocratic Philosophers*, 201.

3. Preserved in Simplicius' commentary on the *Physics* of Aristotle; fragment 101A in Kirk, Raven, and Schofield, *Presocratic Philosophers*, 107.

agency and at what time it will, but it comes as an equal and opposite reaction to whatever has overstepped its proper bounds.

This is very much the view of *dikê* presupposed by the first two plays of the *Oresteia* and modified at last in the third. To put it schematically, *Agamemnon* and *Libation Bearers* show how the ineluctable and destructive power of retributive justice, operating over generations, leads to a profound crisis—familial and civic—that only the final extinction of the house of Atreus seems capable of ending. Up to this point in the trilogy, the story appears to illustrate the workings of what we might call the natural history of justice, a cycle of destruction in which each act feeds off the one before and nourishes the next. *Eumenides* brings the cycle to a different end by forging new institutions for the operation of a justice that can settle disputes within the framework of a legal system and that thereby fosters the survival of human communities rather than their destruction. (The kind of community in question will turn out, not surprisingly, to be the Greek polis, and the institutions to be a mythical version of those found in Aeschylus' Athens.) The natural cycle of *dikê* is not, and cannot be, overturned; rather, it will be transformed, in the end, by the work of gods and mortals who initiate a new, unnatural history of justice.

To see the process of retributive *dikê* at work in the *Oresteia*, let us ask why Agamemnon is killed in *Agamemnon*. Even if the question only means, why does Clytemnestra kill him, the play already offers multiple answers. For Clytemnestra, Agamemnon is first of all the murderer of their daughter, Iphigenia, whom he sacrificed in order to allow his fleet to sail to Troy when Artemis' wrath had stilled the winds. But there is more: Clytemnestra has taken Aegisthus as her lover in Agamemnon's absence and intends to rule with him after Agamemnon's death; and, perhaps paradoxically in the circumstances, but predictably, she is offended by Agamemnon's arrival with his own new concubine, Cassandra, prominently in tow.

The play insistently presents other points of view as well. Cassandra opens up the history of the royal house by evoking infants slaughtered and served up to their father to eat:

> Look there, do you see them? Can't you see them, there
> by the house, so young, like hovering dream shapes, children
> killed by the very ones they loved, their hands
> full of the gore of their own flesh, the vitals,
> all the dripping inner parts—I see
> them holding out that pitiful weight
> of meat their father ate.   (1391–97/1217–22)

Cassandra reminds us that the crimes of the house of Atreus go back to earlier generations. She evokes the horrible strife between Agamemnon's and Aegisthus' fathers, the brothers Atreus and Thyestes. The children she sees are Aegsithus' brothers, killed by Atreus to avenge himself on Thyestes, who had taken Atreus' wife as his mistress. Atreus banished Thyestes from his realm, then called him back with false blandishments and served him a meal of flesh from the boys he had secretly killed. Aegisthus can truly claim that with Agamemnon's death the "kind light of the day of final justice" (1814/1577) has brought vengeance at last for his father and his slain brothers. Adultery, deceit, slaughter of innocent children: the crimes of the house of Atreus appear as an incessant, obsessive repetition of past crimes, repayment "stroke for stroke" (1636/1430) without end.[4] Yet the very repetition makes it clear that each new blow is an act of *dikê*:

> The hand of fate is honing bright
> the blade of justice on another
> whetstone for another act of harm.   (1768–70/1535–37)

Other and even broader perspectives on *dikê* are given vivid voice in the course of the trilogy. The presentation of the Trojan War is perhaps the most perplexing and most illuminating example. Troy's destruction is at once the trilogy's paradigmatic instance of justice and the occasion of horrible injustices that condemn Agamemnon, its triumphant returning hero, even before he reaches home. The Chorus shows us Zeus *xenios* ("Zeus, lord of host and guest," 417/362) ordaining the destruction of the whole city as punishment for Paris's violation of the laws of guest-friendship. In his service, "Kindly Night" (407/355)

> cast down over the towers
> of Troy the smothering mesh, seamless,
> so that in no way could the old

4. This is not the whole sordid story of the House of Atreus, but it is as far back as Aeschylus chooses to go. Prior events in the fuller telling of the tale include Tantalus killing his son Pelops and serving him up to the gods to eat. When they discovered what he had done, they brought the boy back to life. Only his shoulder had been eaten by Demeter, and Hephaestus rebuilt it in ivory. Tantalus was condemned to suffer eternal hunger and thirst in Hades. Pelops won Hippodamia as his bride by winning a chariot race against her father Oenomaus; this he accomplished by the trick of replacing an axle-pin of Oenomaus' chariot with wax. When Oenomaus became entangled in his reins, Pelops killed him. Atreus and Thyestes were among the children of Pelops and Hippodamia. Thus, the family history of treachery, murder of family members, and eating one's own children stretches out for several generations. See Gantz, *Early Greek Myth*, 531–50, for versions of these legends that Aeschylus and his audience might have known.

> or young slip free
> of the enslaving wide net of
>
> all-conquering destruction. (410–15/357–61)

And Zeus himself dispatched the sons of Atreus with their vast armies, and they have conquered and destroyed the city. The Herald who announces Agamemnon's return says that he has "broken her soil / up with the just spade of avenging Zeus" (596–97/525–26). Even Helen, known to one and all as the cause of all the suffering, can be seen as the agent of justice: the lion cub that grows up to become "a priest of death / and ruin, ordained by god" (841–42/735–36), "poisonous deliverer of tears / to brides, the Erinys" (858–59/749).

Yet everything about the war conspires to make it cry out for new punishment, new retribution. Consider, for example, Agamemnon's sacrifice of Iphigenia. He does not choose to kill his daughter; a great goddess, Artemis demands the sacrifice, and by stilling the winds so that the Greek fleet cannot sail to Troy, she makes it a necessary condition of waging war and winning the just victory that the gods have ordained. It is worth noting how this theme is developed. Although the death of her daughter gives Clytemnestra a powerful claim for vengeance against Agamemnon, the emotional burden of the tale is given not to her but to the old men of the Chorus. Their entrance song in *Agamemnon*, a lyric sequence of length and complexity unequaled in ancient drama, begins by invoking the cry for justice raised by the sons of Atreus against the Trojans, but when they compare that cry to the shrieking of vultures whose chicks have been stolen from the nest (56–63/47–54), they conjure up unbidden the slain child of Agamemnon and Clytemnestra. Proceeding to tell the story of the expedition, the Chorus recalls the omen seen by the kings before they set out:

> The king of birds to the kings
> of the ships, black eagle and a white behind it,
>   in full view, hard by the palace,
> by the spear hand, ripped open a hare
>   with her unborn still swelling inside her
> stopped from her last chance ever to escape.
> Sing sorrow, sorrow, but let the good prevail. (133–39/114–21)

Calchas the seer explains that the omen portends victory in the end, but reveals that Artemis (goddess of wild animals) is angry. The slaughter of "the trembling hare and all her unripe young" (156/137) thus foretells the sacrifice of Iphigenia as well as the multitudes of warriors who will fall in battle, and civilians who will die with the death of

Troy. Iphigenia haunts the rest of this song. The old men seem drawn against their will to evoke the scene of the sacrifice. "Sing sorrow, sorrow, but let the good prevail" becomes a refrain, repeated (158/139, 178/159) as they find their words turn more and more ill-omened. Finally, when they reach the moment of Iphigenia's death, we see how Agamemnon

> ordered his men to lift her like
> a goat, face downward, above the altar,
> robes falling all around her, and
> he had her mouth gagged, the bit yanked
> roughly, stifling a cry that would
> have brought a curse down on the house. (267–72/231–38)

Agamemnon's guilt in the death of his daughter has attracted intense scholarly scrutiny, but it is perhaps fair to say that it is a problem for us largely because the trend of Aeschylus' thought here does not square with the familiar Aristotelian logic of the excluded middle. Aeschylus is explicit that Agamemnon is both trapped by fate *and* responsible for his deed, and we must accept that these truths are compatible:

> And when he secured the yoke-strap
> of necessity fast upon him,
> yielding his swerving spirit up
> to a reckless blast, vile and unholy,
> from then on he was changed, his will
> annealed now to mere ruthlessness (248–53/218–21)

There is necessity here — in the world of this drama, like that of the Homeric epics, nothing happens by mere chance — but there is also something about Agamemnon, who will not abandon his ships, his allies, his command even to spare his beloved daughter. Fate in tragedy is often like that, after all. Oedipus has no way to avoid his fated crimes, but the brash, proud young man who kills his father at the crossroads, and who takes as his prize for destroying the Sphinx, a queen old enough to be his mother, is no puppet, but Oedipus to the life, acting entirely in character. Character, in Heraclitus' famous phrase, is destiny.

The Chorus's evocation of Iphigenia shows both Agamemnon's impossible dilemma and its intolerable human consequences. The just cause is tainted from the beginning. And it is only the beginning. If Iphigenia haunts the parodos, the warriors who die at Troy are the central figures of injustice-within-justice in the magnificent first stasimon (407–552/355–488). As we have seen, the song begins on a triumphant note, with the Chorus's evocation of Troy's just destruction, caught in the net of Zeus's retribution for the crime of Paris, but their theme soon turns bitter, becoming a lament for all who died in the struggle, and particularly for the men who will return from Troy only as "dust bitterly wept for, urns packed tight/with ashes that had once been men" (504–5/442–44). The old men give voice to the disproportion between what was lost and what was to be won, the faithless Helen:

> "All this," some murmur to themselves,
> "all this for someone else's wife."
> All through their grief. resentment smolders
> against the champions of justice,
> the sons of Atreus.   (509–13/448–51)

In the end, what began as a hymn of victory ends in fear for the victor, against whom the citizens and the gods are angry for having killed so many. For the first time, the Chorus invokes the Erinyes by name (526/463), the dreaded agents of *dikê* who destroy the proud and prosperous if they have thrived unjustly. To be an Agamemnon, to wage a great and victorious campaign, is to court excess, lose balance, risk the most terrible of falls. Great triumphs bring ruin in their wake:

> The price of excessive glory is
> excessive peril. The thunderbolt
> strikes truly from the eyes of Zeus.   (533–35/468–70)

This lesson is driven home again and again in incident and image. Victory brings sacrilege. Clytemnestra, for example, warns that if the conquerors of Troy destroy the city's shrines and temples, they will be conquered in turn (386–89/338–40). Coming from Clytemnestra, this suggests a surprising sympathy with Agamemnon's cause; hence it is treated as a problem by modern commentators, who tend, in the interest of consistent characterization, to make the warning a hypocritical mask for Clytemnestra's secret hopes. The point, however, is not so much about Clytemnestra's character as about the tainted character of the Trojan War itself. The scene in which the Greek Herald arrives to announce Troy's destruction follows directly on the first stasimon and shares its pattern of moving from triumph to foreboding. Among much else, the Herald confirms—fulfills, as it were—the queen's warning when he asks for a fitting welcome for "Lord Agamemnon, lighting up the darkness" (593/522–23):

> Come give him now the greeting he is owed,
> for he has harrowed Troy, broken her soil

up with the just spade of Zeus.
The altars, too, and all the holy shrines
are leveled, and the seed is dying out
from all that land.   (595–600/524–28)

Aeschylus' audience knew from the epic tradition that the Greeks' atrocities and excesses in sacking Troy drew divine wrath down upon them, but this is not just an allusion to the traditional tales. The complexities of *dikê* in the *Oresteia* are on full display here. No sooner has the Herald shown us Agamemnon as the vicar of Zeus on earth, wielding the spade of *dikê*, when we hear news of divine vengeance still in store for the victors. Clytemnestra's warning serves in retrospect to make the meaning of this moment crystal clear.[5]

Agamemnon's arrival confirms this sense of danger. Prominent among the spoils of war he brings with him is the prophetess Cassandra, now his concubine. She was Apollo's virgin priestess, but Agamemnon has dared to violate her and make her his own. Cassandra's presence underscores the link between the conquest of Troy and the death that awaits its conqueror, the death she will so vividly foresee and then share. Agamemnon's first and final act on his return is to succumb to Clytemnestra's blandishments and tread, against his better judgment, on the sacred cloths strewn before him. Walking this crimson path to his death, he enacts a visual metaphor of the conqueror conquered. The symbolic act that signs his fall is not chosen at random; the trampling down of lovely things also characterized Troy's crime (428–29/371–72). Similarly, Agamemnon "lighting up the darkness" evokes the flames that ravaged Troy, metamorphosed into the beacon-fires that brought the news of Troy's destruction, and then "swooped down on the royal house" of Argos (353). So also the net of destruction cast over Troy (410–15/357–61) will become the net in which Agamemnon is caught and killed.

Agamemnons's death is overdetermined, to say the least, but we are not invited to choose the "real" reason among all those on offer. Rather, we are led to see how they all converge to give his death a sense of inevitability. But what of justice? What difference does it make that

---

5. The technique here certainly owes something to Homer's art of foreshadowing. For example, when Menelaus is wounded in Book 4 of the *Iliad*, Agamemnon in his anger prophesies the fall of Troy. When Hector, Troy's greatest hero, repeats those very same lines then in Book 6, the repetition has an extraordinary force. Here, the language avoids an entirely formulaic repetition, but the foreshadowing technique is the same, putting Clytemnestra's thought into the mouth of one of Agamemnon's own makes it appear strikingly like a fulfillment. Line 598/527 is almost identical to line 811 of Aeschylus' *Persians*, and for this reason has been suspected, but it is surely authentic here.

the Trojan War is both just and unjust, that Agamemnon is both an avenger and a criminal? It is possible to construe this seemingly disorderly and self-contradictory surfeit of *dikê* as an indication that the concept we call justice cannot be given a fixed meaning or a certain referent in the *Oresteia*,[6] but it may be more to the point to recognize that Greek *dikê* encompasses something at once broader and deeper than our word "justice." Indeed, I am arguing that this move is crucial for understanding how the *Oresteia* works. To accept that Agamemnon is both an agent of justice and a perpetrator of injustice in the very act of carrying out justice, need not make *dikê* into something incoherent or incomprehensible; the *Oresteia* seems rather to demand that we recognize the almost mathematical precision of the workings of *dikê*, whether by the hand of a god, a mortal, or nature itself, as it rights one excess by a sharp turn to equal and opposite excess in a seemingly doomed struggle for balance. This is a crucial component of the tragedy of the house of Atreus—the horror of that incessant swing of the pendulum—but also the problem for which the trilogy as a whole will propose a solution.

At the end of *Agamemnon*, Clytemnestra and the Chorus seem to be reaching for some sort of compromise that could bring the balance to rest at last.[7] The queen, fresh from murdering the king and his concubine, stands over the corpses and glories in her deed, daring to turn its horror into something natural and beautiful:

> And so he fell, and panted his life away,
> and breathing out a last sharp gale of blood
> he drenched me in the dark red showering gore,
> and I rejoiced in it, rejoiced no less
> than all the plants rejoice in Zeus-given
> rainfalls at the birthtime of the buds.　　　(1582–87/1388–92)

The Chorus expresses disgust at Clytemnestra's words and the repellent spectacle: "Your tongue astounds us, how you can swagger so / over the butchered body of your husband" (1596–97/1399–1400). Horrified as they are, however, they come to recognize—as must we—that she has indeed done *dikê*, a necessary and even righteous act of revenge, and they try to understand the consequences still to come:

> Charge answers charge, and who can weigh them, sift
> 　　right from wrong? The avenger
> is ravaged, the slayer slain. But it abides,

6. Goldhill, *Oresteia*, 26–37.
7. See the excellent analysis of the final scenes of the play in Taplin, *Stagecraft of Aeschylus*, 322–32.

> while Zeus on his throne abides,
> that he who does will suffer. That is law.
> Who will cast out the seed of curses
> from the house? The race is grafted to ruin.   (1794–1800/1560–66)

Clytemnestra, in turn, comes to see that her deed is not autonomous and final, and counters the Chorus's bleak prospect of killings yet to come by offering to make a pact with the "Spirit of the clan" (1805/ 1569, the curse that has dwelt so long in the house of Atreus) to offer up her wealth in return for his departure from her halls:

> However
> small my share
> of wealth may be, I'll be content
> if I have rid our halls at last
> of our frenzied killing of each other.   (1809–13/1574–76)

Clytemnestra's gesture is manifestly futile, for no such easy bargain can be struck with the implacable Spirit of vengeance, but it is the sign of a new recognition that she owes some price, still to be exacted, for her own act of vengeance. Before the significance of this insight can be tested, however, Aegisthus unexpectedly appears to deliver a speech that interrupts the colloquy, and moves *Agamemnon* toward an abrupt and grating end that promises only more violence. Yet even this treacherous adulterer, Clytemnestra's lover during Agamemnon's absence and now openly her consort, can rightly invoke *dikê* from first phrase ("O kind light of the day of final justice," 1814/1577) to last ("now that I've caught / him here in the net that Justice spread," 1856–57/ 1611), since the death of his brothers at the hands of Agamemnon's father has been avenged at last by Agamemnon's death. Yet Aegisthus' very insistence on blood feud and vengeance points toward the next round of revenge killings. His stated intention to use the wealth of Agamemnon to enforce his rule (1891–96/1638–42) contrasts with Clytemnestra's willingness to let it go in return for an end to the cycle of violence. And the chorus's scorn for their new tyrant leads them openly to wish for Orestes' return in the role of avenger (1901–3/1646–48). If one needed evidence to show how mistaken Clytemnestra is to hope that the Spirit of the house will be induced to choose another family of victims (1806–9/1571–73), the Aegisthus scene would suffice.

Libation Bearers continues the tale of the house of Atreus, but, from the perspective of justice, it is less a sequel than a repeat. What one notices first, however, are the striking differences, particularly in the presentation of the avengers, Electra and Orestes, the surviving son and daughter of the murdered king. Perhaps most obviously, the culturally jarring gender roles of Clytemnestra, the "manly" woman who plots and executes her own vengeance, and Aegisthus, the "womanly" man, who lurks inside the house and plays a passive role, are returned in Orestes and Electra to the cultural norm. Electra prays for Orestes' return, and when he appears cedes the action entirely to him. The changed tone of the play is marked from the start, when Agamemnon's friends gather at his tomb for a rite that evokes only his greatness and the cruelty of his slaughter, his memory marred by no shadow of the guilt that is so prominent in *Agamemnon*. Images from *Agamemnon* recur with their meanings completely reversed in *Libation Bearers*. Recall, for example, the simile we noticed earlier that conjures up the slain Iphigenia by comparing the war cry of the Atreidae to the shrieking of vultures whose chicks have been stolen from the nest (*Agamemnon*, 56–63/47–54); and the omen of the eagles (*Agamemnon* 133–39/114–21) that foretells victory—and all the horrifying destruction to come—by equating Agamemnon with an eagle that destroys a hare and the unborn young in her womb. These images are conflated and transformed in *Libation Bearers* when Orestes invokes Zeus for help:

> Look down
> on the unfledged orphans of a father eagle—
> killed in the viper's coils, her tangling lust;
> see the unfathered nestlings starve, too young,
> too weak to hunt, to bring the prey back to the nest
> the way their father did.   (279–84/247–51)

Instead of parent birds crying for their lost young, Zeus is to heed the cry of chicks who have lost their parent, the father eagle who should nourish and protect his young. Orestes' situation both resembles and reverses that of his father.[8]

Agamemnon in death has become a sacred hero, to be propitiated and called on for help; his tomb is now a hero's shrine. For the Chorus of slave women loyal to Agamemnon, it is "like an altar" (129/106), and Electra calls it a refuge for suppliants and exiles (382–84/336–37). Even Clytemnestra has sent libations to the tomb in hopes of placating the powerful spirit that dwells there. Here Electra and Orestes are reunited in an emotional upwelling of love for their father and desire to avenge his death. Orestes has been commanded directly and unequivocally by Apollo to kill Agamemnon's killer's, and he has come to accept his mother's slaying as an unavoidable act of justice, to be accomplished even at the cost of his own death (499–503/435–38, cf. 339–51/297–

8. Cf. Lebeck, *Oresteia*, 14.

306). Yet, in contrast to Clytemnestra's vaunted delight in the slaughter of her hated lord, when the moment comes, Orestes hesitates until his companion Pylades, silent until now, reminds him of Apollo's oracle and his obligation to the gods (1028–30/900–902). Despite this hesitation, however, it would be inaccurate to say that Orestes is torn between the need for vengeance and revulsion at killing his own mother. His situation is complicated, because *Libation Bearers* offers the same combination of divine and human responsibility, compulsion and freedom, that we found in *Agamemnon*. Like Agamemnon at Aulis, Orestes has received a divine command; like Agamemnon, he is free to disobey. If anything, the tragedy of being damned if you do and damned if you don't is more explicit for Orestes than for his father, since in *Agamemnon* the consequences of refusing to sacrifice Iphigenia (thus failing to avenge the abduction of Helen and ending the Trojan War before it began) are left entirely to the imagination. In *Libation Bearers*, by contrast, Apollo spells out at great lengths what punishments await Orestes if he fails to act. At the same time, there is no doubt that Orestes has accepted the burden of avenging his father's murder in the full knowledge of what it entails.

Orestes cannot be called a puppet of the Olympian gods or the powers of the underworld, as some critics have tried to do; nor is he "an unwilling avenger . . . terrorized by the god [Apollo] into accepting his part."[9] And yet, although his choice of matricide is demanded by justice, by Apollo, and by the spirit of his father, it also makes him guilty of a crime that calls out for punishment in turn. Early in the play, the Chorus assures Electra that she may, indeed she must, pray for an avenger of her father's death:

CHORUS LEADER A prayer for some god or man to come against them—

ELECTRA Someone to judge them or do justice to them?

CHORUS LEADER Say it straight: someone who'll take a life for a life.

ELECTRA Can it be right for me to ask this of the gods?

CHORUS LEADER Can it be wrong to pay back hurt with hurt?
(142–46/119–23)

9. Zeitlin, "Motif of the Corrupted Sacrifice," 496.

Electra's question, "Someone to judge them [*dikastên*, the regular Greek word for juror] or to do justice to them?" [*dikêphoron*, "bringing justice," Aegisthus' word to describe the day of Agamemnon's death, *Agamemnon*, 1814/1577], ironically suggests a legal solution in a world that has as yet no legal recourse, at least in regard to homicide. So she duly includes a "prayer for evil" in her prayer for good (173/146), and the work of justice is duly marked as part also of an unending cycle of wrongs. Orestes' final words to Clytemnestra before he takes her inside to kill her are a kind of summation: "You did wrong, killing; now suffer wrong and die!" (1059/930).

So, despite all the differences of tone and circumstance, the nature of justice in *Libation Bearers* is no different from that in *Agamemnon*. The play reveals this in any number of ways. The most striking thing in the long list of sufferings that await Orestes if he refuses to kill his mother is the promise of pursuit by his *father's* Erinyes (320–23/283–84). At the end of *Libation Bearers*, it is his *mother's* who begin their assault. The choice of evils he must make could not be clearer or more vivid. When Orestes has finished his account of Apollo's command, the Chorus repeats the great lesson of *Agamemnon*: "Who does shall suffer" (360/313; cf. *Agamemnon*, 1798/1564). Aeschylus underlines the continuity of meaning between the actions of the two plays by staging Orestes' display of the bodies of his victims as a "mirror scene" to one in *Agamemnon*.[10] There, Clytemnestra comes into view standing over the corpse of Agamemnon, apparently still wrapped in the robe in which she murdered him, with Cassandra lying at his side. Here, Orestes appears amid the bodies of Clytemnestra and Aegisthus and displays the same bloodied robe as a token of the justice of his deed (1105–51/980–1017).

The essential identity of the revenge action in *Libation Bearers* with that in *Agamemnon* is further emphasized in what now follows. While Orestes is slaying his mother, the Chorus, like Aegisthus at the end of *Agamemnon*, imagines that light—the light of *dikê*—has returned to the house that was shrouded in darkness:

> See how the light has come, and the hard curb
> that held the house is broken!
> Arise, O house, arise, too long you've lain
> in shambles on the ground.   (1087–90/961–64)

---

10. For this concept of "mirror scene" in the *Oresteia*, see Taplin, *Stagecraft of Aeschylus*, esp. 356–59.

Like Clytemnestra, they imagine an end to the reign of the Erinys that has beset it:

> But soon will Time, the all-accomplishing, pass in
>   through the front gate of the house
> when all pollution is expelled
> from the hearth by the cleansing rites which drive
>   out acts of bloodshed.   (1091–94/965–68)

When Orestes appears with the bodies of his victims, he avoids the intemperate excess of Clytemnestra's vaunts, but like her he is soon driven to self-justification. And just as Clytemnestra's offer to give up her wealth to placate the Spirit of the house represented her recognition that the story was not yet over, so Orestes' announcement that he must set off for Delphi to seek purification (1172–77/1034–39) announces further travails to come. Even more strikingly, he begins to feel the madness that is a sign that his mother's Erinyes have already begun their pursuit. Orestes' final self-justification is also a tortured admission that darkness has begun to fall:

>   I'm like a charioteer
> driving his team far off the course, my mind's
> unreinable, it bucks and pitches me away,
> and I'm defeated, and fear near my heart is ready
> to sing and dance now to a raging tune.
> Before I lose hold of my senses, though,
> I openly declare to all my friends,
> not without justice did I kill my mother,
> stained as she was with murdering my father,
> and with the hatred of the gods.   (1157–66/1022–27)

At the end of *Libation Bearers*, Orestes alone sees "the bloodhounds of my mother's anger" (1193/1054) and, despite the Chorus's attempts to calm him, bolts in terror. The Chorus is left to reflect that the justice they prayed for and welcomed has resolved nothing. The play closes with the same question that shadowed the end of *Agamemnon*:

> Where will it end? When will it all
> be lulled back into sleep, and cease,
> the bloody hatred, the destruction?   (1215–17/1075–76)

Justice, visited on mortals as a series of retributions for past crimes that call out for yet more revenge, cannot come to rest at a point of balance. Just as *Agamemnon* forced us to realize that the most dreadful crimes can be acts of *dikê*, so *Libation Bearers* insists that we see acts of just retribution as further crimes that make their own demand for vengeance. The question of how to achieve a lasting balance, one that preserves rather than destroys the social order still lacks an answer.

THE UNNATURAL HISTORY OF JUSTICE AND THE BIRTH OF THE POLIS
The stage has been set for a new turn in the story of death and revenge in the house of Atreus. *Eumenides* moves from Argos to Delphi and Athens, and, as we shall see, from the old world of vendetta to the new world of the polis and its laws. Aeschylus makes it clear that the old world can offer no solution to the dilemma of *dikê*, which in its retributive form is incompatible with stable and prosperous human communities. The ghost of Clytemnestra, who stirs the sleeping Erinyes to continue their terrifying pursuit of her murderer-son, belongs entirely to the old world of retribution. Her Erinyes, for their part, see themselves as the great upholders of justice against the onslaught of younger gods who would trample it down. While they can adopt the language of moderation and restraint (e.g., 619–30/526–37), they are firm believers in the efficacy of fear and wailing (613–18/520–25), and utterly unyielding in the pursuit of just revenge. The punishment they promise Orestes has the balance of an accountant's ledger:

> You'll have to pay with your own blood for hers,
>   you'll feel me suck the half-
> caked gore out of your living flesh;
>   swill from your very veins
> the vile dregs of the drink I crave.
> I'll shrivel you up and drag you, still alive
>   into the underworld
> where you will pay in currencies of torment
>   for the murder of your mother.   (1300–1309/264–68)

For the Erinyes, Apollo's very sanctuary is polluted by the welcome Apollo has given to the blood-stained Orestes (181–92/164–73). Orestes, on the other hand, repeatedly emphasizes the purifications he has received there (265–69/236–39, 319–27/276–83, 528–38/445–53). Apollo confirms that he has purged his suppliant of the stain of guilt (671–74/576–78), and Athena accepts him as "a proper suppliant who is clean, who bears / no danger to us" (563–64/474). Despite all that, the Erinyes still track him by the scent of blood, and it is clear that the old rites designed to return a murderer to a place in the social order, are not sufficiently powerful to overcome their assault. Wander where he may, flee however long he can, Orestes will never escape them. The point is that there is no simple ritual "fix," and no hope either for the mere passage of time to heal all wounds. As Aeschylus tells the story, the only way to force an end to the chain of crime and vengeance is to change the modality of *dikê* itself.[11]

The solution worked out in *Eumenides* brings myth from an imagined bronze-age past into the world of contemporary Athenian experience. Aeschylus provides a new foundation myth—one that cannot be traced to any previous source and is almost certainly of the poet's own devising—for two venerable Athenian institutions: the homicide court known as the Areopagus from its meeting place on the Hill of Ares near the acropolis, and the nearby cult of the *Semnai Theai*—the August Goddesses, a euphemistic name for the Erinyes. The Areopagus was a council of elders that played an important role in Athenian political life over many generations, but had recently (462, only four years before the performance of the *Oresteia*) been reformed to serve exclusively as a court for hearing cases of homicide.[12] Athenian legend explained that the Areopagus had been founded to handle a trial for murder, but in that case the defendant was the war god Ares (whence the court's name), prosecuted before a divine jury by Poseidon for the murder of his son Halirrhothius, who in turn had raped Ares' daughter Alcippe.[13] Aeschylus' substitution of Orestes' trial for the trial of Ares,

---

11. Parker, *Miasma*, 386–88, looks at Orestes' purification and trial in *Eumenides* from the perspective of early Greek religious practice and finds that Aeschylus does not "dispute the importance of ritual purification or deny its efficacy." One may agree, while still pointing out that by making Orestes' trial the one for which the Areopagus was founded, and by putting the trial after, rather than before, Orestes' exile, Aeschylus lays particular emphasis on the inability of purification to bring Orestes' pursuit by the Erinyes to an end. Orestes returns to Argos not because he has undergone the usual combination of purification and purificatory exile that "temporary exiles" underwent, but only after the new dispensation of legal justice has freed him from the Erinyes' power.

12. For the history of the Areopagus, see Wallace, *The Areopagos Council*. There has been a long-standing and inconclusive debate about Aeschylus' attitude toward the reform of Ephialtes in 462. For a summary of the reform and of recent discussion concerning Aeschylus' possible views, see Wallace, 77–93. The drastic limitation of the Areopagus Council's power was part of a number of changes that gave Athens a fully democratic regime. It is clear that this upheaval was accompanied by political tensions and perhaps even factional strife. Athens' alliance with conservative and oligarchical Sparta was terminated and a new one made with Argos, Sparta's traditional rival (see further the note to *Eumenides*, 885–98/762–74). Cimon, the powerful Athenian leader whose foreign policy was pro-Spartan, and much of whose support probably came from the wealthy classes who made up the Areopagus Council, was exiled from Athens for ten years by ostracism. And Ephialtes, an important politician with democratic sympathies who carried the reform of the Areopagus in the Athenian assembly, died suddenly, and was widely assumed to have been murdered by his political enemies. Fortunately, however, Athens avoided further bloodshed, and with Pericles now acknowledged as leader, Athens pursued further democratic reforms.

13. One indication of Aeschylus' conscious replacing of the old foundation myth with his own is the fact that he provides a new etymology for the Hill of Ares at 800–806/685–90. For its significance, cf. p. 24.

and human jurors for the divine jury, transforms the foundation story of the first homicide court into an aetiological myth about the replacement of retributive clan violence with the judicial deliberation of the polis. The second foundation story, explaining how Athens came to worship the Erinyes at a shrine near the Areopagus, is really a corollary of the first. Apparently, there was already a close connection between the cult of the *Semnai Theai*—the August Goddesses, one of the euphemistic names under which the Erinyes were honored—and the Areopagus.[14] Having chosen to make the Erinyes Orestes' persecutors, Aeschylus found it natural to connect his story to their nearby shrine by making his trial the occasion for the cult's foundation.

In any case, Aeschylus' linking of court and cult is anything but fortuitous. Legal justice supersedes private retribution, but the terror that these stern ancient deities inspire is still needed to deter people from committing crimes and to ensure their respect for law. As the jurors prepare to judge the first trial for murder, Athena offers this advice:

> I urge my people to follow and revere
> neither tyranny nor anarchy,
> and to hold fear close, never to cast it out
> entirely from the city. For what man
> who feels no fear is able to be just?   (813–17/696–99)

This is almost precisely what the Erinyes themselves sang as they awaited the beginning of the trial:

> What man, or city even,
> whose heart is not fed on fear,
> would ever again pay Justice
> the reverence she's owed?
>
> Praise no life that no law reins,
> no life a tyrant rules.   (615–20/522–28)

The Erinyes' old law is not obliterated by the new, nor in accepting their new home and honors do they become something entirely different from what they were. The metamorphosis of Erinyes to Eumenides in this play is but the most obvious and important of a whole series of transformations to bring *dikê* firmly into the world of the polis. Nev-

14. Ancient sources from the fourth century onward record that the Areopagus met only on days sacred to the *Semnai Theai*, that both parties to the trials swore oaths by them, and that those acquitted were expected to sacrifice to them. For sources and details, see Sommerstein's edition of *Eumenides*, 10–11.

ertheless, just as the fundamental nature of *dikê* remains the same, but now can reveal itself in another form or aspect, so the transformations are best understood as revelations of new aspects, not complete negations of old identities. In the case of the Erinyes, it is well to remember that blessing is the other side of the coin from cursing. They have a new role, but the powers they embody remain what it always were. Something similar may be said about Zeus, who presides over justice as a kind of master signifier throughout the trilogy. He may or may not evolve during its course (a heated debate on this subject raged in earlier Aeschylean scholarship), but it is fair to say that his dominant aspect shifts in the course of the trilogy from a stern and angry enforcer—for example, Zeus *xenios* ("lord of host and guest," *Agamemnon*, 417/362), who exacts punishment for the transgressions of Paris by sending the Achaeans to raze the city of Troy—to the Zeus who works his will by means of words—Zeus *agoraios* ("Zeus who guides / men's speech," *Eumenides*, 1135–36/973). The epithet *agoraios* makes Zeus patron of the *agora*, the place of public meetings, and implies that he presides over civic deliberation. For all the differences in these aspects of the deity, he does the work of *dikê* equally in both guises.

Such transformations as these involve the relations of men and women, and even of the gods and mortals, aspects of the trilogy to which we shall soon return, and which have to do with a new understanding of human communities as political entities, and how they might survive and flourish. At this level, Aeschylus ties the change in *dikê* to a change in political structure.[15] The world of *Agamemnon* is that of a traditional Homeric aristocracy, with hereditary power belonging to the males of great houses—power here mired in equally hereditary crime and challenged by a wily woman and her subservient male partner. Usurpation by the upstarts Clytemnestra and Aegisthus involves a form of persuasion that we can characterize as temptation or seduction, typified by the honeyed words with which Clytemnestra leads her husband along the crimson path to his death. The usurpers' victory overturns the old hereditary pattern and transforms Argos, as we see it in *Libation Bearers*, into a tyranny, repressive because imposed against the will of the community. To contest this repression, the male heir returns and is joined by his sister, though she plays a distinctly subordinate role. The form of persuasion authorized by Apollo's oracle and used to thrilling effect in *Libation Bearers* is intrigue and deceit, embodied chiefly in Orestes' false report of his own death, which gains

15. My view of this aspect of the trilogy owes a good deal to Rose's stimulating discussion in *Sons of the Gods*, 184–265. For a very different view, see Griffith, "Brilliant Dynasts."

him entrance into the palace and (through a bit of strategic trickery by the Chorus) brings Aegisthus home unguarded and unarmed. *Eumenides* frees Orestes after long wanderings to return to Argos and reclaim his birthright, but the chief focus is now entirely on the transformation wrought in Athens by his trial. In this way, the emergence of the institutions of the democratic polis can be symbolized (or more precisely represented in a kind of metonymy) by the establishment of a court of law. Significantly, the language that effects the transformations of *Eumenides* is no longer that of temptation or intrigue, but persuasive speech, the matrix of legal and political debate in a democratic state.

The complex relation of gender and power in the *Oresteia* has been much discussed in recent years.[16] It is often said that from this point of view the story of the *Oresteia* is one of women's political disenfranchisement, and it is certainly possible to see the political thrust of *Eumenides* as validating a change from the perverted female rule of Clytemnestra to the (real) patriarchy of Athens in Aeschylus' own day, in which women were as far as possible excluded from participating in public life. It must be understood, however, that what is at stake here is not a record of the loss of women's power, but a myth of failed rebellion against a patriarchy that had always been in place. In weighing such views, much will depend on how one frames the issues. Take, for example, the version of the Delphic succession myth presumably invented by Aeschylus as a replacement for the usual story, in which Apollo won control of the most important sanctuary in Greece by the bloody conquest of Pytho, a vicious female monster.[17] According to the very different account in *Eumenides*, Delphi passed peacefully from Mother Earth to her daughter Themis, and then by Themis' own free will to Phoebe, another child of Earth, and from her to Apollo, who thenceforward added "Phoebus" to his name (1–10/1–8). Froma Zeitlin argues that this way of telling the story provides "a direct mythological model for the transference of power from female to male," differing from the traditional story only because Aeschylus wants a peaceful and orderly version of the transfer to foreshadow the orderly, peaceful ending of the trilogy.[18] Peter Rose, on the other hand, points out that the main thrust of the change is to repudiate a particularly misogynist tra-

---

16. See above all Zeitlin, "The Dynamics of Misogyny." If I dissent from some of her conclusions, it is not without grateful recognition of her groundbreaking work in bringing to the fore the many ways in which the "myth of matriarchy" and its attendant anxieties permeate the trilogy.

17. The best known and most striking account of this version is in the *Homeric Hymn to Apollo*, 224–384. For the likely originality of Aeschylus' version, see Sorvinou-Inwood, "Myth as History," 231.

18. Zeitlin, "The Dynamics of Misogyny," 102.

dition of violent male triumph over the very embodiment of female viciousness. From this perspective, the prominence in Aeschylus' version of a whole succession of female figures evoked in very positive terms, the device of Phoebe's friendly transfer of Delphi to Apollo as a birthday present, and Apollo's adoption of her name as a gesture of recognition are distinctions with a difference, even if the outcome (a given) remains the same. Rose concludes:

> It is legitimate to see in this version a model of willing acquiescence in female subordination; but the fact of subordination was not Aeschylus' doing, whereas the myth he offers to explain it maximizes the enduring positive contribution of females to the new order and specifically rejects a version that represented them as the threat to be beaten and obliterated.[19]

Female submissiveness is normative in the *Oresteia*. Nothing makes this clearer than the disparaging and evidently disturbing portrayal of Clytemnestra's androgyny, the kind that most threatens men through the woman's assumption of "male" mastery and "male" freedom to speak and act. She is firmly in charge during Agamemnon's absence, and after killing him on his return, she rules with her new man, but as the dominant partner. Despite the overt ugliness of her portrayal, however, Aeschylus insists that we understand her motives and recognize the justice in her actions. Indeed, the depiction of women in the *Oresteia* is everywhere complicated and nowhere reflects unproblematic misogyny. Cassandra is a fascinating example. In her unbridled hostility toward Clytemnestra and her concomitant loyalty to the man who has destroyed her city and taken her as part of his spoils, she takes the side of patriarchy. Yet, her very presence and, after her long silence, the mighty torrent of her words and cries testify to the horror of her suffering at the hands of males. Unlike Iphigenia, whom the chorus depicts as gagged at the moment of her sacrifice, wanting to speak but able to appeal to her killers only with her eyes (*Agamemnon*, 270–79/235–43), Cassandra can shout out the horror and pathos of the victim. Aeschylus seems to insist that we feel the pathos of those who do not attack the patriarchy, but are made the victims of its brutality.

It is, then, of some significance that *Eumenides* begins with an account that makes Apollo's rule in Delphi not the result of destroying a monstrous female, but of a gift willingly made by benign female deities. The trilogy is working its way toward a transformation of the relations of men and women from hostility to a form of mutual respect and acceptance. The context of accommodation remains the patriarchy, to be sure, but Athena's persuasion will win the Erinyes a home and rites of honor in Athens as "kindly ones" (1158/992), "venerable ones" (1218/1041) who will protect and bless the city's lands, crops, and people. The model of women's submissiveness that this ending suggests is not a model that we can readily approve, but it is not simply misogynist. Exclusion of females from political power leads in the *Oresteia* to their incorporation into the community through a cult that benefits the city as a whole.

In that light, the contrast implied by Athena's allusion to the legend of the Amazons' attack on Athens (800–806/685–90) is telling. Orestes' acquittal and restoration to power will come at the spot where these warlike barbarian women challenged the men of Athens in battle, threatening their sovereignty and their very lives. The battle returns almost obsessively in the art and literature of the fifth century, suggesting both overt attachment to and unconscious insecurity about an ideology of male domination.[20] Like Clytemnestra (with whom Apollo associates them, 730–32/627–28), the Amazons attempted to overthrow patriarchy and were destroyed. But a different end awaits the Erinyes. Their suit is defeated in court, but they are neither demolished nor dismissed. They are coopted and made to serve the interests of the polis, rather than the narrower ones determined by ties of blood.

The most glaring instance in the trilogy of what many have taken to be misogyny is Apollo's argument before the Athenian court that Orestes should be acquitted because a mother is no true parent, merely "a sort / of nursing soil for the new sown seed" (770–71/659). What are we to make of this argument? It will inevitably strike a modern audience as absurd, but many scholars have assumed that it must have sounded compelling to Athenians of the period. I am inclined to doubt this, and indeed to doubt that the argument itself has any great weight for the trilogy as a whole. It is worth noting that the way Apollo introduces the idea has a certain quality of desperation about it; he pulls it out of the hat when the Erinyes have effectively cornered him (748–67/640–56). They answer his contention that Zeus was more concerned about a father's than a mother's death by challenging Zeus's *bona fides*, pointing out that he locked up his own father in chains. But chains are a different thing from death, says Apollo, for once the earth has drunk up a dead man's blood, nothing can bring him back. Just so, reply the Erinyes, so how can Orestes, who has shed his mother's blood,

---

20. See duBois, *Centaurs and Amazons*, and Tyrell, *Amazons*.

go back to Argos with that blood on his hands? Ah, replies Apollo, *she* wasn't the real parent.

Making the father the sole parent serves Apollo's purpose by underlining the primacy of the male line in defining the properly patriarchal family. But we can say with assurance that his biology was far from uncontested. Aristotle gives it support a century later, but all the evidence we have (much of it collected for us by Aristotle himself) leads to the conclusion that there were strongly divergent views in circulation about how procreation worked, in Aeschylus' day as well as in Aristotle's. Indeed, we have less early evidence in support of Apollo's view than we do for the theory that women also produced semen and that a child's sex was determined by the relative contribution of each seed.[21] It looks as though Aeschylus has deliberately chosen a rather arcane argument, and one about which people could and did disagree. After all, it is a crucial part of his plan to make the acquittal of Orestes the result of an evenly divided vote, and thus he has no desire to give Apollo what might seem to his audience an overwhelmingly decisive argument.

The chief value of Apollo's view turns out to be its appeal Athena, who uses it to make a final decision based on what might be called personal, and to that extent arbitrary, grounds (854–60/735–40). Apollo had supported his theory of the male as sole parent by reference to the goddess, whose birth from the head of Zeus proves, he claimed, that a child can be born without a mother.[22] Athena confirms Apollo's story about her birth, though not necessarily his generalization of it to human biology, when she justifies her vote to acquit Orestes of killing his mother by her own motherlessness. All this conspires not so much to produce a coherent case for the primacy of the male parent as to render the decision to acquit Orestes one about which contemporary Athenians, like the jurors on stage, could disagree. If this is so, then the point of raising the argument is not to focus on the politics of gender as much as on the politics of the law court: no matter how arbitrary or contested the verdict, once it is delivered it must command the respect and assent of all. And, as a political comment, it must be considered a reflection on democratic institutions, where popular con-

---

21. For the sources, see Lloyd, *Science, Folklore, and Ideology,* 86–94.
22. Athena was said to have sprung full-grown from the head of Zeus, after Hephaestus split it open to let her emerge. Aeschylus' version of the myth implies that Athena had no mother at all; however, the fullest and best known account (Hesiod, *Theogony,* 886–900) says that Metis (Good Counsel) was her mother, but that Zeus swallowed Metis before the child could be born in the usual way.

sent is of the essence. All this stands in the greatest possible contrast to the "trial" held to decide the fate of Troy (*Agamemnon*, 933–38/813–17): there the pleas come "not from any mouth but from force of arms" and the jurors are the gods, who cast their ballots "into the urn of blood" in a unanimous death sentence for Troy.

The role of Athena in *Eumenides* brings questions about the relations of male and female together with questions about the relations of gods and mortals. As a warrior goddess, Athena shares androgyny with Clytemnestra, but as a permanent virgin, she exists apart from the conflict of the sexes. Clytemnestra, Helen, and Cassandra can be seen in various ways as rebels against the constraints of marriage; Athena has no part in marriage[23] but can serenely recognize its importance to the prosperity and stability of the polis. She sees to it that those other virgin goddesses, the Erinyes, will receive sacrifices for marriage and the birth of healthy children (970–74/834–36). Indeed, the most important thing about Athena in *Eumenides* is her role as mediator between gods and mortals. It is fundamental to the trilogy that mortals cannot establish lasting justice by themselves, and gods cannot impose it. Only collaboration between them will achieve it. Athena, wise as she is, understands this and eagerly accepts her part. Although both the Erinyes (516–18/433–35) and Orestes (555–57/468–69) explicitly accept Athena's right to judge their case by herself, and both welcome her decision, Athena refuses:

> No, even I don't have the right to rule
> on a murder trial like this one, one
> that calls down such fierce anger either way.   (559–61/471–72)

In the end, as we have seen, Athena does cast the decisive vote, and does so on personal, seemingly arbitrary grounds. It is not the grounds, however, nor perhaps even the decision, but the process she has set in motion and the institution she has created, that matter most. The process may not be perfect (many scholars have labored to show how flawed this one is), but it brings balance by its finality.

If *Eumenides* represents the emergence of polis institutions, and specifically those of the Athenian democracy, as the only means to resolve the impasse of the old clan justice, it is Athena's founding of the Court

---

23. There is a tale (preserved by the mythographers Apollodorus and Hyginus) that makes Athena mother of the Athenian king Erichthonius: pursued by Hephaestus, she ran from him, but he caught her in an embrace and spilled his seed on her leg. Athena wiped it off and threw it on the ground, and from it was born Erichthonius, whom she regarded as her son. Her virgin status remained, however, unchallenged.

of the Areopagus that embodies that new solution. Athena says that she will appoint to it "my ablest citizens," so it is not, as it was not in historical times, a democratically chosen body. On the other hand, as has often been observed, these judges are consistently addressed as if they represent the entire citizen body, and both Orestes' grateful offer of alliance with Athens (885–98/762–74) and the Erinyes' threats of pollution of the entire land (906–17/780–87) indicate clearly that the court has acted for the city as a whole.[24]

Athena's work of mediation is not over when the court returns its verdict, for she must still face the question of how to neutralize the Erinyes' potential for harm and win them instead to the side of the polis. (As goddesses, and ancient pre-political ones at that, the Erinyes are not bound by the social contract that empowers human law.) Again, one may say that Athena's wisdom is harnessed to an essentially democratic process, for she has decided to use persuasion, the defining tool of democratic political leadership, in what amounts to an open negotiation. She takes the Erinyes and their ancient wisdom (987–88/848–49) seriously, and has the patience to understand and the resourcefulness to meet their deepest needs. In the face of the Erinyes' apparent intransigence, Athena persists— "Let me persuade you" (923/794); "I'll put up with your anger" (987/848), "I'll never tire of telling you the benefits / I'm offering" (1025–26/881)— until at last she hears them say, "You might persuade me; I feel my anger is easing" (1047/900). Only once does Athena threaten force, but if the threat is unmistakable, so also is her resolve not to resort to force:

> I have Zeus on my side and—
> why even bring it up?—I'm the only one
> among the gods who knows where he keeps the key
> to the chamber in which the lightning bolt is sealed.
> No, we won't have need of that. Please,
> let me persuade you . . .   (960–65/826–29)

In winning over the Erinyes, Athena heals the breach between the older and younger generations of gods, a matter of deep and bitter concern to the Erinyes. They are among the oldest of the gods, and having seen Zeus chain Cronus underground (cf. 750–51/641) and the Olympian gods ascend to supreme power, they are keenly aware that their old honors and powers are in danger of disappearing. Thus, when Athena first offers them a new home "in a vast cavern / deep in this land of justice" (934–35/805), they imagine that they will be impris-

24. See Rose, *Sons of the Gods*, 247–48.

oned, like Cronus (975–78/837–39 = 1013–16/870–72). Only gradually do they come to realize that this will be a place of honor, and that there will be a new and vital role for them to play as guardians of the soil of Attica and its fertility, patrons of marriage and birth, bestowers of the blessings of peace and plenty, and protectors from the scourge of civil strife. *Eumenides* ends with a solemn ritual procession that will bring the Erinyes to their new home, accompanied by torch light and robed in the crimson cloaks that metics (resident aliens) wore in the great Panathenaic processions held in honor of Athena (1196–99/1022–25). The symbolism is both obvious and effective. The Erinyes have become honored guests, essential to the civic cohesion and good order of the new polis. The blood-red fabric evokes the cloths that Agamemnon trampled down and the cloths he was caught in, cloths so memorably displayed in the first two plays of the trilogy; it evokes the blood that was shed at Troy and in Argos, and the blood that the Erinyes themselves once drank in the house of Atreus. The torch-fire that sees the Erinyes on their solemn way evokes the flames that engulfed Troy and then flew across the sea as beacon-light to presage Agamemnon's homecoming—and yet more ruin. Now, the meaning of these symbols has been transformed and resolved into new promise, reminding us of the long and arduous path that the trilogy has taken and where it has brought us.

LANGUAGE AND IMAGERY, FORM AND MEANING

The language of the *Oresteia* can be pithy and direct; more often it is dense, sometimes almost to the point of inaccessibility. Its use of imagery and metaphor is particularly rich and striking, and at times (as in the example we have just noticed) figures move from verbal to visual realization on stage, to wonderful effect. Aeschylus adapts and extends the language of Homer and the Greek lyric poets, but he also invents new words and startling periphrases, tests the limits of Greek syntax, and plays brilliantly with ambiguity and enigma. The choral lyrics are particularly rich in such experiments. The language of prophecy and dream, though often only partially understood by those to whom the words are addressed, has a special and compelling power. And there are moments when the power of words per se seems to overtake their speakers (or singers). In the great opening chorus of *Agamemnon*, for example, the elders of Argos attempt to sing of "the good omens / shown to the two kings" (124–25/104–5), but again and again words of ill omen rise unbidden to their lips as they are drawn, almost against their will, to evoke the sacrifice of Iphigenia. "Sing sorrow, sorrow, but let the good prevail" becomes a kind of refrain chanted against the

implications of their own song (**139/121, 158/139, 178/159**). And when
the Chorus has heard the Herald's story of Troy's fall, the power of
language reveals itself in the discovery that Helen is truly named. The
Chorus finds the "truth" of the name in the Greek verb stem *hel–*
(seize, destroy):

> Helen: destroyer. The name
> became her, suited her,
> it seemed, as much as the soft
> luxuries of the bower
> she sailed from, destroyer of ships,
> destroyer of men, destroyer
> of cities.   (**782–88**/687–91)

In Aeschylus' startling wordplay, *Helene* metamorphoses into *hele–nas*,
hel–andros, *hele–ptolis*.

The verbal texture that results from elements such as these is un-
surpassed in magnificence and complexity, but is almost impossible to
elucidate without direct reference to the Greek text. Rather than continue with generalized description, I shall pursue one strand of dramatic imagery that runs through all three plays and illustrates important
features of Aeschylus' figurative language. Anne Lebeck suggests some
important principles for the study of his imagery:

> The images of the *Oresteia* are not isolated units which can be ex-
> amined separately. Each one is part of a larger whole: a system of
> kindred imagery. They are connected to each other by verbal similarity
> rather than verbal duplication. . . . [A]ssociative or reminiscent repeti-
> tion . . . may evoke several different passages, yet correspond exactly to
> none. Each recurrence adds a new element to those with which it is
> associated. . . . The significance of a recurrent image unfolds in suc-
> cessive stages, keeping time with the action of the drama. . . . Signifi-
> cance increases with repetition; the image gains in clarity as the action
> moves to a climax.[25]

Since Aeschylus' characteristic method is to interlock related images
that are repeated and varied over the course of the trilogy, strictly speaking one cannot isolate a single element from the whole system of imagery. For the purpose of exemplifying Aeschylus' way of working, however, it will be useful to focus on a set of closely associated images that
move gradually from riddle to clarity, and from conflict to resolution.
These images are grounded in a well-known Greek custom of pouring
three drink offerings after a meal, the first (in the most usual version)

25. Lebeck, *Oresteia*, 1–2.

to Olympian Zeus and the Olympians, the second to the Heroes, the third (always) to Zeus Savior.[26] The libations were generally followed by the singing of a hymn called the *paean*, In the *Oresteia*, the references to this rite are highly allusive until the final one, in *Eumenides*. The Greek audience will have had no trouble, however, in deciphering the allusions and detecting both the bitter irony with which the rite is perverted and distorted, and the residual promise of a saving Zeus, who crowns the meal with blessings and may yet bring the murderous vengeance in the house of Atreus to some good end.

The first appearance of the motif in the trilogy is slight but almost programmatic in its complexity. The Argive elders juxtapose to the painful picture of Iphigenia about to be sacrificed on the altar a remarkable evocation of happier days. Iphigenia has been gagged, so that she cannot cry out, and is being held "like / a goat" (267–68/232) above the altar.

> And with her saffron robe now streaming
> down from her shoulders to the ground,
> with pitiful arrows from her eyes
> she shot each sacrificer, vivid
> as in a picture, wanting to speak,
> to call each one by name, for often
> at the rich feast in her father's halls
> the girl had sung before the men
> and with the pure voice of a virgin,
> at the third libation, lovingly
> had given honor to her loving
> father's paean for healing luck.   (273–84/239–47)

The contrast between the images is a sharp as possible. Approaching the moment of Iphigenia's death, which they cannot bring themselves to mention, the Chorus moves further back in memory to evoke the maiden appearing freely among her father's friends and taking part in the joyous ritual of the libations. The most obvious point of this picture of serene, unsuspecting piety, with its emphasis on Iphigenia's purity and love for her father, is its contrast with the pathetic image of the child about to be slain. More is at stake, however, in "third libation," which evokes Zeus the Savior and the "healing luck" that should come from this rite. In the Greek text, the words translated "third libation" and "healing luck" are juxtaposed and have similar terminations: *tri-*

26. These images are a subset of a larger group associated with rites of sacrifice, central to the trilogy's insistent figuration of murder as a ritual act. The definitive treatment is Zeitlin (note 9), 463–508. The discussion here draws on material published in Burian, *"Zeus Sotêr Tritos,"* to which the reader is referred for further details.

tóspondon eúpotmon. Their juxtaposition marks for Chorus and audience the gap between prayer for blessing and the unspeakable horror that answers it, and in the end can be referred to none other than Zeus, no savior now.

A far more direct and more glaring perversion of the accepted meaning of the third libation comes when Clytemnestra, standing over the corpse of her victims, recalls in a kind of ecstasy the slaughter of Agamemnon:

> I struck him twice, and while he cried two cries,
> his legs gave way. Then soon as he was down,
> I struck him yet again, and the third stroke fell
> as a votive offering for the Zeus
> below the ground, the savior of the dead.
> And so he fell, and panted his life away,
> and breathing out a last sharp gale of blood
> he drenched me in the dark red showering gore,
> and I rejoiced in it, rejoiced no less
> than all the plants rejoice in Zeus-given
> rainfalls at the birthtime of the buds.   (1577–87/1384–92)

Here, Agamemnon's blood is the wine of offering, the three blows are the three libations, and the third and final blow, delivered when the victim's limbs have already gone slack, is a welcome "votive offering" not to Zeus Savior, but to Hades, the Zeus of the underworld whom Clytemnestra ironically calls "the savior of the dead." The blasphemy is simply stunning, and is increased, if possible, in the final lines by the implicit perversion of the primeval creation myth of the mating of Heaven and Earth—with Clytemnestra cast as Earth and Agamemnon's blood becoming the rain-semen of creation and symbolizing not love's consummation, but the fulfillment of Clytemnestra's hatred.[27] A similar, though less blatant, blasphemy informs the oath with which Clytemnestra claims support for her deed: "I swear by Justice, completed for my child, / by Ruin, by the blood-crazed Erinyes" (1637–38/1432–

---

27. Herington, *Aeschylus*, 123–24. For the myth of the mating of Heaven and Earth, cf. this beautiful fragment from Aeschylus' lost *Danaids*, spoken by Aphrodite:

> Holy heaven longs to pierce the land,
> and longing for marriage seizes earth. Rain,
> falling from the liquid sky, impregnates earth,
> and she, to benefit mankind, gives birth
> to grass for the herds and to grain, Demeter's gift
> of life. From the showers of this wedding flow
> the seasons when trees bear their flowers and fruits.
> Of all these things I also am the cause.

(Fragment 44 Radt [*TrGF*]; translation quoted from Peter Burian, *Aeschylus: The Suppliants* [Princeton, 1991], xxi.)

33). Here, the traditional triad of libation is supplanted by a personal and sinister constellation of divinities that culminates not in the saving Zeus but in the vengeful Fury whom Clytemnestra will shortly identify as "the triple-glutted / spirit of this race" (1692–93/1476–77). Zeus's absence in this triad is all the more striking because the epithet *teleios* (translated here by "completed") belongs, particularly in this trilogy, to Zeus. Clytemnestra herself invoked Zeus Teleios just before entering the palace to murder her husband: *Zeu, Zeu teleie, tas emas tuchas telei*, "Zeus, Zeus, sovereign accomplisher / accomplish this my prayer" (1116–17/973–74). Ironically, the next "completion" of *dikê* will be Clytemnestra's own death.[28]

Libation Bearers is punctuated by three striking references to Zeus Savior and his third libation. The first concludes Electra's joyous response to Orestes' revelation that he is her long-lost brother. Greeting him as "hope of saving [*soteriou*] seed, much missed, long wept for" (268/236), Electra turns to a triad of gods for aid in accomplishing the salvation that now seems possible. Like Clytemnestra's triad in the *Agamemnon*, Electra's is a personal one, but she restores Zeus to his rightful place, third and last: "May Power and Justice / and Zeus the third, supreme, be on your side!" (277–78/244–45). Having recognized Orestes as the agent of salvation, Electra invokes its ultimate source, the saving Zeus. Something similar can be said about Orestes' reference to the impending murder of Aegisthus as a third libation:

> And then
> the Erinys, full as she is with blood, will still
> guzzle his unmixed gore, poured out in a third,
> a last libation. (657–60/577–78)

This is reminiscent of Clytemnestra's libation of blood, but without her blasphemous perversion of the figure of Zeus Savior. Orestes dedicates Aegisthus' murder as an offering to appease the Fury, the Spirit of the house that cries our for vengeance. In calling this new death the third libation, Orestes might be supposed to be reckoning (like the Chorus

---

28. *Telos* and its compounds are used in the *Oresteia* with a frequency and complexity akin to that of *dikê*-words. There is a good, though partial, discussion in Lebeck, *Oresteia*, 68–73; see further Zeitlin, "Motif of the Corrupted Sacrifice," esp. 464–67 and 475–80. Another irony latent in *Agamemnon*, 1637–38/1432–33, and elsewhere in the trilogy where *telos* is used in connection with death and the destruction of the family, is that *telos* is commonly used to refer to the consummation of a marriage rite, and thus to marriage in general. Hera, as the presiding goddess of marriage is often given the epithet *teleia*, and she appears in this guise ("Hera, the fulfiller") at *Eumenides* 238/124. Apollo is there accusing the Erinyes of "spitting on" marriage vows, but Athena will at last persuade them to accept sacrifices on behalf of "the fulfillment [*telos*] of the marriage rite" (*Eumenides* 973/835).

at the end of the play) Thyestes' banquet as the first libation and the assassination of Agamemnon as the second. Primarily, however, "third" here seems to connote "third and last," implying the hope that this will indeed be the final outpouring of blood.[29]

But salvation will not come quickly or easily, and Orestes attempt to placate the Spirit of the house is no more successful than was Clytemnestra's (*Agamemnon*, 1802–9/1569–73). The contradiction in Orestes' crimes of vengeance is apparent in the shocking paradox that identifies the blood of the victim with the third libation to the saving god. Other Erinyes will rise from his mother's blood to pursue him, will seek to drink his blood in exchange for hers. The radical ambiguity of Orestes' situation is nowhere more forcefully put than in the startling variation of the motif of the third savior with which *The Libation Bearers* ends:

> Again, for the third time, on the royal house
>   the storm has crashed,
> its curses blowing through the blood,
> and run its course. First came the feast
> of children's flesh, Thyestes' anguish;
> next came the grim fate of the man,
>   the king, the warlord
> of the Achaeans—killed in the bath;
> Now once again for the third time
>   from somewhere comes
> a savior, or should I say a death?
> When will it end? When will it all
> be lulled back into sleep, and cease,
> the bloody hatred, the destruction?   (1204–17/1065–76)

Electra had invoked Zeus Savior for vengeance; now that vengeance has been achieved, the Chorus momentarily identifies Orestes with Zeus Savior. But the first elements of this triad, the most daring of the series, are not deities to be propitiated, but horrible crimes that called out for and received revenge. Orestes' murder of his mother is another such deed, and Orestes has just rushed from the stage pursued by creatures the Chorus could not see, but who can be expected to exact the same price from him that others have paid before. Will Orestes, coming third and last, be the savior (*sôtêr*) of his house or should he be called death (*moron*)? The chorus has no answer, but the expressive equivocation of their question contains not only their greatest fear, but also the one remaining hope, the suggestion of salvation still somehow to emerge from the wreckage of the house.

29. See Clay, "Aeschylus' Trigeron Mythos."

The question receives its answer in *Eumenides*, when Athena announces that Orestes has been acquitted. He responds to the news that his birthright has been restored at last with a final allusion to the three libations:

> O Pallas Athena, you have saved my house!
> When I was stripped bare of my homeland,
> you gave it back to me. Now Greeks will say:
> "The man is Argive once again; he lives
> among his father's holdings by the grace
> of Pallas and Apollo, and of the third,
> the Savior, he who brings all to fulfillment."
> Yes, he himself gave due weight to the way
> my father died, and has delivered me
> to safety from my mother's advocates.   (875–84/754–61)

The disjunction that the Chorus of *Libation Bearers* applied to Orestes, savior or death, is resolved by applying its terms to appropriate referents. The savior (*sôtêr*) is of course Zeus, as the allusion to the third libation makes clear. And Zeus saves Orestes because he honors the death (*moron*) of Agamemnon, and thus permits its vengeance to go unavenged despite the claims of Clytemnestra's "advocates," the Erinyes. Orestes, in short, reclaims his true place as his father's son; in return he recognizes Zeus as his savior by restoring him to the third place, the place of honor, the place usurped by the Erinys to whom Orestes had poured his libations of blood.

Two general considerations emerge from following this single imagistic thread throughout the *Oresteia*. First, we have noticed a pattern in which a distorted and even perverted image is gradually restored to a positive form. In this respect, Aeschylus' evocation of the third libation typifies a procedure that he repeats in many ways and on many levels. To take a prominent example, themes of hunting, taming, and restraining are embodied throughout the trilogy in images of nets, curbs, yokes and entangling cloths. In *Agamemnon*, Agamemnon puts on the yoke of necessity (248–49/218) and Troy has the yoke of slavery fastened to its neck (600–601/529); Iphigenia has "her mouth gagged, the bit yanked / roughly" (270–71/325–26); Clytemnestra, in her shameless speech on Agamemnon's return, says (with what relish we can guess) that if all the rumors of his wounding had been true, "his body now would / be more net than body, pierced with so many holes" (994–95/867–68). The primary vehicle of this imagery, of course, is another kind of net: the blood-red tapestries down which Clytemnestra lures Agamemnon to his death, the robes in which she entangles him in the bath as she kills him. Like the tapestries strewn at Agamemnon's feet, these robes become visible symbols when Clytemnestra displays them in her vaunt over the corpses of her victims. In *Libation Bearers*, Orestes displays them again to justify his own killings, but as he holds them, the blood that stains them seems to symbolize his own pollution as well. He recognizes that his is "a filthy and unenviable triumph" (1151/1017), and begins his descent into madness. *Eumenides* brings Orestes' escape from the entanglement of blood-guilt, and beyond that, the transformation of the bloody robes into another visible symbol: the crimson tunics that the Erinyes now wear as marks of their new honor. An image of treachery, pollution, and death turns into an auspicious sign—one, we should add, whose power comes largely from the long, arduous process of transformation itself.

A similar process can be seen at work in other, interlocking clusters of images. Fire, for example, a prominent part of the trilogy's pervasive themes of light and dark, is given a characteristic twist when the longed-for beacon-fire that announces the Greek victory at Troy becomes a firebrand spreading conflagration through the house, only to reach resolution on stage in the final torchlit procession. There are similar patterns involving, among others, themes of disease, animals (above all, serpents and lions), blood, and rites of sacrifice. Images of sacrificial ritual have mostly ominous connotations from the beginning of the trilogy through the opening of *Eumenides*. That murders can themselves consistently be figured as rites of sacrifice is emblematic of the distortion of values that the bloody chain of crime and retribution has effected. Finally, the procession that ends *Eumenides* restores sacrifice and other rites of propitiation to positive significance and a proper civic role as elements of cult designed to promote general well-being (e.g., 1173–74/1006, 1213–14/1037–38). The restoration of Zeus Savior to his place in the rite of the three libations, and thus in the perpetuation of family and community, is also part of this transformation.

A further reflection arising from the motif of the three libations weaves several strands of imagery and allusion into a larger pattern, leading us back to the question of trilogic structure and its significance. We noticed that "third" in the context of the libation imagery seems to carry with it the common Greek sense of "third and last." However, the attempt of the principles to give their acts of revenge this finality is everywhere opposed by the doubleness of the *lex talionis*, the iron law of blood for blood, which moves by twos and demands apparently endless pairings. The opposition is clearest in the remarkable dialogue between Clytemnestra and the Chorus as she stands over the bodies of Agamemnon and Clytemnestra. The Chorus's predicts that she will "pay stroke for stroke" (1635/1430; the Greek is a wonderful bit of sound-painting: *tymma tymmati teisai*). Clytemnestra replies by claiming that her deed was a sacrifice to the family Erinys, to whom, as we saw, she allots the third place of the Savior in her private triad. It is the Chorus's insistence on the principle of blood for blood ("he who does will suffer. That is the law," 1798/1564) that prompts Clytemnestra to offer most of her wealth to the Spirit of the house as blood-money, in the vain hope of escaping retribution.

The third libation, however, is not the only image in the *Oresteia* for the idea of coming third and last, performing an act of violence that will bring the violence to an end. The paradigm for this pattern is furnished by another aspect of Zeus, embedded in the story of his rise to power. Aeschylus alludes to this story in the great "Hymn to Zeus" of the *Agamemnon*:

> He who was once great, boundless
> in strength, unappeasable, is now
> unnamed, unsung, as if
> he never was, and he
> who threw him, only to be
> thrown in turn, losing
> the third fall, he
> is gone, too, past and gone.
> But he who sings glad praise
> of Zeus's victory
> strikes to the heart of knowledge.   (189–99/168–75)

In typically cryptic fashion, Aeschylus sketches the succession myth, familiar from Hesiod's *Theogony*: Cronus castrated his father Uranus and succeeded to his power. He in turn was overcome by Zeus after a desperate struggle and confined beneath the earth (cf. *Eumenides*, 749–50/641), along with other gods of the Titan generation. The metaphor for Zeus's victory comes from wrestling; Zeus comes third as the *triak-têr*, the wrestler who wins the third and final fall.[30] The allusion to his predecessors is artfully vague, at least in part because the Chorus's attention is fixed upon the finality of the victory.

The metaphor of the third fall recurs in at various stages of Orestes' struggle. In *Libation Bearers*, Electra asks in a moment of uncertainty:

> What here is well?
> What here is free of evil? Who here
> can wrestle Ruin to a third fall?   (384–86/338–39)

---

30. For a systematic treatment of the metaphor of wrestling in the *Oresteia*, see Poliakoff, "Third Fall."

Orestes' return to Argos ensures at any rate that the match will continue. After Aegisthus has entered the palace, where Orestes waits in ambush, the Chorus comments:

> All by himself the brave Orestes
> will have to wrestle now with two
>   opponents. May
> he win out at last and throw them.   (992–95/866–68)

The next sounds heard are Aegisthus' screams. But victory in this round is not final. In *Eumenides*, Orestes must still wrestle the Erinyes, who claim one of the three falls in their match against him when he admits that he did indeed kill his mother:

> CHORUS LEADER The first fall goes to us. Two more to go.

> ORESTES Or so you boast, but no one's thrown me yet.
>   (687–88/589–90)

And he goes on to win. Through the "associative repetition" of images, Orestes unwittingly imitates Zeus's combat, stands to the house of Atreus as Zeus to the house of Uranus, and comes in to his own as *sôtêr* (savior) and *triaktêr* (winner of the third fall) for his troubled line. Needless to say, the analogy is far from complete: Orestes does not defeat and suppress his father; he avenges him, and only thus is he able to succeed him in Argos. So the history of Orestes' family is both like and unlike that of Zeus's. As unexpected as the connection between Zeus and Orestes may be, it is made more interesting if we recall the link the Erinyes make between their own fate and that of the Titans hidden away in caves beneath the earth. Again, the two situations are both like and unlike. Far from being despised and rendered powerless, the Erinyes will have new honors and bestow great blessings in return. Athena's patient mediation finally persuades them to enter their new home gladly, not in chains as victims of superior might.

In this way, the history of the house of Atreus not only replicates but refines the history of the house of Uranus. The *Agamemnon* depicted Zeus's succession by sheer force—the victory of the *triaktêr*. The end of *Eumenides* shows Zeus triumphing through persuasion ("Zeus who guides / men's speech won out," *Eumenides* 1135–36/973) and proving himself indeed the savior who comes third and last. The great triple movement of the *Oresteia* encompasses two contests, two libations of blood precisely matched; then comes a third, a libation to Zeus Savior, no longer bloody, that brings the cycle of blood for blood to an end at long last. The fundamental significance of the trilogic form in which Aeschylus has given us this story of crime and revenge lies in the sense of closure—and of opening—that comes in this hard-won resolution. The trilogy ends, the world has made a new beginning—and the rest is up to us.

PETER BURIAN

ON THE TRANSLATION

In *The Journal of Cardan*, a meditation on (among other things) the inescapable role of impersonal conventions in the expression of personal experience, J. V. Cunningham makes several comments that illuminate for me the experience of translating the *Oresteia*. In a long passage about the tension in any good work of art between convention, or norms of expectation, and subjective experience, he says, "To be successful in this [artistic] enterprise is to integrate the subjectively primary, the immediate, with the objectively communicable, the mediate, to the alteration of both by their conformation to each other." There's more than one way to apply these remarks to the act of translation. The translator could be thought of as the subjectively primary, the irreducibly unique, the immediate, and the text as the objectively communicable. By passing, so to speak, the original text through his or her very nervous system, the translator is "objectifying" his or her subjectivity even as the text itself, the objective, is colored and modified by the translator's own irreducibly unique relation to it. In a way the text is translating the translator at the same time as the translator is translating the text.

We can also think of the text in its original language as the irreducibly unique or primary, as that which is, by definition, sealed off and isolated, at least to most readers who cannot speak or read that language, just as the new language into which the text is being translated can be thought of as the objectively communicable, the mediate, as that which makes the original accessible to readers.

What is useful in adapting Cunningham's remarks to the act of translation is the recognition of a reciprocal metamorphosis between translator and text, old and new language. In the ideal translation both are transformed by their relation to each other: the strangeness of the original is made familiar enough to be available in a new language, and the new language itself, the familiar, is made strange by capturing the original's exotic glow.

Of course no translation could fully realize this ideal. As the saying goes, much is always lost, and, in the case of the *Oresteia*, the losses are probably too numerous to count. As John Herington has written, "There is much we can, or at least might, do with English. We can make speakable and actable verses; sometimes, with luck, we can even make singable songs; and to that extent we can match the effects of the ancient originals. What we cannot do is to reproduce a dialect which was never spoken outside the theater but was mostly as remote from the *language* of the streets as the tragic masks and costumes were from the *dress* of the streets." The richness and variety of Aeschylus' quantitative meters, his verbal, metaphorical density, and the links in tragic poetry of particular meters with particular modes of discourse and levels of feeling, make the music of the ancient poetry nearly impossible to reproduce in English. I was guided in my metrical choices by a desire to mark off the speech and dialogue passages from those of song and chant. I tried to make the lines as sayable or singable as possible without compromising the stylistic elevation and remoteness of the original from "the language of the streets." To make the lines more sayable to English and American ears, I cultivated an idiomatic though still somewhat formal diction, on the one hand; yet on the other I established the long sentence as a sort of syntactic norm to give some flavor of the rhetorical intensity and strangeness of Aeschylus's tone and style.

For the speeches, dialogue, and stychomythia, I used blank verse, that is, unrhymed iambic pentameter. The Greek iambic trimeter becomes, in English, iambic hexameter, because there are four syllables per iambic foot in Greek but only two syllables per iambic foot in English. Iambic hexameter is notoriously hard to write in English because the line tends to break up either into a pentameter unit with an extra foot attached, or into two units of trimeter, or two of tetrameter and dimeter. The line, as a line of verse, is hard to sustain, and even harder to hear. Blank verse, the staple of English verse drama, provides more flexibility and variety of movement as well as more linear coherence. For the choral odes, I used a looser but still discernible iambic cadence in a variety of lines and stanzaic patterns: for the passages in marching anapests, I composed in eight-line units (sometimes divided into stanzas, sometimes not), in which the pattern of line lengths is 4, 2, 4, 4, 4, 4, 2, 4. By often playing long sentences off against these tetrameter and dimeter lines, I attempted to give some hint of the forward motion created by the Greek anapestic pattern without having to resort to anapestic lines, which in English sound less like Aeschylus and more like Dr. Seuss. For the choral songs, I relied on a wide variety of line lengths (from hexameter to monometer) in which the iambic beat is sometimes more sometimes less emphatic. In general, I tried to find a vital equivalent in English for the Greek meters, so that the very sound and movement of the verse, the dance of syntax through and across the lines, would come alive as English poetry even as the rhythms (the modulations of the iambic norm) insinuate without adhering to the sound and movement of the original Greek.

But there's a more important reason why I chose a finely articulated meter for this translation of the *Oresteia*. Broadly speaking, the trilogy is about justice as a sort of cosmic balance that inevitably and inexorably rights itself both by means of *and* despite the evil deeds of characters who claim to act on justice's behalf. If justice is an eternal norm, then unjust human action is a distortion of or departure from the norm. It is the norm itself, however, that defines the distortion as distortion, that measures the extent of the departure. In a sense, this cosmic justice is never more present or active than when it's being warped by some particular evil act and then invoked to justify that evil. This tension between norm and variation on the metaphysical level is echoed in the tension on the metrical level between the underlying but ever recurring norm of the iambic cadence and the rhythmical variations playing constantly around it, variations that the norm itself makes audible as expressive variations even as the variations modify our perception of that norm, muting it at one moment, emphasizing it the next. Since the Aeschylean universe operates on principles consistent with the principles of metrical composition, I felt that the most inclusive way to do "justice" to the Oresteia was to cast the trilogy in a clear but flexible accentual-syllabic line, a line in which repetition and surprise, norm and variation were constantly in play, constantly resisting and defining one another, each becoming what it is, working its own destiny out, in and through its relation to the other.

I relied primarily on both H. W. Smyth's prose translation, and Hugh Lloyd-Jones's translation and commentary. I also found Garvie's commentary to *The Choerophori* indispensable. But the most important and crucial influence on what I've done has been my collaboration with Peter Burian. This work has been painstakingly slow yet thoroughly exhilarating. It is ironic that throughout this process, while I, the poet, worried over issues of historical precision, Peter, the scholar, consistently urged me to push the translation further away from the prose or prose-like translations and line-by-line commentaries on which I relied. Our poetic and scholarly sensibilities consistently met, clashed, informed, and refreshed each other over matters as small and absolutely crucial as tone, metrical changes, particular metaphors, and line breaks. Our work on the great tapestry scene between Agamemnon and Cly-temnestra is perhaps exemplary of the kind of dymanic this collabora-tive process entailed.

Clytemnestra asks Agamemnon to enter the palace by walking over tapestries her handmaidens have spread before him. Agamemnon at first resists, reminding Clytemnestra that such honors should be re-served only for gods, not men. In Hugh Lloyd-Jones's rendering, Aga-memnon says: "I tell you to honor me with honors human not divine. Apart from footwipers and embroideries the voice of fame resounds."

In my initial version of these lines, Agamemnon says: "Honor me like a man, not like a god. / The voice of fame speaks otherwise and elsewhere, / apart from tapestries." Peter was quick to point out that I had stayed too close to Lloyd-Jones, that all I had done, in effect, was to run a thin electrical current through his version. In the same spirit of fidelity, Peter encouraged me to make the text over into something that was more my own, that more freely engaged a more flexible range of idiom. The result was, I believe, closer in spirit to the ancient text: "Revere me like a man, / not like a god. True fame speaks for itself, / it doesn't need to throw its voice like some/ ventriloquist into mats and tapestries."

Every aspect of this process, from the initial, tentative, often embar-rassing attempts at finding an idiom and a music that's analogous to the poetry of the original, to the hardnosed exchanges with Peter, dur-ing which we tested the poetic and scholarly resilience of every line, of every word and phrase, to the multiple revisions in which, at times, I can hear the haunting and challenging echo of Aeschylus' voice in my voice, has dramatized for me the truth of T. S. Eliot's sense that "good translation is not merely translation, for the translator is giving the original through himself, and finding himself through the original." Eliot describes the duality of voice in good translation. In my work with Peter, the translator's voice, already doubled with that of Aeschy-lus, is doubled again in the interplay of scholar and poet.

ALAN SHAPIRO

AGAMEMNON

CHARACTERS

WATCHMAN of the palace at Argos

CHORUS of old men of Argos

CLYTEMNESTRA Queen of Argos

HERALD of the Argive army

AGAMEMNON King of Argos, leader of the Greek forces at Troy

CASSANDRA Trojan captive, daughter of King Priam and priestess of Apollo

AEGISTHUS cousin of Agamemnon, lover of Clytemnestra

SERVING WOMEN

ARMED ATTENDANTS

*The scene is Argos. The stage building represents the royal palace of Agamemnon.
The* WATCHMAN *appears on the roof of the palace, lies down, and gazes out into
the night.*

WATCHMAN I beg the gods to deliver me at last
from this hard watch I've kept now for a year
upon the palace roof of the Atreidae,
dog-like, snout to paws, night after long
night, studying the congress of the stars,
the unignorable bright potentates
that bring down through the night sky to us here
below, the summer now, and now the winter,
eternal even as they wane and rise.

And here I am still watching for the sign,   10
the torch flame, flickering news from Troy,
the bright flare of her capture. These are my orders
straight from a woman's hope-stiffened heart that urges
like a man.
            My bed is hard with restlessness
by night, and damp with dew by morning, and
just fear (no dream or sleep) comes near it,
fear that I'll fall asleep, that my eyes will be drawn
down into sleep, as if sleep were a sickness
I could cure by singing or humming, as I do,
from time to time some little tune or other,   20
and yet the more I sing, the more I have
to weep for all the troubles of this house
that excellence no longer orders now.
Come soon, deliverance from this weight of watching,
come, fire out of black night flashing toward me,
come, happy news I'm ever watching for.

He sees the beacon.

At last!
Day-shining flare of night, I welcome you,
blazing torch that will kindle the torch-lit dance
we'll dance in Argos for the sake of this!   30
   At last! At last!
I call out loudly to Agammenon's wife
to rise from her soft bed and raise a shout
of triumph all throughout the palace halls
to celebrate that far blaze, if, in truth,
as it proclaims, the city of Troy's been razed.
I'll dance a little dance here as a warm-up.
I'll count as mine my master's lucky roll,
since my watch now rolls a triple six for me.

Well, only let the king come home at last,   40
and I will take his much missed hand in mine.
About the rest, I'm mum. A great ox stands
upon my tongue. But, oh, the house, if it
could only speak, the house would tell a tale
all right. Me, my words are meant for those
who know already what I mean to say;
for those who don't, I don't recall a thing.

     The WATCHMAN *exits from the rear of the roof. The*
    CHORUS *of twelve Argive elders enters the orchestra from*
                                the right side.

CHORUS Ten years since the two kings, Menelaus
     and Agamemnon,
  great sons of Atreus, claimed justice   50
from Priam, and in the double name
of throne and sceptre, by the grace
of Zeus, from this land launched
  a thousand warships
bristling with Argives poised for slaughter.

Radical from the heart came the fierce
  cries, shrill
as vultures who in agonies

of sheer grief for their children wheel
and bank above the robbed nest,   60
keening for the long labor, all
    the fretful guarding
of the young, now entirely destroyed.

And who is it hears among the high
    Gods—Apollo,
maybe, Pan or Zeus? Who hears
the birds wail, the grief-struck
tenants of the upper air
and then, at last, late though it is,
    against the   70
violators aims the Erinys?

Just so Zeus, protector of host and guest,
    has sent the sons
of Atreus against the son
of Priam, for one woman's sake,
one woman claimed by many men,
that many grapple for, knees buckling,
    driven into dust,
and the spears shattered in the flickering rite

before the blazing sacrifice,   80
    for Danaans
and Trojans both. The case stands
where it stands. It rides its irresistible
momentum to the destined end.
    And no smooth tongue
of fire, or liquid poured on the ground,
    or tears will now
dispel the quick edge of sharpened rage.

But we, too old to do our share,
    abandoned by   90
the expedition, wait here at home,
leaning on staves, weak as children,
For the fresh force quickening the heart

diminishes, and the war god
   has deserted,
and old age is a withered leaf

propped on three legs and, no stronger
   than a child, goes faltering
forward in daylight like a dream.

>   *The* CHORUS *turns toward the palace, with hands*
>   *outstretched.*

But you, daughter of Tyndareus,   100
   Queen Clytemnestra,
is there some news? What have you heard
that has persuaded you to send
messengers around the city
to order sacrifices on all
   the altars of
the gods that guard us, the gods we woo —

the sky gods and the gods below,
   gods of the gates
and of the marketplace, are all   110
ablaze with offerings — first here,
then there, the torchlights fan
toward heaven, drawn by the sacred oil's
   frank persuasion,
the softest salve from the deepest chamber.

Reveal to us what you can, or will,
   of these things — be
the healer of this worry that
forebodings darken even as hope
flares from each sacrificial fire,   120
hope beating back the heavy inward
   sprawl of unbearable
sorrow crushing the heart.

Mastery is mine to sing of the good omens   *Strophe* 1
   shown to the two kings

along the road; for still from the irresistible
   god-surge of strength within me
breathes persuasion grown old with my years,
   to sing how the twin thrones joined
as one heart in command of the Achaeans,   130
   the youth of Hellas, driven
with spear and arm to Troy by the ominous wing beat.
   The king of the birds to the kings
of the ships, black eagle and a white behind it,
   in full view, hard by the palace,
by the spear-hand, ripped open a hare
   with her unborn still swelling inside her,
stopped from her last chance ever to escape.
Sing sorrow, sorrow, but let the good prevail.

And when the good seer of the army
      saw it,   *Antistrophe 1*   140
   perceiving the two kings
weren't of one mind, he knew that the Atreidae,
   the leaders of the fleet,
were the ravenous destroyers of the hare,
   and so, interpreting
the sign, he spoke: "This campaign will in time
   overrun Priam's city,
and Fate slaughter all of the thick herds
   of the people before the walls.
But let no god's jealousy before this happens   150
   hurl into darkness the vast bit
of the army meant to curb the mouth of Troy.
   For holy Artemis, in pity,
is furious at her father's flying bloodhounds eating in sacrifice
the trembling hare and all her unripe young.
   The bird feast sickens her.
Sing sorrow, sorrow, but let the good prevail.

Beautiful as you are, and kind to the dew slick *Epode*
   cubs of ferocious lions,   160
ever delightful to the teat-sucking whelps
   of all beasts grazing the fields,

grant nevertheless that the signs mean well—fraught
   though they are with evil.
And blessed Apollo, Healer, keep her from sending
   gale winds against the ships,
holding them fast and long at anchor, exacting
   cold, mute sacrifice,
infection of blood strife and faithlessness. For wrath
   waits, ready to rise again,   170
an ever wakeful keeper of the house,
   unforgetting, secret, never
to be denied its vengence for the child."
   These were the mixed words
Calchas shrieked out as he read the bird omen
   by the wayside
for the royal house, and in harmony with these
sing sorrow, sorrow, but let the good prevail.

Whoever Zeus may be,   *Strophe 2*
if it pleases him by this   180
name to be called, by this
name then I call to him.
I have weighed this with that,
and, pondering everything,
discover nothing now
but Zeus to cast for good
the anxious weight of this
unknowing from my mind.

He who was once great, boundless   *Antistrophe 2*
in strength, unappeasable, is now   190
unnamed, unsung, as if
he never was, and he
who threw him, only to be
thrown in turn, losing
the third fall, he
is gone, too, past and gone.
But he who sings glad praise
of Zeus's victory
strikes to the heart of knowledge:

For it was Zeus who set   *Strophe 3*   200
men on the path to wisdom
when he decreed the fixed
law that suffering
alone shall be their teacher.
Even in sleep pain drips
down through the heart as fear,
all night, as memory.
We learn unwillingly.
From the high bench of the gods
by violence, it seems, grace comes.   210

And then the older of the two   *Antistrophe 3*
kings of the Achaean ships,
not blaming the prophet, let
his spirit blow with the hard
winds of luck that blew
in against him when the host
was held fast in port
at Aulis on the shore
opposite Chalcis, where
the tides crash to and fro,   220
their food stores dwindling,

winds from the Strymon driving against
        them,   *Strophe 4*
battering ships, and bringing hunger,
illness, and a dull, undistracted
leisure to the men who wandered,
neglectful of ship and cable, who
by doing nothing doubled the time
of the delay, the flower of Argos
all wasting away now, withering.
And when the seer cried Artemis was   230
behind this, and showed the kings
a salve more hateful than the storm,
so that the Atreidae threw down
their staves against the ground and wept,

51

the older prince spoke out before them: *Antistrophe 4*
"My fate is heavy either way:
heavy if I refuse to obey,
and heavy too if I kill my child,
pride of my house, staining these father's
hands with streams of maiden blood   240
spilled at the altar. Which way is free
from evil? Can I desert my ships?
Fail all my allies? For in the eyes
of heaven, that they, with too eager passion,
should crave a sacrifice, even
of maiden blood, to still the winds,
is right. May it all be for the best."

And when he secured the yoke-strap   *Strophe 5*
of necessity fast upon him,
yielding his swerving spirit up   250
to a reckless blast, vile and unholy,
from then on he was changed, his will
annealed now to mere ruthlessness.
For men are made bold in the throes
of madness urging evil, in love
with cruelty, courting sure disaster.
And so he steeled himself into
the sacrificer of his daughter
to quicken a war waged for a woman
with an early offering for his ships.   260

And all her prayers, her cries of Father,   *Antistrophe 5*
Father, even her girlhood, counted
for less than nothing to the captains
frenzied for battle, and her father,
after praying, though she clasped
his knees, begged him with all her heart,
ordered his men to lift her like
a goat, face downward, above the altar,
robes falling all around her, and
he had her mouth gagged, the bit yanked   270
roughly, stifling a cry that would
have brought a curse down on the house.

And with her saffron robe streaming   *Strophe 6*
down from her shoulders to the ground,
with pitiful arrows from her eyes
she shot each sacrificer, vivid
as in a picture, wanting to speak,
to call each one by name, for often
at the rich feast in her father's halls
the girl had sung before the men   280
and with the pure voice of a virgin,
at the third libation, lovingly
had given honor to her loving
father's paean for healing luck.

What happened next I neither know   *Antistrophe 6*
nor speak. The art of Calchas does not fail
to reach fulfillment. And Justice tilts
the scales to ensure that suffering
is the only teacher. As for the Future,
you will only learn it when it comes.   290
Till then, leave it alone. Pointless
to grieve before there's reason to.
All will come clear when the dawn comes.

*The doors of the palace open, and during the following
lines* CLYTEMNESTRA *and her attendants enter.*

So, may what comes from this be good,
be as this nearest, only breast-
work of our Apian land might wish.

CHORUS LEADER *(turning to address Clytemnestra)* Obedient to your
power, Clytemnestra,
I've come straight here: when the king's gone it's right
to honor the wife who keeps the throne for him.
Whether or not it's good news you have heard,   300
or offer sacrifice in hope of good news,
I'd like to learn, though I won't grudge your silence.

CLYTEMNESTRA   May good news only, as the saying goes,
be born with the dawn that's born from mother Night.
The joy I have to tell you outruns all hope.
The city of Priam is in Argive hands.

CHORUS LEADER   Have I heard you right? Your words outrun belief.

CLYTEMNESTRA   Achaeans hold Troy now. Is that clear enough?

CHORUS LEADER   Joy overwhelms me, swelling my eyes with tears.

CLYTEMNESTRA   Yes, and your eye attests your loyal heart.   310

CHORUS LEADER   What proof, though, is there? Your trust is based on
what?

CLYTEMNESTRA   Of course I have proof, if no god has fooled me.

CHORUS LEADER   Are you persuaded by some dream you've had?

CLYTEMNESTRA   I give no credence to a sleeping mind.

CHORUS LEADER   Or some vague rumor on which your hope has fed?

CLYTEMNESTRA   Do you scorn my thinking as you would a girl's?

CHORUS LEADER   But when exactly? When was the city taken?

CYLTEMNESTRA   Last night, the mother of the light we see.

CHORUS LEADER   What kind of messenger could come so fast?

CYLTEMNESTRA   Hephaestus, flashing a bright flame down from Ida.   320
Beacon to beacon, the fire ran homeward, first
shining above the island, till another shone
from Ida to the rock of Hermes in Lemnos,
on the crag of Zeus on Athos, then another
went soaring out across the arching sea—
unflagging, restless, torch after powerful torch;
the pine now like a sunrise in the dead

of night flared jubilantly to the watchtower
on Mt. Macistus who, in turn, never delayed,
or gave in heedlessly to sleep, so never   330
failed his duty, as the fiery current
ran on unbroken, signaling from afar,
over the waters of Euripus, to
the sentinels upon Messapion.
And they too answered light with light,
setting a bonfire of gray brushwood blazing.
It never dimmed, the flame, or slowed, for now
it overleaped the plains of the Asopus,
bright as a full moon, to Cithaeron's rock,
where yet another convoy was ignited.   340
And far ahead of them the watchmen sent
the light that they received from far behind,
burning a brighter blaze than was commanded;
light shimmered in the water as it passed
over the Gorgon Face, from shore to shore,
and at the mountain of the wandering goats
forged new links in the chain of fire, the men there
gathering so much kindling together
that a high beard of flame now passed beyond
the headland that looks out across the gulf   350
of Saron till at last it plunged all the way
to Arachne's peak, the watch nearest the city.
From there it swooped down on the royal house,
this flame descendent of the fire of Ida.
This is the course of torchbearers I arranged;
each carrying the relay from the one before,
and everyone victorious from the first
to last. This is the evidence and sign
of the news my husband sends to me from Troy.

CHORUS LEADER Soon, lady, I'll give the gods my thanks.   360
But this tale of yours fills me with so much wonder
that I would have you tell it once again,
through to the end, till all my wonder's gone.

CLYTEMNESTRA The Achaeans hold Troy in their hands today.
The city, I think, rings with a sharp clash

of cries that will not blend. Pour vinegar
and oil in one bowl, and you would say
the two like enemies shun one another;
just so you could tell the conquered from
the conquerors, each crying their different fates   370
in different voices. Here are the Trojans bending
down over the bodies of their husbands,
brothers; children embracing fathers, and fathers
children, all wailing in voices no longer free
for the loved ones they will never hold again.
And here the Achaeans, spurred on by the work
that sends them wandering all night, after
the fighting's over, their hunger now unstrictured,
under no one's orders, foraging
for whatever grub they stumble on,   380
taking what quarters chance puts in their way.
And even now they bed down in the houses
that their spears have taken, free of the frost and dew,
the open sky, sleeping the sleep of men
the gods protect, all night, without a watch.
Now if they only reverence the gods
that keep the city, the shrines and holy temples
of the conquered land, then they, the vanquishers,
might not be vanquished in their turn. Let no
unholy passion overwhelm them, taken   390
by greed to ravage what should be left alone.
For they must still win their safe passage back
all down the homestretch of the double course.
Yet even if the army should return
without offending any god, even
if they don't waken the anger of the dead
for what was done to them, yes, even then
some unseen trouble may still lie in wait.

This is my woman's tale. But may the good
win out completely for all men to see.   400
Of all the blessings whose enjoyment I
now pray for, this one surely is the best.

CHORUS LEADER Well said, lady. Like a wise man.
Since I have heard your evidence, I'm ready
to offer thanks up to the gods. Our joy
today is equal to the pain that made it.

                    CLYTEMNESTRA *exits into the palace.*

CHORUS O Zeus, high one, and kindly Night,
        holder of all
the brightest glories over us,
you who cast down over the towers   410
of Troy the smothering mesh, seamless,
so that in no way could the old
        or young slip free
of the enslaving wide net of

all-conquering destruction. I stand
        in awe of great
Zeus, lord of host and guest, who has
accomplished this, had slowly all
along been bending back his bow
on Alexander, so that his bolt   420
        should not fall short
of the mark nor fly beyond the stars.

Let them speak of a stroke from Zeus;   *Strophe 1*
that much can be traced, at least.
What he decides, he accomplishes.
Impiety to say, as some have,
that no god ever deigns to see
to those who trample underfoot
the grace of things untouchable.
The punishment for reckless daring   430
will be revealed to the descendents
of the ones whose pride blows boundless, whose house
abounds with riches far beyond
what's best. May I have wealth
without the taint of trouble, enough
to satisfy a man of sense.

For no gold's blinding glitter
protects him who heedlessly
kicks the high altar of Justice
over out of sight.   440

Rapt by miserable Persuasion,   *Antistrophe* 1
the irresistible daughter of
Destruction, who decides beforehand, the guilty man's whipped on, there's
no antidote, the evil now
shines candidly its garish light.
Like bad bronze blackening when handled
or rubbed, so he too, when brought to justice
shows the black grain of his being
and, foolish as a boy who runs   450
after a flying bird, brings down
against his city a wasting plague.
His fervent prayers will go unheard
by any god, and a man who deals
with him the gods will destroy as well.
    Such was Paris who
    at the house of the Atreidae
    dishonored his host's table
    by robbing his host's bed.

And she now, leaving in her wake   *Strophe* 2   460
among her people the clatter of shield
and spear, the mustering of troops,
the rigging of ships, and bringing, too,
to Troy a dowry of destruction,
daring a deed undarable,
blithely stepped through the gates. And all
the prophets of the royal house
wailed as they watched her, saying: "Alas,
alas for the great house, for the house
and for the princes! Alas for the lawful   470
love-bed she once slipped eagerly into.
See how he sits alone in such
dishonored silence that he neither
implores nor curses; and how, as he longs

for her so far beyond the sea,
a ghost is mistress of his house.
   The chiselled flow of all
   her flowing forms torments him;
   against the void her eyes
   leave, love is powerless.   480

The pleasure brought by dream, because *Antistrophe 2*
persuasive, only deepens pain.
For when the beloved whom he thinks
is there before him slips through his arms,
the vision vanishes, it wings
its way unfollowably down
the disappearing paths of sleep."
These are the sorrows in the house,
the sorrows at the hearth, yes, these
and worse than these; and everywhere,   490
in every house, for every man
who went out from the land of Hellas,
there is a woman mourning, one
whose grief is too great to be told.
Grief upon grief, it cuts the heart.
   The men they sent away
   they know, but what returns
   into the houses now
   are only urns and ashes.

The war god, broker of bodies, he   *Strophe 3*   500
who loads the scales in the spear clash,
sends in return for loved ones only
a heavy dust from the fires of Troy,
dust bitterly wept for, urns packed tight
with ashes that had once been men.
And they keen over them, praising
this one's skill in battle, that
one's glorious death among the slaughter.
"All this," some mutter to themselves,
"all this for someone else's wife."   510
All through their grief resentment smolders

against the champions of justice,
the sons of Atreus. But they
   in all their beauty fell
   by the walls of Troy, and so
   the victors now lie hidden
   under the ground they conquered.

The citizens are talking and   *Antistrophe* 3
the talk is dangerous, enraged,
resentful, every hurled out curse   520
demands full payment for the loss.
Fearful, I wait to hear what now
goes cloaked in secrecy. For the gods
in their own time see to the ones
who kill so many, and the black
Erinyes deliver, piecemeal,
down into darkness one who thrives
unjustly, grinding his life away
until his luck is turned around,
and he, a shade among the swarming   530
shades that close in all around him,
has no strength left to fight them off.
The price of excessive glory is
excessive peril. The thunderbolt
strikes truly from the eyes of Zeus.
   May I provoke no envy:
   be neither conqueror,
   nor eat my life away
   as captive to another.

Fueled by the running beacon, rumor   *Epode*   540
swiftly spreads throughout the city,
and who can say if it is true
or only some godsent deception?

Who is so green or gullible,
so bereft of sense, to let his heart flare
with each bright message, only to feel
new sorrow when the message changes?

So like a woman's sharp spirit to take
what's hoped for as a proven fact.
The rumor she believes, which spreads   550
like brushfire far and fast, will just
as quickly die away to nothing.

CHORUS LEADER Soon we shall learn about these watched for signals,
the beacon exchange of fire for fire, if they
do tell the truth, or if, the way that dreams do,
this joy-delivering light only deceived us.

                              HERALD *enters from the left.*

I see a herald coming from the shore,
olive twigs shading his forehead, and the dust
upon him, thirsty brother of the mud,
convinces me that what he has to say   560
will not be said by kindling mountain brushwood
up into smoky signals, but by words
we either will rejoice to hear, or else—
but I refuse to think of any "else."
May there be good beyond what just seems good.
And may anyone praying a different prayer for our city
reap in himself the spoils of his own intent.

HERALD Hail, earth of Argos, land of beloved fathers!
In the sunlight of this tenth year I've come home;
so many hopes have foundered, but not this one.   570
This one came through. Not once in all those years
did I imagine I should die at home
in Argos, and be buried here at last,
here in this longed for soil. Hail to my country,
hail to this sun's light, and to you, high
lord of the land, Zeus, and to you, bright king
of Pytho, your shafts no longer raining down
upon us—wasn't it enough, the hatred
you brought against us by Scamander's banks?
Be once again our healer and protector,   580
our lord Apollo! I greet all the gods

61

together, and my patron god, Hermes,
beloved herald, whom all heralds honor,
and all the heroes who escorted us,
may they embrace with all due kindness
the army that the spear has missed. And hail,
too, palace of our kings, this cherished house,
these sacred benches, and deities that greet the sun!
If you have ever welcomed him before,
receive him now, your glad eyes brightening,   590
give him a fitting welcome, for now, at last,
after so many years, he has come home,
Lord Agamemnon, lighting up the darkness
for you and for all who gather here together.
Come give him now the greeting he is owed,
for he has harrowed Troy, broken her soil
up with the just spade of avenging Zeus.
The altars, too, and all the holy shrines
are leveled, and the seed is dying out
from all that land. That's just how heavy the yoke is   600
that he fastened to Troy's neck, the oldest son
of Atreus, our king who now has come,
a man the gods hold dear, a man worthy
of honor far beyond all living men,
for neither Paris nor his city boasts
the crime was greater than the punishment.
Convicted of rape and theft, relinquishing
what he had taken, he brought to total ruin
his father's house, and all his father's land.
Double was the reparation that   610
the sons of Priam paid for one son's deed.

CHORUS LEADER Herald of the Achaean host, all joy to you!

HERALD If the gods wished me to die now, I'd die rejoicing.

CHORUS LEADER Did longing for your homeland so oppress you?

HERALD So much so that my eyes well up with joy.

CHORUS LEADER This ailment then must have been pleasing to you.

. HERALD Sorry? I don't quite follow what you're saying.

CHORUS LEADER Because you pined for those who pined for you.

HERALD Do you mean the people longed for the longing
        army?

CHORUS LEADER So much that my dark spirit often sighed.   620

HERALD What was it set your heart to this black brooding?

CHORUS LEADER Silence has long since been my only safety.

HERALD But why? When the kings left were there some you
        feared?

CHORUS LEADER So much, to quote you, that even death was welcome.

HERALD Yes, well, we won out at last. Of all
      that happened in that long stretch of time, one part
      now, you could say, has turned out well for us,
      another, no; but who beside the gods
      can live his whole life free of any pain?
      For if I were to tell you of the labor   630
      and the hard encampments, the tight quarters
         cramped
      with lousy bedding, what groans we didn't groan
      when even our meager rations weren't doled out;
      and worse things, too, on land, more awful, for
      our beds, if you could call them beds, lay up
      against the ramparts of our enemy,
      and thick mist drizzling from the sky, and dew
      from the meadows seeped over us, into and through
      our fraying clothes, our hair aswarm with vermin;
      And if I were to tell you of the winter,   640
      when the birds died in the snow squalls Ida
      kept swirling down against us day after day;

or of the summer heat when the sea at noon
lay windless, waveless, in a flattened sleep . . .
Why chew this over now? All that for us
is past, and past too for the ones who died,
who now will never care to rise again.
Why must I tell the tale of all the lost,
and why should the living live it through again
in stories, groaning over old misfortune?   650
In my view it is right to say a long
goodbye to the disasters that befell us.
For those of us left from the Argive army,
the gain today weighs heavier on the scale
than all the losses: so as our fame flies
over the sea and land, it's right to boast
in this sun's light: "The Argive host, once Troy
was taken, hung up these spoils to the gods
of Greece, past glories for their shrines."
Whoever hears such words will praise the city   660
and the army's leaders; and the grace of Zeus
that brought these deeds to pass shall be exalted.
My story now is told. And you have heard it.

CHORUS LEADER Yours words have overcome my disbelief,
and I believe them, for a willingness
to learn returns youth wisely to the old.
It's right, though, that Clytemnestra and her house
hear the news first, that I share the wealth with them.

CLYTEMNESTRA *enters from the palace.*

CLYTEMNESTRA I cried in triumph a long time ago,
when the first message of the fire came,   670
telling of Ilium's capture and destruction.
Some, scoffing at me, said, "Just on the strength
of beacons do you think that Troy's been sacked?
So like a woman—to be swept away by feeling."
So I was made to look just like a fool,
as if my mind were cracked. Still, I sacrificed,
and here and there throughout the city, women,
as women do, cried out in jubilation,

and in all the houses of the gods,
lulled softly to rest the sweet flame fed on spice.   680

Why do you need to tell me the full story?
Soon I will hear it from the king himself.
But so I'm ready in every way to greet
my honored husband at last on his return—
for what day can dawn sweeter for a woman
than this one when a god has brought her man
home safe from war, and she unlocks the door—
take to my lord this message: may he come
as quickly as he can, the city's favorite,
and may he find his wife now just as faithful   690
as on the day he left, the watchdog of his house,
loyal to him, and him alone, hateful
to all his enemies, in all things steadfast,
having never once in all these years
destroyed the marriage seal he set upon her.
I know no pleasure from another man,
or scandal-mongering gossip, any more
than I know how to dye bronze. Be assured
that what I've said is overflowing with
the truth, with what a good wife ought to say.   700

CLYTEMNESTRA *exits into the palace.*

CHORUS LEADER She's made a seemly speech indeed for those
who know how to interpret what she says.
But Herald tell me now of Menelaus,
a power much loved in this land: what do you know
of him? Did he, like you, return home safely?

HERALD If I give you a false report, though fair,
the joy you harvest will not last, my friends.

CHORUS LEADER If only truth and good news were the same!
It's hard to hide it when the two are split.

HERALD He vanished utterly from the Achaean host,   710
he and his ships alike. This is the truth.

65

CHORUS LEADER Did he leave Troy before you? Or did a storm,
                       battering you all, sweep him away?

HERALD You've hit the target like a expert marksman
              and briefly spoken sorrows too long to tell.

CHORUS LEADER And in the rumors other voyagers
                       passed on to you, was he alive or dead?

HERALD No one could say for sure, except the sun
              that fosters all life everywhere on earth.

CHORUS LEADER And the storm the gods in anger aimed at the ships,   720
                       how did it come upon them, how did it end?

HERALD It is not right to defile a day's joy
              with a grim tongue that spews bad news. Honor
              due to the gods must be kept separate.
              And when a grim-faced messenger brings bad
              news to the city that the city prayed
              never to hear, news of the army's rout,
              news telling how a single wound tortures
              all of the people in the city, how
              the double-pointed scourge that Ares loves,   730
              destruction's two-tipped goad, the blood-drenched
                       twins,
              has harried many men from many homes—
              yes, when a messenger is weighed down with
              a cargo of woes like these, then it is right
              to sing in tribute to the Eryinyes.
              But when with news, at last, of its salvation
              he comes to a city ready to rejoice—
              how can I muddy good with bad, how tell
              about the storm sent down to the Achaeans,
              breaking against them hard with the wrath of heaven?   740
              For fire and sea, the bitterest enemies,
              only for this campaign, declared a truce,
              and gave sure proof of friendship by destroying
              thoroughly the hapless Argive armanent.

Evil rose up at night from the rising waves.
The Thracian winds rammed ship into ship, and they,
tearing each other open, whirled away
in the whirlwind, in the slant rain, vanishing
like sheep sent scattering by an evil shepherd.
And when the sun rose brightly, we could see   750
how the Aegean bloomed with Achaean corpses,
and everywhere the wreckage of their ships.
But as for us and our ship, some god's hand
had to have held the tiller, and by stealth,
or sweet talk, brought the hull through, unscathed.
And luck, our savior, was our helmsman then,
and sailed us on, so that we neither had
to stay at anchor, pummeled by heaving waves,
nor run aground against some rock-strewn shore.
And having then escaped a floating grave,   760
in the bright daylight, dazed by our own good luck,
we brooded over what we just got through,
the suffering of the fleet, the brutal beating.
And now, if any of them still live, they speak
of us as dead, of course, as we do them.
But may all in the end be well for them!
And as for Menelaus, first and above
all look for his return. If some ray of sun
still shines upon him, alive and flourishing,
by the will of Zeus who has not yet determined   770
that his house be all destroyed, there are still grounds
for hope he will come home again. Know that
in hearing this much you have heard the truth.

                              HERALD *exits to the right.*

CHORUS Who can have named her so   *Strophe* 1
        exactly? Someone now
        invisible whose power
        to see, so long ago,
        what far ahead was fated
        to happen, rightly led
        his tongue, his lips, to name

that spear bride, source of killing,
Helen: destroyer. The name
became her, suited her,
it seemed, as much as the soft
luxuries of the bower
she sailed from, destroyer of ships,
destroyer of men, destroyer
of cities, swept ahead
on the breeze that the giant Zephyrus
sent her. And on her heels,   790
fast on the scent of blood-strife,
many shield-bearing huntsmen
followed the disappearing
track of the oars that had
already beached the ships
on Simois's leaf-thick shores.

Inexorable in its aim,   *Antistrophe* 1
Wrath made for Troy
a marriage whose name is mourning,
and then demanded a reckoning   800
for the guest-table, dishonored,
and the dishonor to Zeus,
from those who sang out
in the bride's honor the song
that fell then to the bride-
groom's kin to sing.
But learning a different tune
in a new key fraught with sorrow,
Priam's city laments,
I think, in her old age,   810
laments and calls it evil,
the marriage Paris made.
She has endured destruction,
death, sheer desolation,
and a season of ceaseless keening
caused by the spilled blood
of all her piteous sons.

A man raised as his own   *Strophe 2*
a lion cub, not weaned
yet, robbed of the breast,   820
gentle in the beginning,
the children's pet, and to
the old a quiet pleasure.
And often in his arms
he rocked it like a baby,
its bright eyes ever turned
to the hand it nuzzled
to ease the belly's hunger.

But as time passed it showed   *Antistrophe 2*
the color of its bloodlines,   830
and in return for all
the kindness it received
from those who fostered it,
it made a bleak, forbidden
feast, cruel slaughter of all
the cattle, the house foul
with blood, since no one could
beat back the agony,
and all about them, near
and far, a chaos of strewn   840
corpses. A priest of death
and ruin, ordained by god,
was nurtured in the house.

And one could say there came at first
        to Troy   *Strophe 3*
    a sweet air
of windless calm, and wealth with all its subtle,
    shimmery
ornaments, a soft arrow of the eyes,
    a love-flower
stinging the heart. But who was it who turned   850
    the marriage bed
to ruin, devised such a bitter consummation?
    Who drove on

to the sons of Priam, in the train of Zeus,
   protector of host
and guest, and spread the deadly poison of
   herself among them?
The poisonous deliverer of tears
   to brides, the Erinys.

An ancient saying, still repeated, still   *Antistrophe 3* 860
   believed, proclaims
that great prosperity, once it has reached full growth,
   turns to begetting,
does not die childless—and from the high
   state of a house's
fortune a quenchless misery is born.
   But I'm alone
in thinking otherwise—an evil act
   is all that fathers
more evil after it: the son follows   870
   in the father's footsteps.
For when a house is just, its children are
   the beauty of its fate.

But, soon or late, at the determined time,   *Strophe 4*
   among the impious
old arrogance gives birth to new, brings forth
   that irresistible,
undefeatable spirit of wild daring
   that is itself
the black face of ruin, so like its parent.   880

Even in hovels, under smoke-smeared
     rafters,   *Antistrophe 4*
   Justice shines
her blessings on the ones who live with honor;
   but from grand halls
made radiant with gold by unclean hands
   she turns away,
her eyes drawn back to what is simply good,
   shunning the power
of gold that flattery makes a fool's gold of,

and, always, all   890
things she is guiding to their determined end.

AGAMEMNON *enters from the left in a horse-drawn car,*
accompanied by CASSANDRA.

And now, my king, scourge of Troy,
    son of Atreus,
how should I greet you, how do you justice
and neither shoot beyond nor fall
short of the mark of what suits you,
what you deserve, for there are now
    so many here
among us who prefer the outward
sheen of truth without the substance,   900
    who flout justice
and groan out with the ones who groan
though no pain grips their heart, and then,
among the joyous, with a show
of joy disguise a joyless face.
    But the good
discerning shepherd of his flock
sees through those eyes that brighten with
    a seeming heart-
felt loyalty that's really just   910
a fawning, watered-down affection.
And when you long ago led forth
your thousand warships for the sake
    of Helen, the picture
I painted in my mind of you
(I will not hide it) was disfigured,
    ugly; I thought
the tiller of your mind steered wildly,
trying by sacrifice to bring
back courage to your dying men.   920
But now with love drawn from the deep
    well of the heart,
I say, "Even the toil is sweet
to those who have at last succeeded."

And you will learn,
in time, by careful scrutiny,
which of your citizens have served
the city justly, which have not.

AGAMEMNON I first greet Argos, as is only just,
and all the gods who dwell here in the land,   930
they who have helped me in my safe return,
and in the justice I at last exacted
from Priam's city. For the gods heard pleas
not from any mouth but from force of arms
and unanimously cast into the urn of blood
their vote of ruin, death, for Ilium;
And though a hand drew near the other urn,
and held out hope, the vessel wasn't filled.
Smoke, even now, lifts up a declaration
of the city's fall, the fiery thunderstorm   940
of its destruction goes on living and
the embers, eating down, dying with the city,
exhale the rich fumes of the city's wealth.
For this we owe the gods our gratitude
and remembrance, since what was arrogantly
plundered has been remorselessly avenged,
and for a woman's sake all of the city
was ground down into dust by the Trojan Horse,
the wooden monster that held the Argive host
till they made their fierce leap when the Pleiads set.   950
Over the wall, the flesh-crazed lion leaped
and gorged himself upon the blood of kings.

I've gone on this long in honor of the gods.
But as for your concerns, know I have listened,
and still remember, and think the same as you—
You have my full support. For few men give
by nature honor to a friend's good fortune
without resenting him. For envy burrows
deep in the heart and doubles the sickening weight
of the disease for the man afflicted with it.   960
Weighed down with sorrows all his own, he groans

72

to see someone who's happy in his life.
I speak from hard experience and, knowing
too well the mirror of friendship, comradeship,
call those who only mimic loyalty
the shadow of a shade. Only Odysseus,
who dragged his feet at first, once harnessed, always
pulled his own weight, and more. Whether alive
or dead, he still deserves our praise and thanks.
As to the rest, what concerns the city   970
and the gods, we shall hold assembly and
talk openly about this. And what is well,
we will make sure that it continues well,
But what needs healing, we will heal,
Yes, one way or another, we'll try to thwart
the pain of the disease by some kind means,
burning, or cutting.
                    I'm going inside now
to my halls, my household, greeting the gods who sent
me far away and brought me back. Since Victory
has been with me, may she stay with me forever.   980

                    CLYTEMNESTRA *enters from the palace followed by*
                    serving women holding crimson tapestries.

CLYTEMNESTRA   Elders of the city, I'm not ashamed
to tell you all how much I love my husband.
As one grows older, all shyness dies away.
I am self-taught in suffering. Let me tell you
how hard my life's been these long years my husband
fought beneath the walls of Troy. How hard
and fearful for a woman, her husband gone,
to sit in her house alone, the helpless prey
of deadly rumors, as messenger follows messenger,
each bearing news worse than the one before,   990
all crying devastation for the house.
And if this man had suffered as many wounds
as rumor after rumor of his wounds
poured through the house, his body now would be
more net than body, pierced with so many holes.

Or if he'd died as often as he did
in the tales I heard, you'd have to say he had
three bodies, like a second Geryon,
and could claim he had received a triple cloak
of earth (a mighty weight of earth above   1000
him, not to mention all the earth below)—
perishing three times, once for every shape.
Distraught from deadly rumours such as these,
I often pulled a noose around my neck
and yanked it tight, and would have hanged myself
had others not discovered me, and seized me
and, though I fought them hard, loosened the knot.
And this is why our son is not here with us,
as he ought to be, Orestes, in whom resides
the joint pledge of our love for one another.   1010
Don't be surprised to hear this. For your friend
and ally, Strophius the Phocian, is
looking after him. He urged this on me
for two reasons: the danger you ran at Troy,
and the way the people's clamorous lawlessness
might topple the council, since it's human nature
to want to trample on the man who's fallen.
That's my justification, quite without deceit.
My tears, those fountains that gushed once, have all
run dry, no drop remains, and my eyes are sore   1020
with weeping from the years of nightlong vigils
for the beacon fires set for you that were never lit.
Year in, year out, my sleep was so thin even
the faintest whirr of a gnat's wing was enough
to wake me from the nightmares in which I saw
you suffer more torments than the time that shared
my sleep could hold. Now, these troubles all
        behind me,
with my heart free of sorrow, I can call
my husband here the watchdog of the fold,
the ship's stout rigging, the high roof's central pillar,   1030
sole son to a father, land appearing
to sailors who despaired of seeing land,
bright rill of water to the bone-dry traveler.
Fairest is the weather dawning after storm.

What joy I have at last to elude all need.
These are the greetings he deserves. Let Envy
not begrudge me what I'm blessed with now, for I
endured much in what went before.
                                          And now,
beloved, step down from your chariot,
don't let your foot touch the ground, my king, the foot   1040
that toppled Troy.
                          Handmaidens, I gave you all
the task of strewing with tapestries the ground
he walks on—why the delay? Let his path be
covered quickly over all with purple,
so Justice now may guide him to the home
he never hoped to see. And for the rest,
a vigilant attention will accomplish
everything down to the smallest detail, justly,
with god's help, exactly as it's been ordained.

AGAMEMNON   Child of Leda, guardian of my house,   1050
in one respect, at least, your speech mirrors
my absence, for you have stretched it out too long.
What praise is due me ought to come from others,
not you. What's more, you shouldn't coddle me
like a woman, or grovel, mouth wide with loud
        hurrahs,
as if I were some barbarian; don't draw down envy
upon my path by strewing it with robes.
Only the gods one honors in this way.
A man who walks on fineries such as these
walks fearfully. Revere me like a man,   1060
not like a god. True fame speaks for itself,
it doesn't need to throw its voice like some
ventriloquist into mats and tapestries.
Not thinking basely is the greatest blessing.
Call only one whose life ends happily
a fortunate man. And I am hopeful
if in all things I can behave like this.

CLYTEMNESTRA   Now tell me this: and say what you truly think.

AGAMEMNON Be sure, I never defile what I truly think.

CLYTEMNESTRA Would you have vowed to do this, in fear of the gods?   1070

AGAMEMNON If someone, who knew I should, ordained it, yes.

CLYTEMNESTRA And if Priam had crushed you, what would he have
                    done?

AGAMEMNON He would have trampled on fineries, I think.

CLYTEMNESTRA Don't worry then what other men might say.

AGAMEMNON Yet people talk, and what they say has power.

CLYTEMNESTRA A life unenvied is an unenviable life.

AGAMEMNON And it's unwomanly to love contention.

CLYTEMNESTRA It is fitting for the fortunate to give way.

AGAMEMNON Does winning this fight mean so much to you?

CLYEMNESTRA The gain is all yours, if you let me win.   1080

AGAMEMNON Well, if you want it so badly—someone quick
            loosen these boots that slave on my behalf,
            And as I trample down the god's purples,
            let no envy strike me from a far-off eye.
            Shameful to squander with my feet like this
            the house's substance, ruining such wealth,
            such woven opulence that silver bought.
            But enough of this.

                              (*pointing to* CASSANDRA)

                    Now bring this stranger in,
            and treat her well. From far away the gods
            look favorably upon a gentle master.   1090

For none bows by his own will to the yoke
of slavery. And she came with me as
the choicest flower of abundant treasure,
the army's gift.
                    But since I let my will
be bent to yours in this, my feet will trample
a purple path into my palace halls.

CLYTEMNESTRA There is a sea—and who will drain it dry?—
breeding wave after wave of purple, precious
as silver, inexhaustibly renewed,
in which to dye our garments. Yes, a wealth   1100
of such stuffs by the Gods' grace, king,
is amply here for us: the palace knows
no lack. And anyway I would have trampled
down even more robes than these, as many, then,
as needed, all along, had an oracle
enjoined it, when all I thought of, dreamed of, was
some scheme to get you safely home to me,
body and soul. For while the root still lives,
the leaves bring cool shade to the house again,
uncurling, spreading, against the dogstar's heat.   1110
So coming back to hearth and home, you bring
a summer's warmth to us in wintertime.
And when Zeus presses wine from the green grape,
there is at once a coolness in the house
as the sovereign strolls again all through the palace.

AGAMEMNON *exits into the palace.*

Zeus, Zeus, sovereign accomplisher,
accomplish this my prayer; and may what you
are ready now to do be all your care.

The serving women remove the tapestries and
CLYTEMNESTRA *exits into the palace after them.*

CHORUS Why, even now, this fear, ever   *Strophe 1*
unriddable, hovering   1120

77

near my heart's foreseeing? And why
this, too, this prophecy
that sings unrecompensed, unasked for,
like a perplexing dream
that no hope seated deep within
my heart can ever banish?
Time has grown old since the day they threw
the cables down onto the sand
when the army in its ships
first came to Ilium.   1130

And I have seen him, with my own eyes,   *Antistrophe* 1
    seen him return, myself
the witness, and yet still within me,
    self-inspired, chants
the dirge the lyre shuns, dirge of the Erinys,
    dirge chanted by a mind
bereft of hope, hope's cherished strength.
    And it is not for nothing
that everywhere inside me speaks
    the same disquiet, that   1140
my heart swirls and eddies with
    a sense of justice soon
to be fulfilled, though I still pray
    what I expect may fall
away, and fail to reach fulfillment.

Well-being, at its utmost, chafes against   *Strophe* 2
what bounds it. For disease, its neighbor,
leans hard on the wall they share,
and a man's fate, however straight
the course he's steering, even so   1150
can strike a hidden reef and founder.
But if trembling foresight jettisons
some part in proper measure of all
the wealth a man possesses, then
the whole house overwhelmed with excess
will not sink, nor the hull plunge under.
The great gift of Zeus springs

abundant from the ploughed earth
each year to stave off the plague of famine.

But the lifeblood of a man, once spilled   *Antistrophe 2*   1160
before him, blackens the ground, and who
can enchant it back into his body?
Even Asclepius, skilled in the art
of bringing dead men back to life,
Zeus struck down as a warning to us.
And if one fate didn't block another
from going beyond its god-set bounds,
my heart would overbrim my tongue,
and pour out all of its worst forebodings.
But, as things stand, it only mutters   1170
in darkness, grief-struck, hopeless
of drawing any good at all
from these fires burning through my mind.

CLYTEMNESTRA *enters from the palace.*

CLYTEMNESTRA You go inside now. I'm talking to you, Cassandra.
Zeus, not unkindly, has determined you
should share the lustral water of our house,
standing where all the slaves crowd the altar
of the god who guards the house's wealth—come
         down
now from the chariot and don't be proud.
Why even Heracles, they say, was once   1180
sold into slavery and had to stomach
the gruel all slaves must eat. And yet if bad
luck such as this should fall to anyone,
there's still good cause for gratitude at having
masters whose wealth is old as well as great;
for those who have reaped a harvest that exceeds
their hopes are cruel to slaves beyond all measure.
Here with us you'll be treated as custom warrants.

CHORUS LEADER She's talking plainly to you, and she expects an
         answer.

79

Caught in your tangled fate, you should obey   1190
her if you can, though maybe now you can't.

CLYTEMNESTRA Well, if she's capable of doing any better
than twittering like a swallow, barbarian-style,
then she must understand me, and what I say
will soon convince her that she'd best obey.

CHORUS LEADER Go with her. What she orders you to do
is best, as things stand. Get down from your seat
there in the chariot, and do what she says.

CLYTEMNESTRA I don't have time to dawdle here by the door;
the cattle are standing ready for sacrifice   1200
by the central hearth stone, victims for the fire,
a joy we never hoped to have. And you,
if you would do what I say, make no delay;
but if the meaning of my words eludes
your understanding, then, instead of speech,
give me a sign with your barbarian hand.

CHORUS LEADER I think the stranger needs someone to help
her understand. She's like a captured beast.

CLYTEMNESTRA Yes, she is crazed and given over to
the wayward bidding of a wild mind—   1210
too freshly torn off from her conquered city,
she hasn't learned yet how to bear the bridle
until her rearing up and bucking has all
been broken in a bloody foam. I won't
waste more words on her, to be insulted so.

CLYTEMNESTRA *exits into the palace.*

CHORUS LEADER I can't be angry, though; I pity her.
Poor girl, come on, give up your seat there
on the carriage and, bowing to what cannot be
resisted, yield to this new yoke that's yours.

> CASSANDRA, *who has become more and more restless*
> *through the preceding dialogue, suddenly leaps from*
> *Agamemnon's chariot. She is wearing insignia that*
> *identify her as priestess of Apollo.*

CASSANDRA   OTOTOTOI POPOI DA   *Kommos*   1220
Apollo! My Apollo!

CHORUS LEADER   Why do you cry woe to Loxias?
He is no god to come to with a dirge.

CASSANDRA   OTOTOTOI POPOI DA
Apollo! My Apollo!

CHORUS LEADER   Once more she calls out darkly to the god
who will not stand for any lamentation.

CASSANDRA   Apollo! My Apollo!
God of the roadside, my destroyer,
For you again, this second time,   1230
with what ease have destroyed me.

CHORUS LEADER   She is about to prophesy her sorrows—
the god's gift stays with her, though she's enslaved.

CASSANDRA   Apollo! My Apollo!
God of the roadside, my destroyer!
Ah, where have you brought me?
Where? What house is this?

CHORUS LEADER   To the house of Atreus. If you don't see this,
then I'll tell it to you, and you'll know.

CASSANDRA   No, to a house that hates the gods,   1240
one that knows by heart stories of kin
murdering kin, a slaughterhouse
for men, a killing floor drenched in blood.

CHORUS LEADER   The stranger has the keen scent of a hound,
fast on a trail of blood, and blood she'll find.

CASSANDRA *(pointing to the door of the palace)*   Yes, there they
             are—the witnesses
             I trust—look, the children are wailing
             for their own slaughter, for the flesh
             their uncle roasted, and their father ate.

CHORUS LEADER Yes, your prophetic fame had reached our ears;   1250
             But we are not in search of prophets here.

CASSANDRA O god! What is she plotting now?
             What devastation? What huge evil
             lurks in this house, unbearable
             for friends, beyond all remedy,
             and no help anywhere in sight?

CHORUS LEADER These prophesies I can't quite follow; but
             the others, yes, the city's all abuzz with them.

CASSANDRA Ah, will you see this through, wretch?
             Your own husband who shares your bed?   1260
             You wash him, soothe him, in the bath.
             How can I tell it through to the end?
             It will be done soon. She stretches out
             first one hand, then another, toward him.

CHORUS LEADER I've lost the trail. Her riddles set me down
             bewildered in a dark of oracles.

CASSANDRA Ah! Ah! what apparition shimmers
             into view? It's a net of Hades, yes,
             but a net that is his bedmate, that shares
             the guilt of murder. Let the fierce   1270
             gang ravenous for the house shout out
             in joy over this butchery,
             this sacrifice stoning will avenge.

CHORUS What Erinys is this you call
             to raise her howl over the house?
             Your words drain all joy from me, and
             pale blood seeps back drop

by drop into my heart, dripping
as from a spear gash, when the rays
of life darken as it sets,   1280
and death is near, and hurrying.

CASSANDRA Ah! Look! There! Keep the bull away
from the cow! She has caught him in the robe,
and with the slick device of her black
horn strikes, and he slumps in the roiling water.
Bright blade flashing treachery,
I tell you, in the murderous bath.

CHORUS Though I can boast of no great skill
in judging oracles, this seems
even to me like something evil.   1290
And yet from oracles what good
is ever sent to men? Through veils
of evil, all that these wordy arts
bring to their listeners is fear.

CASSANDRA Oh, oh! The misery of
my miserable fate! For it is my own
affliction that I speak of now;
a new cup has been all spilled out.
Where have you brought me, unlucky one?
For what except to share your death.   1300

CHORUS Your mind is cracked, seized by a god,
and over your own fate you chant
as harshly as, with shattered heart,
each day, each moment of each day,
the tawny nightingale would grieve
throughout a life so dense with sorrow
she could not keep from crying out
alas, lamenting Itys, Itys.

CASSANDRA Oh but to end life as a tuneful,
full-throated nightingale! For the gods   1310
gave her a winged body and
a life immune from wailing, while

83

for me, what waits is only death
by cutting with the sharpened spear.

CHORUS   From where, in the grip of what god
do you suffer seizure after useless
seizure, and with foreboding cries
and sharp notes fashion songs of fear?
From where, and how, have you marked out
the boundaries along this evil-   1320
omened path of prophecy?

CASSANDRA   O, the love bed of Paris, deadly
to his loved ones! O Scamander,
river of home! Long time ago,
ah me! I flourished by your waters.
But soon, by other streams, beside
Cocytus and the endless shores
of Acheron in the world below
I'll wander, wailing my prophesies.

CHORUS   Why have you said this, and so plainly?   1330
Even a child could understand.
Again I'm pierced by the sharp stroke
of your cruel fate, by your shrill cries
of sorrow it shatters me to hear.

CASSANDRA   O sorrow, sorrow of my city,
its utter devastation! O
the sacrifices that my father
made before the walls, reckless
slaughter of our grazing herds.
But what good came of it? There was   1340
no cure to save the city from what
it had to suffer. Now I, too, am
on fire; I, too, will crash to the ground.

CHORUS   These phrases go with those before:
some destroying spirit swoops down,

a dead weight, on you and compells
this dirge, these tears shot through with death,
toward what end I do not know.

CASSANDRA Well, then, my prophecies won't peek again
like some shy newlywed from behind a veil.   1350
No, they will blow clear as a fresh wind
toward sunrise, and surge like a wave against the new
light with a woe far greater than its shining.
No riddles anymore. You be my witness,
running beside me stride by stride as I
sniff out the track of crimes done long ago!
The choir that sings as one, yet sings its tunes
discordantly and only brings on discord,
can't leave this house. Yes, soused on human blood
to utter recklessness, a home-brewed,   1360
rioting band of Eryinyes is dwelling there,
not easily driven out. And what they sing of,
as they carouse from room to room, is that
first mayhem, that ancestral sin, as one
by one each spits on a brother's bed
that brought destruction to its defiler.
Have I shot wide of the mark or have I hit it
like a master archer? Or am I some cut-purse prophet,
a babbler careening from door to door?
On your oath, bear witness that I know   1370
the legacies of crime within this house.

CHORUS LEADER How could an oath, however truly taken,
cure anything? Still it astounds me that,
though bred beyond the seas, you can describe
what happened here, as if you had been present.

CASSANDRA The seer Apollo charged me with this power.

CHORUS LEADER Fired with longing for you, though a god?

CASSANDRA I was ashamed to speak of this before.

CHORUS LEADER While fortune lasts, we have that luxury.

CASSANDRA He grappled hard, breathing his gift upon me.   1380

CHORUS LEADER And did it get as far as making children?

CASSANDRA I gave my word to Loxias, then I broke it.

CHORUS LEADER Were you already in the grip of the god's art?

CASSANDRA Yes, even then I told Troy all its sorrows.

CHORUS LEADER How then did you escape Apollo's anger?

CASSANDRA For my offense, I can never be believed.

CHORUS LEADER And yet to us what you foretell seems true.

CASSANDRA Ah! Ah! O misery! The terrible labor of
true prophecy whirls me around, and I
am shaken to the core with darkening preludes!   1390
Look there, do you see them? Can't you see them,
        there
by the house, so young, like hovering dream shapes,
        children
killed by the very ones they loved, their hands
full of the gore of their own flesh, the vitals,
all the dripping inner parts—I see
them holding out that pitiful weight
of meat their father ate. Because of this,
I tell you, there is one who plots revenge,
a skulking lion panting in the bed,
poised in the house, alas, against the lord's   1400
return, my lord, since I now bear the yoke
of slavery. And the great leader of the fleet,
who leveled Ilium, is unaware
of how the bitch tongue fawns, licking his hand,
her ears drawn back in welcome—yet she
will strike and slaughter with a treacherous stroke.

Such shameless daring: the female kills the male.
She is—what is she? by what name should I call
that rabid beast?—two-headed serpent, or
a Scylla coiled in the rocks, the sailors' scourge,   1410
implacable raging hell-hag breathing war
against her own! And how she trumpeted
her triumph, she who stops at nothing, as if
she herself turned the tide of battle, even while
she seemed to revel in his safe return.
And whether you believe all this or not,
it doesn't matter. What is coming, comes.
And soon you will yourself stand here and say,
in pity, that my words were all too true.

CHORUS LEADER Thyestes feeding on his children's flesh   1420
I understand, and tremble at, and am seized
by terror as I hear it told in truth,
not in deceiving images. But when
I hear the rest I lose the path and stray.

CASSANDRA I say you'll look on Agamemnon butchered.

CHORUS LEADER Hush these bad omens, lull your mouth to sleep.

CASSANDRA And yet there is no healing for these words.

CHORUS LEADER No, if it's meant to be—but may it not.

CASSANDRA And while you pray, they're busy with the killing.

CHORUS LEADER Who is the man who crafts this hateful crime?   1430

CASSANDRA How it eludes you, the track of my prophecies.

CHORUS LEADER I don't see the device of the designer.

CASSANDRA Yet I am all too fluent in the Greek tongue.

CHORUS LEADER So are the Pythian oracles, but hard to follow.

CASSANDRA POPOI! It's like fire, and it burns down over me!
Wolf-god Apollo, ah, OTOTOTOI POPOI!
This lioness on two feet, she who beds
down with the wolf when the noble lion's gone,
will tear me open, wretched as I am;
and as if brewing a black enchantment, she   1440
will mix my quittance in the cup as well,
and as she sharpens the blade edge for the man,
brag that he will pay for bringing me here.
So why do I go on mocking myself, keeping
this staff, these fillets at my neck, these trappings
of prophecy?

(breaking her ceremonial staff)

At least I can destroy you
before my own destruction!

(throwing down her garlands)

Off now, go,
fall to your utter ruin! And as you fall
feel how I pay you back! Make someone else,
other than me, more richly destitute!   1450

(tearing off her priestly robe)

But see, Apollo, yes, his very self,
is stripping me of my prophetic garb,
he who looked on while I was jeered at,
despite my vestments, ridiculed by friends
turned enemies, mocked surely, though in vain,
but like some homeless drifter people taunt
with "beggar," "vagrant," "starveling," I bore it all.
And the prophet has destroyed his prophetess,
escorting me off to meet my fate right here,
right now. No, not my father's altar now   1460
awaits me, but a chopping block my blood
will redden soon, a steaming libation for the dead.

Yet my death, too, will not go unavenged
by heaven, for there will come, in turn, another
to avenge us, a son who will slay his mother, requite
his father; an exile and a wanderer, hounded
far from this land, he will return to put
the capstone on this killing of his kin.
For the gods have sworn a great oath that the stroke
that brings his father down will bring him home.   1470
Why am I keening so, since I have seen
Ilium's city go the way it has gone,
and seen, too, those that made the city suffer
suffer in turn such judgment from the gods.
My turn to die now—I will dare to go.
I call this door I'll enter, the door of Hades.
I pray the readied stroke is swift, and that,
without a struggle as my blood spurts forth
in easy death, I simply close my eyes.

CHORUS LEADER O woman, greatly pitied and greatly wise,   1480
you have spoken much. But if you truly know
your fate, how can you go up to the altar
more calmly than a cow the god escorts.

CASSANDRA Friends, there's no escaping what's here already.

CHORUS LEADER The less time one has, the more one clings to it.

CASSANDRA The day is here; what use is there in fleeing?

CHORUS LEADER Know yours is a brave heart, to endure like this.

CASSANDRA No happy person's ever praised this way.

CHORUS LEADER But a death that brings glory is a blessing.

CASSANDRA Alas for you, father, and for your high-born children!   1490

> CASSANDRA *steps toward the palace,*
> *then starts back in horror.*

CHORUS LEADER What is it? What fear stops you, pulls you back?

CASSANDRA PHEU! PHEU!

CHORUS LEADER Why this cry? Some terror in your mind?

CASSANDRA The stench of slaughter. The whole house reeks of
               blood.

CHORUS LEADER How so? That's just the smell of sacrifice at the
               hearth.

CASSANDRA It's like the exhalation from a tomb.

CHORUS LEADER You smell no Syrian incense in this house.

CASSANDRA And yet I go into the house to mourn
            my fate and Agamemnon's. Enough for living!

                    (*Again she turns suddenly from the
                            doors of the palace.*)

            Ah, my friends, I won't cry any cry   1500
            of terror like a panicky small bird
            caught in a bush. But after I am dead,
            you be my witnesses when a woman is killed
            for me, a woman, and a man dies,
            in turn, for a man unlucky in his wife.
            I ask this as your guest bound now for death.

CHORUS LEADER Poor girl, I pity you for this end you see.

CASSANDRA I want to say one more thing, and not just sing
            my own lament: I pray to the sun's last shining
            that my avengers will exact a bloody   1510
            payment from my foes, for my murder too,
            for murdering a slave, a harmless prey.
            Alas for men and their vicissitudes!
            In good times one may say they're like a shadow;

in bad times like a picture that a wet sponge
brushing against it lightly wipes away.
And these I pity so much more than those.

CASSANDRA *exits resolutely through the palace door.*

CHORUS Whoever says, that is enough
     good fortune? No one
would ever bar it from the high   1520
halls, leaning hard against the door
and saying, "Never come here again."
So to this man the blessed ones
     allowed that he
should capture Priam's city and

come home weighed down with honor
     from all the gods.
But if he must atone for blood
his forebears shed and by dying for
the dead ordain that others die,   1530
in turn, for him, who, among mortals,
     can boast of being
born to a fate immune from harm?

Cries are heard from within the palace.

AGAMEMNON Oh! I've been struck, and the stroke is deep and
     deadly!

CHORUS LEADER Shh! Who cries he's been stabbed and gravely
     wounded?

AGAMEMNON Oh! yet again I'm dealt a second blow!

CHORUS LEADER Hear how the king cries. I think the deed's been
     done.
Let's ask ourselves what we can safely do.

CHORUS MEMBER 1 Here's my idea—we summon everyone
     throughout the city, and we storm the palace.   1540

CHORUS MEMBER 2 I say we break in now, at once, and seize them
     with the blood still dripping from their swords.

CHORUS MEMBER 3 Yes, I agree with that, and vote for acting
     right away, this is no time for dithering.

CHORUS MEMBER 4 It's all too clear from what they've done already
     they're planning to be tyrants of the city.

CHORUS MEMBER 5 Yes, while we waste time, they're alert and busy,
     trampling down the fair name of delay.

CHORUS MEMBER 6 I can't tell which plan would be best. Someone
     readier to act could think this through more clearly.   1550

CHORUS MEMBER 7 I feel the same way, for I don't see how
     by mere words we can raise the dead again.

CHORUS MEMBER 8 Yet just to save our skins shall we bow down
     and kneel to those who have defiled the house?

CHORUS MEMBER 9 No, anything but that; better to die,
     for death's an easier fate than tyranny.

CHORUS MEMBER 10 Yet can we say for sure, just on the strength
     of hearing the king cry out, that he's been killed?

CHORUS MEMBER 11 We need to know the facts before deciding
     what we should do; guessing isn't knowing.   1560

CHORUS LEADER All my votes go for this course: that we learn
     for certain how it is with Atreus' son.

          The palace doors open, and CLYTEMNESTRA
     is seen standing over the dead bodies of AGAMEMNON,
          wrapped in a crimson-colored robe, and of
               CASSANDRA *at his side.*

CLYTEMNESTRA I tailored much of what I said before
     to suit the time. But now I feel no shame

to say I lied. For how else could I give
my enemies (even when they're disguised
as friends) what they deserve, how else set up
the nets of harm so high no one can over-
leap them? I have been brooding for a long time
over this strife bred from an ancient feud,   1570
and now at long last it's come; and here I stand,
here where I cut him down, my aim achieved.
My aim was so exact—I won't deny it—
that he could not outrun death, or fend it off
once I ensnared him in a deadly wealth
of robes, escapeless as a fishing net;
I struck him twice, and while he cried two cries,
his legs gave way. Then soon as he was down,
I struck him yet again, and the third stroke fell
as a votive offering for the Zeus   1580
below the ground, the savior of the dead.
And so he fell, and panted his life away,
and breathing out a last sharp gale of blood
he drenched me in the dark red showering gore,
and I rejoiced in it, rejoiced no less
than all the plants rejoice in Zeus-given
rainfalls at the birthtime of the buds.
Now things stand where they stand, my honored lords
of Argos; if you will rejoice, rejoice;
but know I revel in it. If it were ever   1590
right to pour libations joyfully
over a corpse, it would be more than just
to pour them over him! Such is the curse-
brimmed mixing bowl he filled up in the house
and, now he's home, has swilled down to the dregs.

CHORUS LEADER   Your tongue astounds us, how you can swagger so
                over the butchered body of your husband.

CLYTEMNESTRA   You test me as if I were a witless woman;
               but I speak with undaunted heart to you
               who know, and it's all one, whether you praise   1600
               or blame me. This is Agamemnon, my husband,

now a corpse, the work of this right hand,
a righteous workman. There's nothing more to say.

CHORUS   Woman, what foul food nursed
deep in the earth, or what drink drawn
from the flowing sea could you have tasted
to take on yourself so horrible
a sacrifice and the people's curse?
You have cast away, you have cut away,
and away will you go from the city, under   1610
the full weight of the city's hate.

CLYTEMNESTRA   Now I'm the one you would condemn, would cast
out from the city, with the people's hate
and loud curses all about me, though before,
back then, not one of you said anything
against this man, when easily, with no
compunction, as if it were a beast he slaughtered,
plucked from a wide field swarming with fattened
      sheep,
he slit his own child's throat—the child I carried,
in pain bore, loved—and all for what, to charm   1620
the winds of Thrace? Why wasn't he the one
you banished from the land in punishment
for that foul act? Yet now you hear my case
and all at once you are a ruthless judge.
Well, I warn you: threaten me all you want,
and know that if you bring me down in a
fair fight I am prepared to let you rule;
But if by god's will it goes otherwise,
you'll learn discretion, though you learn it late.

CHORUS   Your daring's outrageous, your words   1630
too cocksure; your mind is maddened
by your blood-dripping deed; your eyes
shine, speckled with blood. Your honor gone,
deserted by your friends, you'll pay
at last for this, pay stroke for stroke.

CLYTEMNESTRA   Listen: there's more—hear my solemn oath!
I swear by Justice, completed for my child,
by Ruin, by the blood-crazed Erinys,
to whom I sacrificed this man that my hopes
will never pace the corridors of fear   1640
so long as the fire on my hearth is kindled
and kept bright by Aegisthus, just as loyal
to me as ever; for in him I have
a shield of trust nothing can ever shatter.
So here he lies, the one who wronged me, playboy
of each Chryseis beneath the walls of Troy!
And here beside him is his spear bride
and fortune-teller, the trusty sybll of his bed,
whore of the sailors' benches! Now they receive
the honor they deserve. For here he lies,   1650
and here, too, after singing her last lament
like a swan, she lies beside him as his lover.
For me, she only brought an added relish,
a saucy garnish to my bed's delight.

CHORUS   Ah! If only quickly,   *Kommos / Strophe 1*
painlessly, free of the drawn
out vigil of the sickbed,
some fate would bring to us now
the sleep no one will wake from
ever, now that he is slain,   1660
the best of guardians
who in a woman's name
suffered so much, and by
a woman's hand is dead.

Ah, ah, crazed Helen—   *Mesode 1*
you who alone brought down
so many, those numberless many
lives beneath Troy—now you've crowned yourself
with this last, this perfect garland through the
willing of the blood not washed away.   1670
So it was true, all along
unshakable strife dwelled in the house,
a husband's misery.

CLYTEMNESTRA Don't pray for death because of this!
Don't train your wrath
on Helen, making her alone
the man-destroyer, the one who turned
so many Danaan lives to wreckage,
and made a grief no one can master.

CHORUS Furious Spirit, you swoop   *Antistrophe 1*   1680
down on the house, on the two
heirs of Tantalus, and
hold sway through women
of like mind, and through them
press such crushing
weight against my heart!
You stand over the body
like a famished crow
and caw in brash abandon
your harsh discordant cry.   1690

CLYTEMNESTRA You talk sense now by calling on
the triple-glutted
Spirit of this race! He feeds the lust
for blood deep in the belly, the thirst
to lap it up, and before the old
wound heals, the fresh pus swells and oozes.

CHORUS The Spirit whose praises you sing   *Strophe 2*
has the house gripped tight;
truly his wrath is heavy.
Ah, you praise sheer evil   1700
that fills its maw with misfortune,
feeds and is never full.
Woe, unassuagable woe,
and all through the will of Zeus,
source of all that is,
doer of all that is done,
for without Zeus what
is accomplished among us? What
of all these things is void
of god, not god-ordained?   1710

O my king, my king,   *Refrain*
how will I weep for you?
How can I speak
love from a shattered heart?
You lie snared in this spider's web,
heaving your last breath in a sacrilege of death,
alas, like a cowering slave,
killed by the treacherous two-
edged blade your own wife's
hand brought down.   1720

CLYTEMNESTRA You're so sure that this was my work.
            No longer see
     me as the wife of Agamemnon!
     Masquerading in the image
     of this dead man's mate, the old and
     pitiless avenger of Atreus,
         in a manic feast,
     cut him down as payment, a grown
     man butchered for the butchered young.

CHORUS That you yourself aren't stained   *Antistrophe 2*   1730
     with slaughter—who would bear witness?
     How? How can it be?
     But an avenger from
     his father's time may well
     have led you on. And down
     through streams of kindred blood
     black havoc pushes his way
     to where he will exact
     atonement for the caked gore
     of the devoured children.   1740

O my king, my king,   *Refrain*
how will I weep for you?
How can I speak
love from a shattered heart?
You lie snared in this spider's web,
heaving away your last breath in a sacrilege of death
alas, on a slavish bed,

killed by the treacherous two-
edged blade your own wife's
hand brought down.   1750

CLYTEMNESTRA There's nothing slavish, I think, in this
  man's death. Didn't
he wreck the house with his treachery?
But now what he has suffered is
as just as it was unjust what
he did to her, my child, the child
 he fathered, the child
I weep for still, Iphigenia.
Let him not preen and boast in Hades,
 now that he's paid   1760
by dying for what he began.

CHORUS Thoughts scatter every which way and
  I don't   *Strophe 3*
 know where to turn while the house teeters.
I fear the rain that pummels down on it,
 hard rain of blood against the house,
rain beating every moment even harder,
 thicker, long past the drizzling
first drops. The hand of fate is honing bright
 the blade of justice on another
whetstone for another act of harm.   1770

O earth, earth, if only you had drawn
  me down   *Mesode 2*
into your sunlessness before I saw
 my lord inhabiting the slick
bed of the bath, hemmed by its silver walls!
 Who now will bury him? Who now sing
his lament? Will it be you? Will you now dare
 to do this, to strike your husband down
and then bewail him, and for his shade unjustly
 pay ill-favored favor
for his great deeds? Who sob-choked at the tomb   1780
 will praise him, the godlike man,
sorrowing in all honesty of heart?

CLYTEMNESTRA This duty is no concern of yours.
    He fell by my hand,
by my hand he died, and by my hand
he will be buried, and nobody
in the house will weep. But she, his daughter,
Iphigenia, happily,
    as is only right,
will meet her father at the swift ford   1790
of sorrows and cast her shadowy arms
    around him and kiss
him just as sweetly as he deserves.

CHORUS Charge answers charge, and who can weigh
    them, sift   *Antistrophe 3*
right from wrong? The ravager
is ravaged, the slayer slain. But it abides,
while Zeus on his throne abides,
that he who does will suffer. That is law.
Who will cast out the seed of curses
from the house? The race is grafted to ruin.   1800

CLYTEMNESTRA Now you have found a true prophecy.
    But as for me
I gladly give my promise to
the Spirit of the clan that I
will bear all this, however hard,
if only he will go from the house
    for good and grind
some other family out by bringing
kin to murder kin. However
    small my share   1810
of wealth may be, I'll be content
if I have rid our halls at last
of our frenzied killing of each other.

                  AEGISTHUS *enters from the left with*
                  a group of armed followers.

AEGISTHUS O kind light of the day of final justice,
now I can say at last that the gods on high

are avengers of mankind, and do look down
upon earth's misery, now that I see,
to my delight, this man who's lying here,
robed in the tangling mesh of the Erinyes,
paying for what his father's hand devised.   1820
For Atreus, the ruler of this land,
and this man's father, drove my father from
the city and his very home — Thyestes,
my father and (to say it clearly) his
own brother who challenged his right to rule alone.
And when he came back as a suppliant
there at his own hearth, poor Thyestes found
a kind of safety, since he wasn't killed
and didn't stain his birthplace with his blood.
But Atreus, this slain man's godless father,   1830
an eager but not a loving host, with feigned
good cheer, as if in celebration of
a festive day, served my father up
a feast of his own children's flesh. First he chopped
the toes and fingers off, and over them
he lay the flesh in strips, and placed the dish
before my father as he sat apart.
And lifting to his lips unknowingly
this or that indistinguishable part,
he ate his family's ruin, as you can see.   1840
And when he realized what a horrid deed
he'd done, he screamed and fell back, and spewing
        out
the chewed up meat, called down on Pelops' clan
a fate as horrible, kicking the table over
to double now the fierceness of his curse:
may all the race be overthrown and fall.
From causes such as these this man lies slain
before you, and I'm the one who planned this murder,
planned it with Justice, for he drove us out,
my wretched father and myself, his third born,   1850
still just a swaddled babe. But when I grew
to manhood, Justice brought me back again,
and from afar I carefully laid my hand

upon this man, stitching together, piece
by fatal piece, the whole cloth of this plan.
So even death would please me, now that I've caught
him here at last in the net that Justice spread.

CHORUS LEADER Aegisthus, to gloat amid such misery
like this is something I would never do.
Do you claim you slew this man deliberately,   1860
that you alone conceived, directed every
step of this awful murder? I tell you
in no uncertain terms that on the day
when justice is meted out you won't escape
the people's curse, and stoning at their hands.

AEGISTHUS And do you dare to speak to me like this,
you who are seated at the lowest oar
when those on the bench above you steer the ship?
Old as you are, you'll learn how hard it is
at your age to be taught discretion. Bonds,   1870
and whips, and hunger with its gnawing pains
are wonderfully efficient healers and
instructors of delinquent minds. Can you
have eyes and fail to see this? Don't kick
against the pricks, or strike them and be struck.

CHORUS LEADER You woman! So while you kept yourself safe
here in the house, and waited for the men to return
from battle, you befouled the husband's bed,
and plotted death for the supreme commander?

AEGISTHUS From these words, too, will spring a race of tears.   1880
The tongue of Orpheus was not a tongue
like yours, for he led all things in the wake
of his voice's ecstasy, while you, who stir
up rage, puling and barking, will be led
away and, once broken, will be tame enough.

CHORUS LEADER So you would be our tyrant here in Argos,
               you who had plotted death against this man
               yet wouldn't do the deed with your own hand?

AEGISTHUS Yes, the entrapment was the woman's role,
           of course, since I, old enemy of the house,   1890
           was suspect. But with his wealth now I will try
           to rule the citizens, and anyone
           who fights me I will bridle with a strong bit,
           and he will be no pampered trace-horse fed
           on barley! But the bitter intimate
           of darkness, hunger, will see him yield at last.

CHORUS LEADER A coward to the life—why didn't you kill
               this man yourself instead of leaving it
               to her, a woman, to do your dirty work,
               defiling the country and its gods?   1900
               Oh, does Orestes see the light somewhere?
               Will he come home at last, with fortune's favor,
               and slay these two with overpowering strength?

AEGISTHUS If that's the way you're going to act and speak,
           you'll learn your lesson soon, and learn it well.

CHORUS LEADER Come, friends, to arms, our work is here at hand.

AEGISTHUS *(to his guards)*
           Come, men, hands on hilts, ready your swords!

CHORUS LEADER Ready for death, my hand too clasps the hilt.

AEGISTHUS We cheer the omen: death for yourself you mean.
           We'll take our chance, whatever it may be.   1910

                    AEGISTHUS' *guards move toward the Chorus, but stop*
                                    on CLYTEMNESTRA's *words*

CLYTEMNESTRA No, love, enough, let's work no further damage.
              Already there is too much here to reap,
              a sad abundance. There's been enough destruction;

let's have no more bloodshed. Go honored elders,
go to your homes, and yield to destiny
before you suffer; what we had to do
we did—all you can do now is accept it.
If we could say "enough" to troubles, we
would be content, for we have all been kicked
by the Spirit's hard hoof. Such is a woman's   1920
saying, if any thinks it fit to listen.

AEGISTHUS Can I stand by, though, while these old men pelt me
with flowers from their wayward tongues, hurling
words that tempt their fate and miss the mark
of sense, and self-restraint, as they abuse their master?

CHORUS LEADER Argives will never fawn on an evil man.

AEGISTHUS If not today, then soon, you'll feel my vengeance.

CHORUS LEADER Not if the Spirit brings Orestes home.

AEGISTHUS I know myself how exiles feed on hope.

CHORUS LEADER Gorge and grow fat, soil justice, since you can.   1930

AEGISTHUS Oh you will pay in time for this arrogance.

CHORUS LEADER Brag on bravely, like a cock by his hen.

CLYTEMNESTRA Ignore these harmless barkings; you and I
will rule the house, and set it all in order.

> CLYTEMNESTRA and AEGISTHUS *enter the palace, fol-*
> *lowed by the guards; the* CHORUS *exits to the right.*

LIBATION BEARERS

CHARACTERS

ORESTES son of Agamemnon and Clytemnestra

ELECTRA their daughter

CHORUS of captive slaves, serving women of Clytemnestra

ORESTES' NURSE named Cilissa

AEGISTHUS lover of Clytemnestra, now ruler of Argos

SLAVE of the household of Aegisthus and Clytemnestra

CLYTEMNESTRA Queen of Argos

PYLADES son of Strophius of Phocis, companion of Orestes

The scene is in Argos, at the grave of Agamemnon. ORESTES *and* PYLADES *enter from the left.*

ORESTES   Hermes of the dark earth, go-between,
overseer of my father's power,
rescue me, fight by my side, I pray, for I've
come home at last to this land, come home from
    exile.

On this grave mound I cry to my father: Father
your son is calling you, listen to me.

I cut this strand of hair now for Inachus,
the stream that gave me life, a second strand
for the death I couldn't mourn: I wasn't here
to grieve, my father, when you died, I couldn't   10
reach my hand out when they bore you away.

ELECTRA *enters with the* CHORUS *of slave-women
carrying libations to offer at the tomb.*

What's this? a band of women coming this way,
in black robes that the bright day seems to blacken
even more? What bad luck could it mean?
Has some new blow been struck against the house?
Or is it, could it be, they bring libations
in my father's honor in the hope
of quelling the angers stirring underground?
That must be it, of course, for isn't this
Electra, my own sister, who approaches?   20
Wan, wasted, wraith-like, her grief declares her.
Zeus, Zeus, let me avenge my father's death,
and when I do, fight gladly at my side!

Pylades, let's hide here out of the way
so I can learn exactly what this band
of black-robed women might be praying for.

ORESTES *and* PYLADES *hide.*

CHORUS   I was sent marching from the house   *Strophe 1*
with these libations, my every step
timed to the sharp blows of my own hands,
my cheeks scarred like a field my nails   30
rake red with fresh furrows, anguish
my only heart's food, and the only
sound the sound of my garments ripping
as in grief I rip them down,
down to the breast I can't not strike
for all countless sorrows in my life,
a life no laughter ever nears.

For terror, dream-seer of the house,   *Antistrophe 1*
with every hair-end bristling, every
sleeping breath now breathing wrath,   40
cried out its shrill cry in the dead
of night, deep from within the palace,
falling heavy on the women's quarters,
and those who unriddle dreams declared
with the gods' assurance that the dead,
stirring in anger underground,
are mad with bloodlust for the killers.

Yet with ill-favored favors such   *Strophe 2*
   as these, to fend off harm—
O Mother Earth!—she sends me here,   50
   the godless woman. But I
am terrified to speak the words
   she's ordered me to speak.
Can it be scrubbed away, the spilled
   blood pooling on the ground?
O hearth blaze of misery!
   O great house in shambles!

Sheer sunlessness that all men hate
   now covers the house
in shadow, since the Lord's been killed.   60

Antistrophe 2

And the sovereign awe no one could tame,
   fight off, defeat in war,
awe that resounded everywhere,
   in every mind and heart,
has slipped away. Now there is only fear.
   For though men idolize
success as if it were a god,
   no, more than a god, Justice
finds a way to right the balance.
   And some it swoops down on   70
suddenly in the bright day;
   some it waits for, tensing,
in the twilit shadows, and some it grabs
   only after black night
has wrapped them in its useless shroud.

Because the earth that nurses life   Strophe 3
   has drunk up so much blood,
the gore clots, vengefully hard,
   and will not wash away.
And sickness worms its slow and ever   80
   painful course all through
the guilty's person's heart and brain
   till he is nothing but
his own disease.

Defile a virgin's bed, and there's   Antistrophe 3
   no remedy at all.
And even if all streams could flow
   into a single stream
to clean the blood-stained hand, the hand
   would stay red while the blood   90
reddened the water.

For me, however, since the gods cinched tight   Epode
   the noose the army

strung around my city, and led me from
   my father's house
here into slavery, what can I do
   now but obey
the ones who rule me, whether right or wrong,
   obey and beat
down all the hatred that I feel — obey   100
   and weep discretely,
behind my sleeve, for my masters' pointless fate,
   while grief in secret freezes
deep in the heart.

ELECTRA You servant women who keep the house in order,
since you've come here to pray with me, tell me,
please, what you think I ought to do. What should
I say as I pour these sad libations? What words
would cheer my father, what prayer would move him?
     Do
I say they come from a devoted wife?   110
From her? My mother? That I'll never do,
and yet I don't know what else to say when I pour
this honeyed stream out on my father's tomb.
Should I speak the customary prayer?
"Bring equal honors to the ones who bring
these honors to you." What a worthy gift
for all their evil! Or do I say nothing,
just stand here in disgraceful silence, the way
my father died, and pour these offerings out
for the dirt to drink, and then just go away   120
like someone dumping filth, some foul remains,
my head averted as I toss the cup aside?
Help me decide what I should do, my friends.
We hoard a common hatred in this house.
Don't be afraid to tell me what you think,
One destiny is waiting for us all,
free man and slave alike. So tell me, please,
tell me if you've a better idea than mine.

CHORUS LEADER Your father's grave is like an altar to me.
I'll tell you my deepest feeling, just as you wish.   130

ELECTRA Say it, with all your reverence for his tomb.

CHORUS LEADER Say blessings as you pour for all your friends.

ELECTRA And who among us should I call my friends?

CHORUS LEADER You first, and then whoever hates Aegisthus.

ELECTRA You mean I'm praying for the two of us?

CHORUS LEADER You know. You don't need me to spell it out.

ELECTRA Who else can we consider on our side?

CHORUS LEADER Remember Orestes, though he's far away.

ELECTRA Orestes, yes. That's excellent advice.

CHORUS LEADER As for the murderers, be sure to say—   140

ELECTRA Say what? I'm just a child, untutored. Tell me—

CHORUS LEADER A prayer for some god or man to come against
                                  them—

ELECTRA Someone to judge them, or do justice to them?

CHORUS LEADER Say it straight: someone who'll take a life for a life.

ELECTRA Can it be right for me to ask this of the gods?

CHORUS LEADER Can it be wrong to pay back hurt with hurt?

ELECTRA Greatest herald of the world above,
and world below, O Hermes of the dark
earth, help me now. Call on the nether spirits,
the spirits who oversee my father's house,   150
to hear my prayers. Call on the very earth
herself who gives birth to all things, nurtures them,

makes them strong, then gathers what she grows
back to herself again. And as I sprinkle
these waters on the dead, I call on my father,
"Pity me, pity our own Orestes, make him
a saving light you kindle in the house.
For we are homeless now, mere drifters, sold
by our mother who bartered us away—for that
husband of hers, Aegisthus, who helped her kill you.   160
I live a slave's life, and Orestes, stripped
of all he owns and cast out, lives in exile,
while they are wallowing in the bed of wealth
your labors bought.
                              O Father, can you hear me
praying? Bring Orestes home to us
somehow or other, and me—make me more chaste,
more decent than my mother, and in all
I do more pure. This is my prayer for us.
And for our enemies, I pray that someone soon
appear and avenge you, father, killing the killers,   170
exacting justice, paying life for life.
So in the middle of my prayer for good
I place this prayer for evil against them both.
For us, however, draw up your blessing now
into the daylight, graced by the gods, by the earth,
and by justice that brings triumph in the end."
These are my prayers.
                              Over them I pour libations.
And now it's your task to wreathe them with the
          flowers
of mourning, to sing praises of the dead.

CHORUS   Shed tears, let them fall and die   180
          for our dead lord,
     into this earthwork of the good
          that turns back
     evil, the spreading stain of evil,
          now that we've poured
     these offerings out. Hear me O lord!
          O majesty hear

from your muffled shade-enshrouded spirit!
   OTOTOTOI, oh
let him come soon, poised with spear,   190
   savior of the house,
the Sythian bow bent backward in his hands
   to scatter arrows,
or a very Ares, hilt held firm
   and bright blade flashing!

ELECTRA My father has received what the earth has swallowed.

                (noticing a lock of hair on the tomb)

What's this? There's news here, friends. Come here
   and see.

CHORUS LEADER Tell me. My heart is leaping up with fear.

ELECTRA A lock of hair—see? see it?—on the grave.

CHORUS LEADER Is it a man's or a slim-figured girl's?   200

ELECTRA Easy enough—anyone can tell.

CHORUS LEADER Then tell me. Let the old learn from the young.

ELECTRA Nobody could have cut this hair but me.

CHORUS LEADER Yes, those who should've cut theirs are his foes.

ELECTRA And from the look of it it almost seems—

CHORUS LEADER Like whose? Whose hair? That's what I want to know.

ELECTRA Like mine. It's hard to tell the two apart.

CHORUS LEADER You mean Orestes? A secret gift from him?

ELECTRA It does seem like his. Who else could it be from?

CHORUS LEADER How in the world could he have risked returning? 210

ELECTRA He sent it here in honor of his father.

CHORUS LEADER Then there's even more to grieve for, if you're right:
to think he won't step foot here on this ground again.

ELECTRA Yes, the salt-surge of bitter bile sweeps up
through me too, it's as if a rough blade splits me
open;
tears flood wildly from my eyes that cry
their own thirst for this lock of hair I see.
For how can I think that anybody else,
one of the townsmen, has such hair? Could she
have cut it, the murderer herself, my mother 220
who is no mother to her children now?
And yet for me to say without a doubt
that it's the precious gift from him, the most
beloved of all men to me, Orestes. . . .
No, no, hope's playing me for a fool. If only
this lock could speak to me like a messenger,
so that my mind was not turned, pushed, pulled
this way and that, and knew once and for all
that I should throw it away, that it was cut
from a head I hate, or that it came from him, 230
my brother, and could sorrow with me here,
an honor to our father and his grave.

We call on the gods who know well the storms
that batter us like sailors lost at sea.
And if we manage to come through somehow
to safety, from a small seed there just might spring
a giant tree.

(noticing the footprints)

Wait! Look! Another sign,
these footprints, see? They match each other, and
they look like mine. Two outlines, yes, two pairs,

his own and a companion's. The heel and the   240
ball of the foot, and the arch, too, when I step
beside them are the same as mine. Oh god,
this is unbearable, I don't know what to think!

ORESTES *and* PYLADES *emerge from their hiding place.*

ORESTES As you now thank the gods for the fulfillment
of old prayers, pray for success in what's to come.

ELECTRA Give thanks? Why? What have I won yet from the
            gods?

ORESTES The sight of him you've prayed so long to see.

ELECTRA And how would you know who that man might be?

ORESTES I know Orestes, what he means to you.

ELECTRA And how is that an answer to my prayer?   250

ORESTES Because I'm here, the one who loves you most.

ELECTRA What is this, stranger? Some snare to catch me in?

ORESTES If so, then I ensnare myself as well.

ELECTRA Can you be laughing at me, at my pain?

ORESTES At my own pain only, if I laugh at yours.

ELECTRA Are you really—can I use the name—Orestes?

ORESTES You see me in the flesh and don't believe it,
yet when you saw the hair I cut in mourning
and traced my footprints, your heart jumped,
        quickened,
and you believed it was my very self you saw.   260
Here lay this lock back on the spot I cut it from,

you'll see how well it matches yours. And here,
look at this piece of weaving your own hand made,
striking the loom, the beasts you pictured there!
Now careful! Don't forget yourself with joy!
Our closest kin will kill us if they get the chance!

ELECTRA   Most precious darling of your father's house,
hope of saving seed, much missed, long wept for,
trust in your strength and you'll win your father's
          house
once more.
                    Bright face in which four faces shine: 270
face of the only father I now have;
face of the only mother I can love
now that I justly hate the face of the one
who bore me; loved face of the sister, too,
so cruelly slaughtered, and, finally, trusted face
of a true brother who coming back to me
gives back my self-respect.
                              May Power and Justice
and Zeus the third, supreme, be on your side!

ORESTES   Zeus, Zeus, guide everything we do. Look down
on the unfledged orphans of a father eagle—   280
killed in the viper's coils, her tangling lust;
see the unfathered nestlings starve, too young,
too weak to hunt, to bring the prey back to the nest
the way their father did. See us, my sister
Electra and me, two young ones robbed of our father,
cast from the house, and if you let us die,
the nestlings of a father who never failed
to sacrifice to you, who gave you all
the honors you deserved, who'll pay you homage
with holy banquets opulent as his?   290
Allow the eagle's brood to perish and
no one will ever trust your signs again.
Allow the royal family, like a great tree,
to wither away, and it won't serve your ox-
strewn altars on the days of sacrifice.

Look after it, and you can raise the house
back up to greatness, though it lies low now.

CHORUS LEADER Hush, children, hush! You're the last to save
your father's hearth. Someone might hear you,
        someone
who loves to gossip and might repeat all this   300
to those in power. O may we see it soon:
their bodies hissing as the black pitch burns!

ORESTES Apollo's great oracle never will betray me,
ordering me to see this dangerous work
through to the end; with sharp cries it described
the arctic ills that would blow in against me,
piercing my warm heart, if I failed to kill
my father's killers—spurred to a savage rage
by being stripped of all I own—to kill the two
of them as they killed him, in the same way.   310
He said that otherwise I'd pay the debt
with my own life, and it would be a life
of torment that would never end. He revealed
to me all the secrets of the angry spirits
below the earth, the plagues they send against us:
he spoke of sores and chilblains, boils that swell
on the flesh, and burst, and eat away at it
till all the living tissue's been devoured,
and over the oozing puss a white fur forms.
He warned of how the Erinyes would come   320
to torture me in other ways as well,
worse ways, and all brought to fulfillment by
my father's blood. For he can still see me, my father,
even in darkness his glance is following me.
No one can escape that upward shower
of arrows from the spirits underground,
aimed by the murdered kin who call for vengence;
it'll drive you mad, night terrors you can't explain
or shake won't let you sleep, and you'll be harried,
hounded from the city, a brass goad   330
lashing your flesh raw. Men like that

have no part whatsoever in the festal bowl,
in the drink poured out in friendship. Their father's
     wrath
comes upon them, unseen, out of nowhere,
and drives them far away from any altar,
so that shunned everywhere, with every door
closed shut against them, honorless and loveless,
they die a slow, cruel, painful, withering death.
Why shouldn't I trust oracles like these?
But even if I didn't, I'd still be driven   340
to carry out the work, for many longings
move inside me toward a single end:
the god's commands aside, there's the great sorrow
I feel for my father, and the way the loss
of my possessions eats away at me;
and then there's also seeing how the people
of the most glorious city in the world,
the very ones, so proud in heart, who brought
Troy to her knees, now kneel before a pair
of women—for he has a woman's heart,   350
and, if he doesn't, we'll know it soon enough.

CHORUS Now, far reaching Fates, let it   *Kommos*
            be done, accomplished
        now, by the will of Zeus, even
        as Justice takes the path she takes,
        crying aloud for what is owed her:
        "Let words spit out in hate be paid
            with words spit back.
        Let blow atone for deadly blow.
            Who does shall suffer."   360
        So it goes, the story three times old.

ORESTES Father, unhappy father, what   *Strophe 1*
             word can I say, what act perform
         to reach you like a favoring breeze
         where your deep bed holds you fast?
         The sphere of darkness stands opposed
         to the sphere of light. And yet the lament

that glorifies brings joy, they say,
to the sons of Atreus who lie
here before the palace door.   370

CHORUS   My son, the dead man's spirit is not
                      devoured   *Strophe 2*
              by the fierce jaws of the fire;
          no, later on he lets his anger spring—
              the dead man is lamented,
          the avenger brought to light, and the just dirge
              owed to forebears and
          to fathers, stirred to action on every side,
              hunts the guilty down.

ELECTRA So hear us, father, as each one   *Antistrophe 1*
              cries out for grief with many tears: 380
          now we, your children, sing this dirge
          for you over your tomb, this tomb
          that's welcomed us as suppliants
          as well as exiles. What here is well?
          What here is free of evil? Who here
          can wrestle Ruin to a third fall?

CHORUS   But, bad as things are now, a god,
              if he wills it,
          still could alter all our crying
          to a happier key, and then   390
          instead of keening by a grave
          a paean in the royal halls
              will usher in the much-
          loved mixing bowl full of new wine.

ORESTES If only, father, you had fallen   *Strophe 3*
          at Troy, run through by a Lycian spear,
          you would have left behind such glory
          in your halls! You would have left your children
          such a life that men would turn
          to look at them with admiration   400
          when they walked; you would have had

119

a great tomb heaped with earth, a burden
easier for your house to bear.

CHORUS A friend to the friends who died at Troy
            so nobly,   *Antistrophe 2*
        greatest and most revered
    among the heroes there below the earth,
        and minister to those
    who rule the dark! For while he lived he was
        a king of kings, a king
    over those who wield in their hands the awesome   410
        power that destiny
    allots, the sceptre citizens obey.

ELECTRA Not even there at Troy, father,   *Antistrophe 3*
        would I have wanted you to die
    and be buried by Scamander's stream
    with all the other spear-fallen host!
    If only your killers could have been killed
    first, killed in the same way; if only—
    far off in Argos—we could have heard
    the news of their death, and never had   420
    to know the troubles we know now!

CHORUS These things you speak of, child, are better
        than gold, yes, better even
    than the great good fortune of
        the blessed race that lives
    beyond the North Wind's lair. For there's
        no end to wishing, you
    can do it all you want. But come now—
        since the sharp snap of this
    double lash strikes home—our side   430
        already has its allies
    underground, and the hateful ones
        in power have unclean hands.
    Time now for you to act, his children.

ORESTES This pierces straight through my ear like an
                        arrow: *Strophe 4*
                Zeus, Zeus, you deliver late-
                avenging devastation from below
                to the over bold and reckless, and
                it will be paid at last, one way
                or other, the debt that's owed to parents!   440

CHORUS May it be mine—the shrill triumphant cry   *Strophe 5*
                when the man at last
        is cut down, and the woman slaughtered! Why?
                Why do I try to hide
        what nevertheless flies around and sets
                my mind to shaking; so
        my heart's prow pushes hard against the wrath
                that blows back in against it
        just as hard, heavy with all my hatred.

ELECTRA And when will Zeus, all flourishing,   *Antistrophe 4*   450
                bring his hand against them and at last
                cut off their heads? Now let a pledge
                be given to this land: I demand
                justice from the unjust! Hear me,
                Earth, and the dark lords underground!

CHORUS But it is law: that each and every
                drop of blood spilled
        on the ground calls out for more blood spilled.
        Yes, murder cries for the Erinys
        who rise from those who died before   460
        to bring ruin on the heels of ruin.

ORESTES POPOI! Look at us now, you powers   *Strophe 6*
                who rule the underworld, great curses
                of the dead, behold the last remnants
                of the Atreidae, dishonored, helpless,
                cast out from their very home!
                Where, Zeus, which way can we now turn?

121

CHORUS My heart in its turn is shaken as I listen *Antistrophe 5*
    to this keening
so that I'm stripped of hope, my mind all darkened   470
    by these words I hear;
but when its strength renews, hope brightens till,
    all pain eclipsed,
it suddenly shines before me in its sheer
    loveliness.

ELECTRA What do we say to prevail? Must we   *Antistrophe 6*
    tell over again the miseries
we've suffered, yes, at our mother's hands?
Fawn all she wants, it won't soothe us,
not ever. For from all she's done   480
my heart's become a savage wolf,
enraged, and unappeasable.

CHORUS I mourned him the way a Mede would do,
    I beat   *Strophe 7*
    my breast in the strains
of a wailing woman from Susa. You would have seen
    wave after wave
of blows that my outstretched arms, my two hands,
    striking
    now, now clutching,
brought down from above, from high above, blood
    splattering
    all over me   490
as my battered head resounded with the sound
    of pummeling.

ELECTRA IO! IO! Cruel, shameless mother!   *Strophe 8*
Cruel burial, burying a king
without his people, without the dirges
he deserved, a husband you had
the heart to bury and not mourn!

ORESTES Everything in your story tells dishonor.   *Strophe 9*
    But I swear
with god's help, with the help of my own hand,   500

         she'll pay for having
done this to my father. Just let me kill her,
   then I can die myself!

CHORUS And he was mutilated, did you know
          that?   *Antistrophe* 9
      Cut apart,
disfigured? And she who buried him like that
    did it to make
his death impossible for you to bear.
    Your father died
horribly dishonored. Now you know.   510

ELECTRA You speak about my father's death; that
          day,   *Antistrophe* 7
     though, I was far
away, humiliated and ignored,
    locked up inside
a dark room like a vicious dog, crying
    great streams of grief
as readily as someone else might laugh. Hear this
    and write it in your hearts!

CHORUS Write it, and let the words pierce   *Antistrophe* 8
through your ears to where your mind is quiet.   520
All we have told you up to now
is true; now burn to know the rest!
Keep your heart clenched tight
with anger for the fight ahead!

ORESTES Father, listen to me! Come to your loved
          ones!   *Strophe* 10

ELECTRA Drenched in tears, I join my voice to his!

CHORUS Our band cries out, too, in one voice:
      come back into the light!
Hear us now my king, side with us
    against our enemies!   530

ORESTES Now force will battle force, and justice
                  justice!   *Antistrophe* 10

ELECTRA O gods, answer my just prayer with your justice!

CHORUS I shiver as I listen to them pray!
                  Though it's waited long,
            let what is destined find its way at last
                  to those who pray for it.

            O trouble bred in the bloodlines,   *Strophe* 11
                  and blood-drenched stroke
            striking discordant notes of ruin!
                  Ah, the festering wound,   540
            the hideous cry, unbearable,
                  the pain no one can soothe!

            Only the house and no one else   *Antistrophe* 11
                  outside it, none, can stop
            the festering; only the children can
                  do this bloody healing!
            We sing this harsh hymn to the gods
                  alive below the earth!

            So hear us now, you blessed ones
                  beneath the ground,   550
            answer our prayer, and send the strength
            we need to bring triumph to these children.

ORESTES Father, who didn't die a king's death, grant me
                  the power to be the ruler of your house!

ELECTRA I, too, father, ask your help in this:
                  to cut Aegisthus down, and get away.

ORESTES This way you'll have the customary feasts;
                  If not, among the richly feted dead,
                  as offerings steam and burn, you'll get no honor.

ELECTRA And I will bring wine from my cherished store,   560
         my bridal wine from your house, father, and
         of all tombs I will honor your tomb most.

ORESTES O earth send up my father to guide the battle!

ELECTRA Persephone, grant us his transfigured power!

ORESTES Remember the bath in which they killed you, Father!

ELECTRA Remember the strange net they cast to catch you in!

ORESTES You were tangled in chains forged by no blacksmith,
         father!

ELECTRA Shrouds made to shame you as they held you fast!

ORESTES Don't these taunts rouse you to awaken, father?

ELECTRA Now won't you lift up your beloved head?   570

ORESTES Send Justice to fight beside us, those you love,
         or help us catch them in the same grip—if
         you'd like to see the ones who threw you thrown.

ELECTRA Father, hear this too, my final cry:
         Look at your nestlings at your tomb, and pity
         our sorrows, the woman's and the man's alike.

ORESTES Don't wipe away the seed of Pelops. So long
         as we live, you yourself can't die, though dead.
         For children keep a man's fame living on
         after he dies; like corks that buoy a net up,   580
         saving the flaxen meshes from the deep.

ELECTRA Hear us! This keening has been all for you.
         You save yourself by honoring our words.

CHORUS LEADER Surely, no one would reproach you for a drawn-
         out prayer that compensates the tomb for tears

125

unwept before. But now it's time to act,
since you're poised to act. It's time to test your luck.

ORESTES And we will, too. But I don't think it's straying
from our path to ask why she would send libations.
What made her try, too late, to cure a sickness   590
long past curing? Such puny solace now
to send to the dead who hates her. What was she
    thinking?
The gift is so much less than the offense.
Besides, a man who pours out everything
he owns to make atonement for a life
he's taken only throws his wealth away,
or so the saying goes. So tell me why
she's acted as she has. I want to know.

CHORUS LEADER I know, child, I was there. I saw her shaken
by dreams and terrors that would wake her, keep her   600
wandering through the house all night. That's why
the godless woman sent libations here.

ORESTES Do you know the dream? Can you tell me what it
    was?

CHORUS LEADER She gave birth to a serpent. That's what she said.

ORESTES What happened next? How did her story end?

CHORUS LEADER She swaddled it like a baby, and laid it down.

ORESTES What did it want to eat, the little monster?

CHORUS LEADER She gave it, in the dream, her breast to suck.

ORESTES How could the creature's fangs not tear her nipple?

CHORUS LEADER They did. And the beast sucked blood in with the
    milk.   610

ORESTES No idle dream, this vision means a man.

CHORUS LEADER And scared to death she screamed herself awake,
and torches the dark had blinded now were kindled
everywhere through the palace for the queen's sake.
It was after that she sent libations here,
hoping some sharp cure could cut away her panic.

ORESTES Then, I pray to the dark earth, and to my father's
tomb,
that this dream will be realized for me.
Look how I read it, and make it all cohere:
for if the snake slipped out of her, as I did,   620
and lay there swaddled in the very bands
that swaddled me, and opened its big jaws
wide for the nipple I was nurtured from,
and sucked in blood clots with the loving milk,
and she cried out in terror, then it follows:
just as she gave suck to this violent sign,
by violence she'll die. I am the serpent.
I am her killer. That's what this dream predicts.

CHORUS LEADER I make your reading of this dream my own.
Let it come true! Now tell your friends just what   630
their roles are, what they should and shouldn't do.

ORESTES The plan is simple: Electra, you go inside,
and keep what we've arranged to do a secret,
so that the ones who killed an honored lord
by treachery, will by treachery be killed,
caught in the tangling net they caught him in,
just as lord Apollo promised, seer
who's never said a false word in the past.
Disguised as a stranger, with a traveler's gear,
I'll go to the gate of the courtyard with Pylades,   640
this man here — a friend and ally to the house.
And we'll both speak a Parnassian accent,
copying the way they talk in Phocis.
Then if no one at the door should welcome us
(given the curse that's blackening the house)
we'll wait till people passing back and forth
before the gate have noticed us, and start

to wonder why we're kept outside and say,
"Why does Aegisthus shut the suppliant out,
if he's at home, and knows the man's been waiting?"   650
Now listen: if I step through the courtyard gates
and find him on my father's throne, or if
when he returns he meets me face-to-face,
before he can so much as look away,
before he can say, "Where do you come from,
      stranger?"
know that I'll strike him dead, ensnare him here
along the quick edge of my sword. And then
the Erinys, full as she is with blood, will still
guzzle his unmixed gore, poured out in a third,
a last libation.
                      You, Electra, keep   660
a careful eye on everything inside,
so everything turns out the way we want;
and all you women, watch what you say: say nothing
when nothing need be said, and only speak
what words will suit our plans. As for the rest,
I pray to the god who stands there at the door,
watch over me, and guide this sword of mine
straight home in the struggle I'm about to face.

                    ELECTRA *enters the palace.* ORESTES *and*
                         PYLADES *move to one side.*

CHORUS No one can count the terrors that the
                  earth spawns,   *Strophe 1*
              catastrophic,   670
        gruesome, and the vast arms of the sea swarm
              with brute monsters
        bent on harm, and everywhere between
              the sky and ground
        lights bloom by day in flares and sudden bolts;
              and birds and beasts
        alike can tell of the whirlwind's whirling wrath.

        But who can describe the overweening
                  pride   *Antistrophe 1*

of men? Or women
mad with passion, reckless in their hearts,   680
    soulmates
to every kind of ruin that befalls us?
    Wild passion,
unrestrained, boundless, that overcomes
    the women, perverts
the yoke of wedlock for beasts and men alike.

Let anyone whose mind is steady   *Strophe 2*
remember this, once he has learned
the story of Thestius' daughter,
ruthless Althaea, who killed   690
her own son. She contrived a plot
to burn the brand that fate assigned
to span his life; it had been kept
since the day he came out crying
from his mother's loins. Deliberately,
deceitfully, she set on fire
what was to have kept pace with him
from birth to death. It glowed bright red
before the fire blackened it.

And they tell of another woman,   *Antistrophe 2*   700
a hateful maiden, the bloody Scylla,
friend to her enemies, murderous
enemy to her dearest friend,
her father; lured by a gold-forged necklace,
a gift from Minos, ruthlessly,
deliberately as Nisus kept
on sleeping unsuspecting as
a baby, she snipped off his lock
of immortality, and all
at once dark Hermes led him down.   710

Since I'm recalling hatreds that stopped   *Strophe 3*
    at nothing, it is right
I come at last to this hateful marriage,
    this heartbreak for the house,
and the outrageous work of cunning

129

hatched in a woman's mind
against the warrior, her husband,
   against a husband even
enemies had reason to revere.
   I honor a low and steady   720
burning hearth within the house,
   not one that flares up wildly;
and a woman's sharp, unwarlike spirit
   that would never dare.

Of all the storied crimes, the crime   *Antistrophe 3*
   of Lemnos is the worst;
yes, people everywhere all groan
   and spit out their disgust at
the very thought, and even call
   every new horror that happens   730
a Lemnian crime. For such a foul
   deed hateful to the gods,
that race has utterly died away
   in stark dishonor, since
no one respects what the gods despise.
   Which of these tales I've told
here is beside the point, unjust?

The sharp point of the sword is poised   *Strophe 4*
near the lungs and driven down
and through them by the force of Justice   740
that strikes back at all who defy her,
flouting the majesty of Zeus,
trampling justice underfoot.

The base of justice is firmly set,   *Antistrophe 4*
and fate, the swordsmith, hammers out
her sword beforehand. Now a child
is brought to the house of ancient bloodshed by the far famed Erinyes
to pay for the pollution at long last.

ORESTES *goes up to the gateway,*
accompanied by PYLADES.

ORESTES Boy! Boy! Hey, don't you hear me knocking? Once
                        more,   750
                is anybody home? For the third time
                won't anyone from the house come out to greet me
                if Aegisthus would have it welcome strangers?

SLAVE All right, all right. I hear you. Where are you from,
                stranger?

ORESTES Tell the masters of the house that someone
                is here with news for them. Now hurry! The night's
                dim chariot is rushing on to darkness,
                it's time for travelers to drop anchor
                some place where a host will welcome them.
                Call whoever's in charge inside the house   750
                to come out here to us, the mistress, maybe,
                who runs the place, or better yet the master,
                for, out of respect, a man must veil his words
                when talking with a woman, but with a man
                he can frankly say whatever's on his mind.

                                        Enter CLYTEMNESTRA.

CLYTEMNESTRA Strangers, just say whatever it is you need,
                for we have all a house like this should have,
                warm baths, and beds to charm away fatigue,
                and the attention of judicious eyes.
                But if you two have come on graver business,   770
                requiring more serious thought, well, that's the work
                men do, and we will let them know about it.

ORESTES I am a stranger, from Daulis, a town in Phocis.
                As I set out for Argos shouldering
                my own pack (at long last I can put it down),
                I fell in with a stranger who wanted to know
                my destination, and he told me his. Strophius,
                a Phocian, was the name he gave me. "Friend,"
                he says, "since you are headed anyway
                for Argos, do me this favor, won't you? Tell   780

the parents of Orestes that he is dead.
Don't let it slip your mind. And what his people
now want to do—if they want to bring him home,
or bury him in a foreign land, an outcast here
forever—carry their wishes back to me.
For as it is, the smooth walls of a bronze
urn now enclose the ashes of a man
we greatly mourned." I've told you all I heard.
Whether I'm speaking with someone who may have
authority in any of these matters,   790
I couldn't say. His parent, though, should know.

CLYTEMNESTRA Ah me! Your news destroys us top to bottom!
O curse that stalks the house, that we can't throw,
is there anywhere your seeing doesn't reach?
Striking with well-aimed arrows from afar
even what's been so carefully hidden away,
you strip me in my anguish of those I love.
And now Orestes—prudent as he was
to steer clear of this slough of butchery:
you can write off whatever hope we had   800
in him to be the doctor who would rid
the house of all your hideous carousing.

ORESTES I wish, with hosts so wealthy, it could have been
good news that made me known to you, and
        welcomed,
for what kindness is greater than the kindness
between a host and guest? And yet I felt
it would have been a grave impiety
not to have seen this task through to the end
for Orestes' friends, when I had promised to,
and since I'm taken in as guest-friend here.   810

CLYTEMNESTRA Put your mind at ease. You'll be no less
deserving of our hospitality,
no less a friend to us, because of this.
Another messenger could just as easily
have brought the news. But now you must be tired

from traveling all day. Time for the rest
you've earned.

(To an attendant)

Take him and his fellow traveler
to the men's guest-quarters; give them everything
a house like this can give. See to it all
as if your very life depended on it.   820
In the meantime, I'll give the ruler of the house
all the particulars you've told me, and we
will not lack friends as we deliberate
about this terrible, sudden stroke of fate.

Exit CLYTEMNESTRA *with the others.*

CHORUS Handmaidens faithful to the house,
    when shall we sound
the strength of our tongue to serve Orestes?
O sacred earth, and sacred barrow
raised high over the king's body,
the master of the fleet, now hear us,   830
    now help us! Now
is Persuasion's time with all
    her slick deceit
to be his second as he steps out
onto the field, and Hermes' time,
lord of the dark earth, lord
of stealthy night, to over see
    and guide the contest
of the swift, death-dealing sword!

Enter ORESTES' NURSE.

CHORUS LEADER The stranger must be busy causing trouble: 840
    for here's Orestes' nurse, in tears.
                 Cilissa,
where are you off to through the outer gate,
with grief your unpaid traveling companion?

NURSE The mistress orders me to tell Aegisthus
          to come and see the strangers right away,
          so he can hear for himself, man to man,
          in more detail, the news they have to tell.
          You should have seen her, the phony look of sorrow
          she put on in front of the servants, and the way
          she hid behind those sad eyes a gloating laugh   850
          of triumph for the work done well enough
          for her—but for the house, what is it but
          the final insult of an evil that
          the stranger's story has made all too clear.
          And that one will be glad at heart, I tell you,
          when he hears the news! O god, god! it
          was hard enough to bear, all those miseries
          mixed up together to assault the house
          of Atreus, that kept the shattered heart
          within my breast forever shattering.   860
          But no agony I suffered was as bad as this!
          I braved the storm of all my other troubles
          best I could. But now my own Orestes!
          How I wore my life away, caring for him
          right from the moment when he came out bawling
          from his mother's womb, oh how I nursed him,
          reared him, walked the floors with him at night,
          when his loud cries would wake me, that and more,
          the endless chores, the headaches, all of it
          I did—and for what?—that's how you nurture such   870
          a helpless thing, like a dumb beast, you have to
          learn how to read the weather of its moods.
          A baby still in swaddling bands can't say
          in words whether it has to eat, or drink,
          or pee, its stomach needs what it needs when it
                  needs it.
          I had to be a prophet to guess what to do,
          and often I guessed wrong, and had to scrub clean
          the baby's clothes, both nurse and washer-woman,
          both handicrafts required of this one hand, my hand
          that took charge of Orestes for his father.   880
          And now, O god, they tell me he is dead,

and here I'm fetching the very man who's ruined
the house! He'll savour the news, that one. You'll see!

CHORUS LEADER Does she tell him to come prepared in any way?

NURSE What do you mean "prepared"? I don't follow you.

CHORUS LEADER With his bodyguards, I mean, or by himself.

NURSE She says his henchmen are to come with him.

CHORUS LEADER Don't tell him that, not if you hate our master;
tell him instead that he's to come alone
to hear the news, tell him to come quickly,   890
that he doesn't need to take precautions.
And say it cheerfully. The messenger
can make the bent word look as if it's straight.

NURSE What, are you happy after news like this?

CHORUS LEADER But what if Zeus should make our bad wind good?

NURSE How so? Orestes, hope of the house, is gone.

CHORUS LEADER Not yet. Only a poor prophet would say that.

NURSE What are you saying? Have you heard something else?

CHORUS LEADER Go give your message. Just do as you're told.
The gods will care for what the gods will care for.   900

NURSE All right, I'll go then and do just what you say.
And, please god, may it all be for the best.

NURSE *exits to the left.*

CHORUS Now hear my prayer, O Zeus,   *Strophe 1*
father of the Olympian gods,
grant that the house may prosper, bring

the just light of deliverance
to those who long to see it. My
every word's been spoken for
the sake of Justice. Protect her, Zeus.

Zeus, Zeus, set the one inside the house   *Mesode 1*   910
   over his enemies,
for if only you raise him up to greatness,
   twofold, three-
fold will he pay you back, and do it gladly!

See how the colt of a man you loved   *Antistrophe 1*
is yoked to a chariot of struggle;
keep a firm hold on the reins
to help him hit his stride and keep it
so that we can see him surge
straining forward as he gallops   920
down the homestretch of the course.

And you gods within, who inhabit   *Strophe 2*
the inner rooms piled high with wealth,
delighting in their glitter, you gods
who feel what we feel, hear us, come
wash clean the blood of past crimes with
a fresh-kill act of justice! May
old murder no longer breed in the house!

And you, Apollo, who dwell in the
     magnificent
   great cave, grant   *Mesode 2*   930
that this man's house stand tall again, and that
   he see with glad eyes
the light of freedom shine out from its dark veil.

May Hermes help him too, in justice,   *Antistrophe 2*
he who best can see the deed
to port, blown on a favoring breeze;
whenever he wants, he will reveal
what's kept obscure, or speak obscurely;
he is the dark before our eyes
by night, and no less dark by day.   940

And then we'll sing a far-famed song   *Strophe 3*
to celebrate our deliverance
from bloodshed, a woman's tune
sung on a favoring breeze, sung shrill
and clamorous; "Our ship goes well,"
we'll sing, "and our gain grows, while ruin
keeps away from those we love."

And you, Orestes, when it's time to act,   *Mesode 3*
   be strong, and when
she says to you "My son," cry in return,   950
   "My father" and
accomplish a destruction none can fault.

Harden your heart into the heart   *Antistrophe 3*
of Perseus, and for the ones
you love below the earth, and those
above, exact some joy at last
from all that anger; make the house
run red with Gorgon gore, and kill
the man whose hands are red from killing.

AEGISTHUS *enters from the left.*

AEGISTHUS I've come as I was bid, and the summons   960
tells me there are strangers here with news
no one would welcome of Orestes' death.
To add this fearful burden to the house
still stung and festering from earlier bloodshed
would make its deep wounds ooze and drip again.
But how do I know the story's really true,
and not just words ignited by a woman's fear,
flaring in air a moment before it dies
away to nothing? Can you say anything
about this that might make it clear to me?   970

CHORUS LEADER Yes, we did hear the story, but you go in
yourself and ask the strangers. A messenger's
report is a poor substitute for hearing
one's questions answered by the man himself.

AEGISTHUS That's what I want: to see the messenger
and grill him carefully: was he there, did he see
Orestes die? Or is he just repeating
some second- or third-hand rumor? One thing's for
        certain,
he can't deceive a mind that's open-eyed.

                    AEGISTHUS *exits into the palace.*

CHORUS Zeus, Zeus, what can I say, where   980
        can I begin
my prayer to the gods for help?
How, with all goodwill, can I speak
words adequate to all I need?
For now the blood-smeared blades of slaughter
        will either cut
down the whole of Agamemnon's house,
or else the son will kindle up
        the torch, the light
of freedom, and regain the throne   990
        and all the great wealth of his fathers.
All by himself the brave Orestes
will have to wrestle hard with two
        opponents. May
he win out at last and throw them.

AEGISTHUS *(off)* EH! EH! OTOTOTOI!

CHORUS Ah! Ah!
What does that mean? How has it all turned out?
Let's lie low while the work is being done,
so we're not blamed for any of these troubles.   1000
For, look, the outcome's clear, the battle's over.

                    SLAVE *rushes from the palace.*

SLAVE Ah grief, sheer grief, my master's murdered, killed!
Grief yet again I cry for the third time:
Aegisthus is no more! Open up,   ——

come open quick, slide back the bars
on the women's doors! We need a strong arm—but
    not
to help the one who's dead, too late for that.

I'm shouting to the deaf, I'm squandering
my voice on those who waste their time asleep!
Where's Clytemnestra? What's she doing? Now   1010
it seems her neck is on the block, and soon
will fall to the blade of just revenge.

                CLYTEMNESTRA *enters from the palace.*

CLYTEMNESTRA What's wrong? Why the hue and cry all through the
           house?

SLAVE I tell you the dead are killing off the living.

CLYTEMNESTRA Ah, me. A riddle. I can guess its meaning:
           We killed by treachery, by treachery we're killed.
           Get me an axe to kill a man. Quick!

                    SLAVE *reenters the palace.*

Let's see who I am—winner or loser, for that's
what it's come down to now, how far I've slipped!

          ORESTES *enters from the palace, brandishing a blody*
                    sword and followed by PYLADES.

ORESTES You're the one I want. This one's had his fill.   1020

CLYTEMNESTRA Ah, you are dead, beloved, great Aegithus!

ORESTES You love the man? Then lie with him together
           in the same grave and don't ever again desert him.

CLYTEMNESTRA Easy, my son, take pity on this breast, child,
           that you so often, half-asleep, would suck
           with soft gums for the milk that let you grow!

ORESTES What do I do, Pylades? How can I kill my mother?

PYLADES What then would become of Apollo's oracles
declared at Pytho, and the oath you swore?
Better that all men hate you than the gods!   1030

ORESTES I judge you winner. Your advice is sound.

(*to* CLYTEMNESTRA)

Come here. I want to kill you by his side,
and, since you thought he was, in life, a better
man than my father, you must sleep with him
in death. Since this man is the one you love,
and the one you should have loved you only hate.

CLYTEMNESTRA I bore you, reared you. Let me grow old with you!

ORESTES What! Kill my father, then make your home with me?

CLYTEMNESTRA Fate had a role to play in this, my son.

ORESTES If so, then your death, too, is no less fated.   1040

CLYTEMNESTRA Aren't you afraid, child, of a mother's curse?

ORESTES No, you gave me birth, then threw me out to suffer.

CLYTEMNESTRA How so when I had sent you to a friend's house?

ORESTES Son of a free man, I was sold, disgraced.

CLYTEMNESTRA If so, then where's the price I got for you?

ORESTES I'm ashamed to taunt you openly with that.

CLYEMNSTRA Go on, but name your father's lusts, as well.

ORESTES Don't you dare judge him: he suffered, you sat at
home.

140

CLYTEMNESTRA A woman suffers, kept from her man, my son.

ORESTES But it's his hard work that keeps her safe at home.   1050

CLYTEMNESTRA You seem, child, bent on murdering your mother.

ORESTES No, you'll be murdering yourself, not I.

CLYTEMNESTRA Watch out for the mad dogs of a mother's curse!

ORESTES What about my father's, if I don't do this?

CLYTEMNESTRA I'm singing my own dirge to a deaf tomb.

ORESTES Yes, my father's fate is bringing you your death.

CLYTEMNESTRA Ah, you are the snake I bore and suckled! Yes,
it was prophetic, the terror from my dreams!

ORESTES You did wrong, killing; now suffer wrong and die!

> ORESTES *pushes* CLYTEMNESTRA *into the palace,*
> *followed by* PYLADES.

CHORUS LEADER I pity even these two their double fall.   1060
But since Orestes has battled hard and long
to reach at last this pinnacle of bloodshed,
we prefer to have it go this way,
so the eye of the house doesn't altogether die.

CHORUS Justice in the end came to the sons of Priam,   *Strophe 1*
came and it crushed them,
and to the house of Agamemnon
a double lion came, a double god of slaughter.
The Pythian-guided exile drove the whole
course by himself, spurred on by the god's just
counsel.   1070

Shout out in triumph for the master's house, *Mesode 1*
how it fought free

at last of evil, of the wearing away
    of its wealth by those two
stained with blood, free of its wretched luck!

And crafty Punishment has come, conducting
        war   *Antistrophe 1*
    in secret. In the fray
his hand was guided by the trueborn
daughter of Zeus—we speak truth when we name her
        Justice—
she breathes a withering wrath against her foes.   1080

Apollo, he who haunts the great cave of
        Parnassus,   *Strophe 2*
    declared it loudly:
this trickery that is no trick.
He roots out ingrown evil; and the will of god
somehow prevails, so we don't help the wicked.
The power that rules in heaven should be feared on
        earth.

See how the light has come, and the hard
        curb   *Mesode 2*
    that held the house is broken!
Arise, O house, arise, too long you've lain
    in shambles on the ground.   1090

But soon will Time, the all-accomplishing,
        pass in   *Antistrophe 2*
    through the front gate of the house
when all pollution is expelled
from the hearth by cleansing rites which drive out acts
        of bloodshed.
Everything's ready, fortune's fair face is shining,
and we can cry, the alien tenants will be evicted.

> *The palace doors open, and* ORESTES *is seen
> standing over the dead bodies of* CLYTEMNESTRA *and*
> AEGISTHUS. *With him are servants who hold the bloody
> death robe of Agamemnon*

ORESTES Look on these two, these tyrants of the land,
who killed my father and despoiled my house.
How stately for a time they were, and true
to one another, and they are faithful still,   1100
as you may judge, imagining their fate.
And their oath too has been faithful to its pledges.
They vowed as one to murder my poor father;
as one they vowed to die: they've kept their vows.

Now as you hear me tell new sorrows, look
at the device they used to snare him with,
my poor father, to manacle his hands
and fetter both his feet.

(to the servants)

Here spread it out,
gather around me and unfurl the mesh
that caught the man. This way my father (not   1110
my father but the one that looks on all
things everywhere on earth, the Sun) may see
my mother's godforsaken work, and so
bear witness for me on my day of judgment
that it was with justice I pursued this death,
my mother's death. As for Aegisthus' death
it's not worth mentioning—an adulterer,
he got what he deserved. The law's the law.

But she who helped to craft this foul act
against her husband, whose children she carried   1120
in her womb, in pain bore, loved for a while,
but then, as you can see, had come to hate—
what is she? If she had been an eel, or viper,
wouldn't her touch alone have had the power
to rot someone she hadn't even bit;
isn't that how far her spirit went
in shameless daring?

(gesturing toward the bloody robes)

                              And this, what should I call this,
              speaking as "nicely" as I can? A lure
              for beasts? bath curtain? coffin shroud to wrap
              a dead man with from head to toe? No, no,   1130
              a net, a hunting-net would be more apt,
              a robe-made foot-trap, what any thief would have
              to draw a traveler in and steal his money,
              plying an outlaw's trade. Yes, with a snare
              as slick as this, he easily could kill
              any number of men, and so warm his heart.
              May I never share my house with such a woman!
              I'd rather die first childless, so help me god!

CHORUS   O god, god, the awful work!
                    Miserable   1140
              the death that ended you. For the
              survivor pain is poised to bloom!

ORESTES Did she commit this crime or didn't she?
              This robe's my witness, dyed by Aegisthus' sword.
              See how the blood-gush worked with time to spoil
              the blended colors of the embroidery.

              Now I can praise him; now I am here to mourn,
              holding this web that killed my father. Still,
              I grieve for what was done, for what was suffered,
              and for all our race, shouldering, as I do,   1150
              a filthy and unenviable triumph.

CHORUS   No one can live his whole life long
                    immune from harm.
              O god, god, trouble has come
              here, and trouble is still to come.

ORESTES But I, I'd have you know this, I can't see
              how it will end. I'm like a charioteer
              driving his team far off the course, my mind's
              unreinable, it bucks and pitches me away,
              and I'm defeated, and fear near my heart is ready   1160
              to sing and leap up to a raging tune.

Before I lose hold of my senses, though,
I openly declare to all my friends,
not without justice did I kill my mother,
stained as she was with murdering my father,
and with the hatred of the gods.
                              Besides,
among the charms that brought me to this daring,
I put Apollo first, the seer of Delphi,
who told me I could do this guiltlessly,
and if I failed to—I can't name the punishment.   1170
No arrow could ever scale that height of pain.

Look how I go now, armed with this branch and
     wreath,
a suppliant, making for earth's naval-stone,
Apollo's shrine, and to the fire called
Forever Burning, an exile from this bloodshed that's my own. Apollo ordered me
to turn to his hearth, to his alone. I tell
all men of Argos, as time goes on:
remember how this evil work was done;
bear witness for me when Menelaus comes.   1180
So now I go, an outcast from the land,
leaving behind, in life, in death, this story.

CHORUS LEADER No, you did well. Don't yoke your mouth to evil.
Don't let ill-omened words now cross your lips.
You set all Argos free when you lopped off
the heads of these two snakes with one swift stroke.

ORESTES *sees the Erinyes, invisible to everyone else.*

ORESTES Ah! Ah! these hideous women, they're like, like
Gorgons, black-robed, snakes swarming over them,
braiding and unbraiding. I can't stay here any longer!

CHORUS LEADER What figments whirl you about, truest of all   1190
to your father? Stay calm, don't fear. You've won so
     much!

ORESTES These troubles aren't figments, no, they're flesh and
     blood,
I see them, the bloodhounds of my mother's anger.

CHORUS LEADER Well, yes, the blood's still dripping from your hands—
see, that's what put this madness in your mind.

ORESTES Ah, Lord Apollo, how they come, they grow
and swarm and their bloodshot eyes drip hatefully!

CHORUS LEADER There's only one way you can cleanse yourself:
Apollo's touch will free you from these troubles.

ORESTES You can't see them, can you? but I can,   1200
they dog me, I can't stay here any longer!

CHORUS LEADER May good luck go with you, and may the god
guard you with kindness, so that your fortune thrives.

    Orestes rushes off left, as the CHORUS *exits right to the
            marching measure of their final lines.*

CHORUS Again, for the third time, on the royal house
   the storm has crashed,
its curses blowing through the blood,
and run its course. First came the feast
of children's flesh, Thyestes' anguish;
next came the grim fate of the man,
   the king, the warlord   1210
of the Achaeans—killed in the bath;
Now once again for the third time
   from somewhere comes
a savior, or should I say a death?
Where will it end? When will it all
be lulled back into sleep, and cease,
the bloody hatred, the destruction?

EUMENIDES

CHARACTERS

THE PYTHIA priestess of Apollo at Delphi

APOLLO son of Zeus, god of prophecy and purification

ORESTES son of Agamemnon and Clytemnestra

CLYTEMNESTRA killed by Orestes, now a ghost

CHORUS of the Erinyes of Clytemnestra

ATHENA daughter of Zeus, patron goddess of Athens

ATHENIAN CITIZEN-JURORS

ATHENIAN WOMEN

The scene is at Delphi, before the oracular temple of Apollo. His priestess, the PYTHIA, *enters from the right.*

PYTHIA   Among the gods I honor in my prayer,
        I give first place to the first prophet, Earth,
        and second place to Themis, the second one
        to hold her mother's seat of prophecy,
        or so the story goes. Then third in line,
        by Themis' own choice and not by force,
        another Titaness took her place: Phoebe,
        child of earth, and she in turn gave it
        to Phoebus for his birthday, which is why
        he added her name to his own.
                             Leaving   10
        the pool and spiny ridge of Delos, he sailed
        into the ship-hive coast of Pallas and came here
        to this land to make his home on Mount Parnassus.
        The children of Hephaestus, road-makers
        who tamed the land that was untamed before,
        escorted him with deepest reverence.
        The people honored him greatly at his coming,
        as Delphus did, the country's king and helmsman.
        And Zeus infused him with the prophet's art,
        and put him as the fourth seer on this throne.   20
        Apollo, then, is spokesman for his father Zeus.

        I make these gods the prelude of my prayer,
        yet in all I say I also honor Pallas
        whose shrine stands there, apart, and revere the
            Nymphs
        whose dwelling is the hollowed Corycian rock,
        sweet haunt of birds and spirits lingering.
        And Bromius too (I don't forget) has held
        sway in this region ever since the day
        he, in his true form, led his troop of women,
        his wild bacchants, to hunt down Pentheus,   30

149

to snare him like a hare in a net of death.
I call on the streams of Pleistus in the gorge below,
and on Poseidon's power, and on Zeus,
who brings all to fulfillment, the Most High.
And as I take my seat to prophesy,
may they all grant me foresight that exceeds
whatever foresight I have had before.
If there are any Greeks here, let them enter
in order of the lots they drew, as the custom is.
My prophecies will follow where the god leads.   40

The PYTHIA *enters the temple, then immediately returns,*
            but now crawling at first on hands and knees.

Terror for tongue to tell of, for eyes to see,
sheer terror has driven me away, again,
from Apollo's house, so that my strength falters,
and I can't stand on my own two legs, and
I go on all fours, trembling, inch by inch,
because a terrified old woman's nothing
at all, no better than a child.
                                        I was
making my way into the inner chamber
where the air glows green from the garlands left there
when I saw a man polluted before the gods   50
sitting the way a suppliant would sit
on the navel stone, blood dripping from his hands,
blood also dripping from his just drawn sword;
he held a tall branch of an olive tree
wreathed as it should be with a shock of wool,
the white fleece radiant—this I can say for sure.
But an astounding gang of women sleeps
around him, all slouched in chairs. Women?
No, not women. Gorgons maybe, but, no,
not even Gorgon shapes could do them justice.   60
I saw a painting once of flying female-
creatures snatching food from Phineus,
but this gang has no wings, and they're all black,

disgusting, and their phlegmy snores spew out
a stink that blinds and repels, and their eyes drip
a sickening ooze. Their dark rags, too, aren't fit
to wear before the statues of the gods,
or even right to bring into the house.
I've never seen the tribe this crew belongs to,
or known a land that could rear a brood like this   70
and not be damaged and regret the labor.
How this will end up now is his concern,
the master of the house, great Loxias
himself, the wily one. He is the prophet,
the healer; he scans the signs to see what is
to come; he has the power to purify.

> The PYTHIA *exits to the right.* APOLLO *and*
> ORESTES *enter from the temple.*

APOLLO   I won't betray you. Your guardian to the end,
both when I'm here with you and far away—
I won't ease up against your enemies.
See how I've tamed, for now, these crazed hags,   80
lulled them to sleep, these maidens of filth, these
      wrinkled
children no god, or man, or any beast
would want to touch: born evil, born for evil,
their only dwelling place the evil darkness
of the deepest underground, despised
alike by men and all the gods above.
They're tamed for now. But flee them, don't let up,
for they will dog you, there at your heels, as you run
on from horizon to horizon, fast
at your pounding heels, over the vast mainland,   90
and across the sea to sea-encircled cities.
Don't tire or lose heart till you've shepherded
your hard task all the way to Pallas Athena's
city. Once there, sit as a suppliant,
holding her age-old image in your arms.
And we'll have judges for your case, and words

that spellbind; we will find the means to free you
from this toil you've been caught in, once and for all.
For I persuaded you to kill your mother.

ORESTES   My lord Apollo, you know how not to be   100
unjust; learn, too, how not to be neglectful.
Your strength assures me of your power for good.

APOLLO   Remember, don't let fear overtake you.
Now, Hermes, my brother, son of my father too,
watch over him; be your own namesake and
escort him, guide him well, for he's my suppliant,
and Zeus honors the rights of outcasts who are blessed
with such a guide back to the world of men.

> ORESTES *exits to the left and* APOLLO *enters the*
> *temple. After a brief pause,* CLYTEMNESTRA'*s*
> *ghost appears, perhaps on the roof*
> *of the stage building.*

CLYTEMNESTRA   Keep sleeping! You there! Ah, what good are you
to me asleep? Because of you I go   110
dishonored among the other dead. The spirits
of those I killed won't stop accusing me,
I wander in disgrace. I tell you, day
and night they hector me with blame. And though
I too have suffered from my blood relations,
none of the gods is angry on my behalf,
though I was slaughtered by my own son's hands.
Picture my wounds in your heart (for the sleeping
          mind
can see more clearly than the mind awake).
Remember where they came from, and don't forget   120
how many offerings I made to you,
how you would lap them up, the wineless pourings,
sober propitiations, holy feasts
burned in a hearth pit in the darkest recess
of the night, at an hour not shared by other gods—
And all for what? To see my offerings trampled

while I watch him slip away so easily
and vanish like a fawn, watch him leap free
out from the middle of your net, and taunt you,
mock you, winking, as he bounds off? Hear me!   130
My very being hinges on my plea.
Wake up now, goddesses from beneath the ground,
for I am Clytemnestra, the dream that calls you.

                              (whining from within the temple)

The more you whine, the farther away he gets,
for *his* friends, unlike mine, know how to help.

                                          (more whining)

More sleep's in you than pity for my pain.
Orestes, who ran me—his mother!—through, is gone.

                                              (moaning)

How can you sleep and moan like this? Get up!
Get up! Ruin's the job you're meant to do!

                                          (more moaning)

Sleep and exhaustion, those arch-conspirators,   140
have drained the poison from the dread snake's tooth.

CHORUS (moaning twice as loud, still from within)   Get him!
        Get him! Get him! There! Over there!

CLYTEMNESTRA The quarry you keep hunting's just a dream,
and yet you still bay like a hound that can't
stop sniffing out the bloodtrail. What are you doing?
Get up! Don't let exhaustion overcome you!
Don't let sleep slacken your pace, make you forget
my misery! Let my just accusations
sting your heart awake, for they are sharp
goads to the sensible. Breathe over him the blood-   150
reek of your breath, shrivel him in the sizzling

153

gust of your belly's fire! Get after him,
wither him away with a fresh pursuit!

(CLYTEMNESTRA'S GHOST DISAPPEARS. *The* CHORUS
enters from the temple by ones and twos.)

CHORUS Up now! Wake her, just as I wake you!
Still sleeping? Come on, get up! Kick sleep away,
let's see if this dream is a truthful prelude.

IOU! IOU! POPAX   *Strophe 1*
Wronged, sorely wronged, my sisters,
Oh I have suffered so much, and for what?
  Yes we have suffered   160
such searing pain, oh yes, a hurt
  no one could bear,
the beast has slipped free of the net and vanished:
sleep took me, and the prey is lost.

O child of Zeus, you thief! So young   *Antistrophe 1*
yet you have trampled down the gray gods
  by guarding the suppliant,
the godless, the mother-hating man.
  A god yourself,
you've spirited away the mother-killer.   170
Could anyone call these actions just?

Blame came to me in my dream — over
      and over   *Strophe 2*
it struck me like a charioteer,
  with the goad gripped
tight in his fist; in the heart, in the guts,
  it struck, and I feel
the cold sting of the scourger's cruel
  quick public lash.

This is what all of you do, you younger
      gods,   *Antistrophe 2*
your power knows no bounds, respects none.   180
  Gore oozes over

Apollo's throne, from the top, to the bottom,
   it drips, and I see
the earth's stone navel smeared with filth
   from bloody deeds.

A prophet himself, he's dirtied his own
         shrine,   *Strophe 3*
      defiled his hearth
at no one's bidding but his own,
   invited blight
by placing men above the god-   190
   set limits, breaking
the age-old power of the fates.

Although he hurts me too, he still won't
         save   *Antistrophe 3*
      Orestes, never;
for even hid beneath the earth,
   this suppliant
will not escape, but come stained,
   cursed, to where
a new avenger will rise against him.

                    APOLLO *enters from the temple.*

APOLLO Get out of this house, right now, I order you!   200
      Away from my temple's deep prophetic chamber
      or you'll be bitten by a flying snake
      shot from my bowstring's beaten gold, and retch
      in agony, coughing up all the black
      scum sucked from men, the clotted gore you guzzled.
      You have no rights here, no business in this house,
      your jurisdiction is where heads are lopped off
      in retribution, eyes gouged out, throats slashed;
      where the manhood of mere boys is cut away,
      their seed squandered, and men—their hands, their
            feet,   210
      their ears and nose—are maimed, and they are stoned
      to death, and where they feel the sharp stake driven
      into their backs and groan out loud and long.

Don't you hear then what sort of feasts you crave
that make the gods despise you? Your very shape
and dress explain it. Creatures like you belong
in caves with blood-befouled, blood-lapping lions;
you have no business in this prophetic place,
rubbing your stinking dirt off on those near you.
Get out of here, you herd without a herdsman!   220
No god would ever tend a flock like this.

CHORUS LEADER It's your turn now to listen, lord Apollo.
You are no mere accessory to this crime;
From start to finish, the blame is yours alone.

APOLLO How so? Say just enough to make it clear.

CHORUS LEADER You told your guest-friend he should kill his mother.

APOLLO I told him to avenge his father. What else?

CHORUS LEADER You took him in, blood still wet on his hands.

APOLLO I told him to come for cleansing to this shrine.

CHORUS LEADER And you malign us for serving as his escort?   230

APOLLO You aren't fit creatures to come near my house.

CHORUS LEADER But we as well have our appointed task . . .

APOLLO Appointed? You? Crow on about this noble job.

CHORUS LEADER We hound all mother-killers from their houses.

APOLLO And what about a wife who kills her husband?

CHORUS LEADER That isn't killing one's own flesh and blood.

APOLLO Why, then, you spit on, treat as less than nothing,
the solemn vows of Hera, the fulfiller,
and of Zeus; and Aphrodite, too, is thrown

away like something worthless by your words,   240
yes, Aphrodite who gives to humankind
the deepest and most intimate bond of all.
Marriage is a thing of destiny,
greater than any oath, and Justice guards it.
And so if you let spouses kill each other
and overlook it, neither punishing them
nor looking on them with a wrathful vigilance,
then I maintain this hounding of Orestes
isn't just. It's clear to me you're stirred
to utter outrage by the one crime while   250
the other doesn't move you in the least.
But Pallas, goddess of wisdom that she is,
will oversee the issue of this case.

CHORUS LEADER We'll never stop harassing him, not ever.

APOLLO Go on, then. Make more trouble for yourself.

CHORUS LEADER Don't try to steal our rights with clever words.

APOLLO If someone gave me your rights, I wouldn't take them.

CHORUS LEADER Why should you, high and mighty as you seem
near Zeus's throne? But the scent of motherblood
        drives us,
and we will hunt the man down, get our justice.   260

The CHORUS *exits to the left.*

APOLLO And I will help my suppliant and save him.
A suppliant's wrath's a dreadful thing for gods
and men alike. I never will betray him.

APOLLO *exits into the temple. There is a*
brief pause. The scene is now set in Athens.
ORESTES *enters from the left.*

ORESTES Queen Athena, I have come at Apollo's
command. Receive me graciously, a cursed,
a hounded man, but one no longer stained,
my hands now clean, my guilt's keen edge now
    dulled,
worn down to nothing by the crowded paths
I've traveled, by the homes I've sheltered in.
Holding a firm course over both sea and land,   270
obedient to Apollo's orders, I've come
at last, goddess, here to your house, your image,
watching and waiting for justice to be fulfilled.

> *The* CHORUS *enters by ones and twos,*
> *miming hounds tracking a scent.*

CHORUS LEADER So, finally, a clear sign of the man.
Here, this way, this is where the voiceless snitch
is leading! Like a blood hound on the scent
of a wounded fawn, we track him by this trail
of blood drops. And he's panting out his guts
from all the endless deadly labors, driven
like a sheep over every stretch of land   280
while we flew wingless, faster than any ship,
across sea after sea, pursuing. I know
he's cowering somewhere near here, for the scent
of blood is like the warm smile of an old friend.

CHORUS Look! Look again!
Check everywhere—
don't let the mother-killer slip through our clutches
and get away unpunished.

There he is, himself, there in the flesh!
   and once again   290
protected, his arms around the image
   of the immortal goddess,
eager to stand trial for his crime.
But that won't happen. Once a mother's blood
   is spilled on the ground,

it can't return again, not ever.
   POPOI! The red
stream pools there, seeps into earth, and then
   it's gone for good.
You'll have to pay with your own blood for hers,   300
   you'll feel me suck the half-
caked gore out of your living flesh;
   swill from your very veins
the vile dregs of the drink I crave.
I'll shrivel you up and drag you, still alive,
   into the underworld
where you will pay in currencies of torment
   for the murder of your mother.
And there you'll see all other mortal sinners,
   the ones who flout   310
the honor owed to gods or guests,
   or loving parents—
you'll see them get the justice they deserve.
For Hades holds men mightily to a strict
accounting down below the earth;
he sees all things, inscribes them
   within the book
of his remembering.

ORESTES I have been schooled by my own suffering:
         I've learned the many ways of being purged.   320
         I know where words are proper, and when silence is,
         and that on this occasion a wise teacher
         has ordered me to speak. For the blood drowses,
         sloughs from my hand, the stain of having killed
         my mother has been entirely washed away:
         when it was still fresh at Apollo's hearth,
         he cast it out by sacrificing swine.
         My story would be a long one if I told it
         right from the start, the many men I met
         and mingled with, not one of whom was harmed.   330
         Time cleanses what it touches over time.
         So now with clean lips and well-omened words
         I call Athena, this land's queen, to be

my savior. Not by force of spear or sword,
she'll claim me, my land, and all the people of Argos,
as her true allies till the end of time.
Wherever she is—whether in distant Libya,
there by the stream of Triton where she was born,
enthroned or on the march to help her friends,
or whether like a dauntless leader she over-   340
sees the Phlegrean plain—O let her come
(a god can hear even from far away),
and save me from the troubles that hound me still.

CHORUS LEADER No, not Apollo's, not Athena's strength
can save you, keep you from going down in disgrace,
forgotten, no place in your heart for joy, all blood
sucked from your body till it's nothing but
death's vaporous feedbag, shadowy husk of air.

So you have nothing to say? You just spit at my
      words—
calf fattened all for me, my living feast,   350
my calf not butchered first over any altar?
Hear the spell we sing to bind you fast:

CHORUS Let's dance as well as sing around him,
      hand in hand,
and let's reveal the terrifying
power of our dark melody
and tell the way our company
fulfills the offices assigned
      to us, our given
right to guide the lives of men.   360
We keep straight on the path of justice,
      that's our belief:
our wrath is never aimed at the one
who holds up hands no blood has stained—
for *that* one lives out his life unharmed.
But the man, like this one here before us,
      who tries to keep
his red hands hid, yet reeks of guilt,

will find us ever at his side,
   bearing witness   370
truthfully for those who died,
the court of last appeal, the final
   blood avengers.

Mother, O mother Night,   *Strophe* 1
who bore me as a scourge
to those under the sun,
and those in sunlessness,
hear me. Leto's child,
Apollo, steals my honor,
he's trying now to steal   380
out of my rightful grasp
this trembling hare whose blood
alone is the atonement
for the motherblood he spilled.

Over our victim's head,   *Refrain* 1
this is the song we sing,
this is the maddening song,
the raging song of fear
that twists the brain, that binds it,
the lyre-shunning song   390
of the Erinyes, draining,
withering life away.

When Fate, the all-directing,   *Antistrophe* 1
spun the unchangeable, ever-
piercing thread of life,
this was the task she gave
us to be ours forever:
those whom rage seizes, who
willfully kill their own
kin with their own hands, we   400
will hound them, drive them down
beneath the earth, and even
in death they'll find scant freedom.

Over our victim's head,   *Refrain 1*
this is the song we sing,
this is the maddening song,
the raging song of fear
that twists the brain, that binds it,
the lyre-shunning song
of the Erinyes, draining,   410
withering life away.

Yes, at our birth, we were given this holy
        task.   *Strophe 2*
So the high gods steer clear of us, and we of them.
None of them would feast with us at the same table;
we have no part in festivals where white robes are
        worn.

The calling I've made my own   *Refrain 2*
is the destruction of houses
when the spirit of Ares, reared,
tamed, pampered in the home,
cuts down a loved one. Then   420
we hunt the doer down,
strong though he is, we suck
his blood away to nothing
for all the blood he shed.

We are all keen to spare others these troubling
        cares,   *Antistrophe 2*
keen, too, to keep the gods from meddling with our
        prayers.
But Zeus despises our band as being soaked in blood
and calls us unworthy to be part of his high company.

The calling I've made my own   *Refrain 2*
is the destruction of houses   430
when the spirit of Ares, reared,
tamed, pampered in the home,
cuts down a loved one. Then
we hunt the doer down,
strong though he is, we suck

his blood away to nothing
for all the blood he shed.

But the self-preening conceits of men, swelling
    so big   *Strophe 3*
under the sun, rot away into earth, all dishonored,
    driven
down by the gale of our black robes rushing upon
    them,   440
by the quick kicks of our raging dance.

For leaping from a great   *Refrain 3*
height I bring the full
force of my foot down
more heavily upon him;
unseen, I thrust out my leg
and even the swiftest runner
stumbles and falls down
to ruin beyond enduring.

But as he falls, his mind so crazed he doesn't know
    it—   *Antistrophe 3*   450
this the miasmal dark that hovers about the man,
and rumor passes its groan from voice to voice to say
that a dense fog has shrouded his house.

For leaping from a great   *Refrain 3*
height I bring the full
force of my foot down
more heavily upon him;
unseen, I thrust out my leg
and even the swiftest runner
stumbles and falls down   460
to ruin beyond enduring.

This stands fixed. Adept at devising,   *Strophe 4*
unmatched alike in remembering wrong done
    as in repaying it;
awful to men, deaf to their pleas,
detested and dishonored we fulfill

our given office; cut off
from the gods, we in the dark slime make
the path rough both for those who live in sunlight
    and for those in sunlessness.   470

Who among mortals is immune   *Antistrophe 4*
to feeling awe and fear when I describe
    the covenant that fate
assigned me, that the gods made final?
My privileges, ancient as they are,
    remain still no less mine.
And I am no less honored for
the station that I hold beneath the ground
    deep in the sunless slime.

                              ATHENA *enters from the left, in full*
                                armor and wearing her aegis.

ATHENA From the Scamander far away I heard   480
        your call for help, as I took possession there
        of land that the Achaean chieftains gave me,
        all completely and forever mine,
        a rich allotment from the spoils of war,
        and a precious gift for Theseus' sons.
        From there I sped, my stride unwearied, wingless
        but for the flap and billow of the folds
        my aegis made.
                      But now I see a strange
        and motley crew of visitors to this land.
        Though I feel no fear, my eyes grow wide with
            wonder.   490
        Who are you? I mean all of you together—
        you stranger with your arms around my image,
        and you who look like nothing ever born—
        not seen by gods among the goddesses,
        or shaped in any human form. But, no,
        it isn't just to speak ill of another
        when he's done nothing wrong; Right won't abide it.

CHORUS LEADER Daughter of Zeus, you'll learn all, in a few words:
we are the children of the never-dying Night.
In our homes beneath the earth we're known as
"Curses."   500

ATHENA I now know your descent, and your true names.

CHORUS LEADER And soon you'll learn our privileges as well.

ATHENA I will, yes, if you tell them to me plainly.

CHORUS LEADER We hound from home the ones who kill their own.

ATHENA Do you chase the killer to some final place?

CHORUS LEADER A place where all joy is unknown to him.

ATHENA And this man here, you howl him on that far?

CHORUS LEADER Yes, since he thought it right to kill his mother.

ATHENA Was he made to do it, fearing some other anger?

CHORUS LEADER What spur's so sharp to make one kill his mother?   510

ATHENA The case has two sides; so far we've heard just one.

CHORUS LEADER He won't swear he's innocent, or yield if I swear to his
guilt.

ATHENA So you would rather seem just than act with justice?

CHORUS LEADER How so? Tell me. For you are rich in wisdom.

ATHENA Injustice shouldn't triumph on an oath.

CHORUS LEADER Then question him yourself. And judge him fairly.

ATHENA You'd take my verdict as the final one?

CHORUS LEADER Yes. We pay you the respect you pay to us.

ATHENA It's your turn, stranger. How will you answer them?
Say first where you come from, who your family is.   520
Explain your circumstances, and then refute
these accusations. If you're sure you sit
in justice near my hearth, clutching my image—
as a holy suppliant, like Ixion before you,
then answer clearly, so I understand.

ORESTES Queen Athena, let me speak first
to the keen anxiety your last words hold.
I'm not a suppliant in need of cleansing.
When I took my seat here at your image,
my hands weren't stained with blood. And I can prove   530
my claim with powerful evidence: by law,
a killer is forbidden to speak a word
till someone with the power to purify
has washed away his blood-guilt with the blood
of a young beast. I have been long since purged
at other houses, both in the blood of sucklings
slain to cleanse me, and in clear-running streams.
My hands are clean. Put your mind at ease.
Now I can tell you straight out where I come from,
who my family is: I am from Argos,   540
and my father, Agamemnon, you know well
as warlord of the fleet who helped you turn
the city of Troy into no city at all.
When he came home, he died an ugly death:
my black-hearted mother cut him down,
wrapped him in her subtle net, a net that
bore witness to the blood bath of his murder.
So I returned, after my years of exile,
and killed the very woman who gave me life—
I don't deny it—killed her for killing him,   550
the father I loved—although Apollo, too, had
an equal hand in this, for he had goaded

me on with warnings of heart-piercing pain
if I failed to get revenge on the murderers.
But it's all up to you now to decide
whether I've acted justly or not. However
the case turns out, I will accept your ruling.

ATHENA This case is too hard for one man to judge.
No, even I don't have the right to rule
on a murder trial like this one, one   560
that calls down such fierce anger either way,
especially as you've come here to my house
a proper suppliant who's clean, who bears
no danger to us, and I welcome you.
And yet these, too, have their appointed task
that can't be shrugged off lightly. If they fail
to get their way, the poison of their outrage,
dripping on the land, will soon become
a deadly everlasting sickness. But since
the problem's up to me to solve, I'll choose   570
a panel of judges to preside at murder
trials like this, and put them under oath,
and so set up a court to last forever.
Now call your witnesses, prepare your proofs,
bring forth whatever evidence you have
that best supports your case. Meanwhile, I'll pick
my ablest citizens, and then return
to deal with this matter fairly, once and for all.

ATHENA *exits to the right.* ORESTES *stands aside during
the following song.*

CHORUS Catastrophes will come,   *Strophe 1*
disasters of new laws, if   580
the mother-killer's mayhem-
making plea prevails.
This deed, from this time on,
will make men poised for any
and all outrageousness.
Truly, parents will await

in time to come the keen
edge of a blade thrust
home by their own child's hand.

And we, wild revelers, who keep   *Antistrophe 1*   590
a close watch over all
men do, will never again
attack them in anger. We'll
let any murder pass:
and one man, seeing his neighbor
suffer, will ask another,
"When will the sickness ease,
or end?" Poor wretch, the balm
he hopes heals evil won't,
and he'll hope in vain.   600

From now on let no one   *Strophe 2*
struck by disaster cry
for help, call out in terror:
"O Justice! O Erinyes,
enthroned in majesty!"
Caught unaware by pain,
some father or mother now
will cry like this, because
the house of Justice falls.

There is a place where dread   *Antistrophe 2*   610
is good, and must abide
to keep watch over all
men think. It's for the best
that wisdom comes from wailing.
What man, or city even,
whose heart's not fed on fear,
would ever again pay Justice
the reverence she's owed?

Praise no life that no law reins,   *Strophe 3*
no life a tyrant rules.   620
   God gives

victory always to the middle way,
    even while seeing to it
differently in different spheres.
Be moderate, I say:
truly, sacrilege
gives birth to recklessness,
but a well mind breeds
what we all love and pray for—
    a lasting, a rich well-being.   630

I tell you, then, revere,   *Antistrophe 3*
in all you do, the altar
    of Justice.
don't kick it over in a wild forgetfulness,
    fixing your hungry gaze
on some brief gain beyond it.
Vengeance will track you down.
The inevitable waits.
Knowing this, first honor
your parents, then respect   640
    the guest you welcome in.

And doing this you will be just   *Strophe 4*
by choice, not by compulsion, and never lack
    well-being—you and yours
will never be dragged down into dirt.
But the wild man, I tell you, shamelessly defiant
    in the face of justice, hauling
his plunder off—he'll be compelled,
in time, to lower his sails when the storm grips him
    and his yardarm snaps and shatters.   650

He calls to those who will not hear him *Antistrophe 4*
as he wrestles to get a grip on whirling water,
    and the god howls with laughter
to see him there, the bold and cocky man
who'd brag that no bad thing could ever touch him
    and now flails, battered by sorrows,
waves rising insurmountably around him.

His lifelong wealth breaks up on the reef of Justice,
and he sinks, unwept, unseen.

ATHENA *enter from the rights, accompanied by a group*
of Athenian citizen-jurors.

ATHENA Herald, declare the court in session, call   660
the people to their places, and let the piercing
Etruscan trumpet, dense with human breath,
blare out its shrill voice to the assembly.
While the court is filling, it is right
that everyone be silent, so that both
the city and these jurors learn the laws
I've fashioned for all time; in that way those
who stand here will receive a just decision.

APOLLO *enters from the left.*

My lord Apollo, take charge of your own affairs:
What role have you played in this matter? Tell us.   670

APOLLO I am here as a witness: when this man
came in supplication to my house
and hearth, as is the custom, I purged him
of the blood he shed. And I am also here
to represent him, for I ordered him
to kill his mother. I am responsible.
Now start the trial, Athena. Take it in hand,
as you know how to do, and set it right.

ATHENA The case is now before us. Plaintiffs speak first.
It's only right you should, for the pursuer,   680
telling the story from beginning to end,
can best explain the nature of the case.

CHORUS LEADER Though we are many, we'll keep our speeches short.

(*addressing* ORESTES)

Answer our charges, each one, as we present it:
First, did you kill your mother? Yes or no.

ORESTES Yes, I killed her. I never said I didn't.

CHORUS LEADER The first fall goes to us. Two more to go.

ORESTES Or so you boast, but no one's thrown me yet.

CHORUS LEADER Then tell us how you killed her, since you must.

ORESTES Yes. I drew my sword and slit her throat.   690

CHORUS LEADER By whose persuasion? By whose sage advice?

ORESTES By this god's oracle. He is my witness.

CHORUS LEADER The god taught you it's right to kill your mother?

ORESTES Yes, and till now I have nothing to complain of.

CHORUS LEADER But when the verdict snares you, you'll change your
                tune.

ORESTES I trust him; and my father will help me from the
                grave.

CHORUS LEADER Good, kill your mother, and then trust in corpses!

ORESTES Yes, I killed her since she was doubly defiled.

CHORUS LEADER How exactly? Explain it to the judges.

ORESTES She killed my father when she killed her husband.   700

CHORUS LEADER Death freed her from her guilt, but you're still living.

ORESTES Why didn't you hunt her down while she still lived?

171

CHORUS LEADER The man she killed was not her flesh and blood.

ORESTES You think I have the same blood as my mother's?

CHORUS LEADER How else could she have fed you in her womb,
you killer? You spurn the mother blood you live by?

ORESTES Now testify, Apollo, on my behalf
and teach the law to show whether I did
or didn't act with justice when I killed her—
for I did kill her, that I don't deny.   710
But you determine whether or not this blood
was justly shed, so I can make my case.

APOLLO I say to all of you, to this high court
established by Athena, he acted justly.
I am a prophet; I can never lie.
Not once from my far seeing throne have I
said anything concerning a man, a woman,
or even a city that Zeus himself, father
of the Olympians, did not command.
Be mindful of how powerful this plea   720
for justice is. Follow my father's will.
No oath is stronger than almighty Zeus.

CHORUS LEADER So you want us to believe that Zeus gave you
this oracle to pass on to Orestes,
told him to avenge his father's murder
and, in the process, cast aside, trample
to nothing, the respect he owed his mother?

APOLLO Yes, I do. For it's a different thing
entirely when a noble man who holds
the scepter Zeus bestows is murdered, struck down   730
not even by the far-shot arrow of
some Amazon, but by a woman's hand,
and in a manner I'll describe to you,
Athena, and to all you seated here

to judge the case by vote. Once he returned
from war where he did well enough, on balance,
the woman made a show of being kind,
seemed anxious to please him, fuss over him like a
    wife,
until, as he was stepping from the bath,
there at the very end, she swaddled him   740
in a winding cloth, tangling him up from head
to toe within the endless fold on fold
of the embroidered robe, then struck him down.
This is how wretchedly he died, a man
all men revered, commander of the fleet.
I've spoken as I have to whip up anger
in you who are called to set this matter right.

CHORUS LEADER So it's your view that Zeus's main concern
is for a father's death. Yet didn't he
himself chain up his aged father, Cronus?   750
How do you square this with your argument?
Heed what you just heard, judges. Remember it.

APOLLO You stinking, hideous filth, shunned by the gods,
we can break bonds, we can slip out of shackles!
    There's
a cure for ills like those, yes, countless ways
of getting free. But once a man is dead,
and the ground has sucked dry all his blood,
nothing can ever raise him up again.
My father made no healing spell for that,
though he can turn all other things, at will,   760
inside and out, and not pant from the effort.

CHORUS LEADER See where your way of pleading for this man
has led you: he has spilled his mother's dear
blood on the ground—so how can he live in Argos,
take possession of his father's house?
What public altars could he use? How can he touch
the cleansing water at his kinsmen's shrine?

173

APOLLO I'll tell you something else, to show how right
        I am: the so-called mother of the child
        isn't the child's begetter, but only a sort   770
        of nursing soil for the new-sown seed.
        The man, the one on top, is the true parent,
        while she, a stranger, fosters a stranger's sprout,
        if no god blights it. And I can prove it to you:
        a father can give birth without a mother.
        And here before us is our witness, child
        of Olympian Zeus, daughter who never fed
        and grew within the darkness of a womb,
        a seedling that no goddess could bring forth.
        In all things, Pallas, and with all my power,   780
        I'll glorify your people and your city;
        for that's the very reason I sent this man
        here to your house and hearth so he could be
        a constant friend to you for all time to come,
        a friend and ally, goddess, he and his heirs,
        each one of their descendents who will keep
        this sacred bond, this covenant forever.

ATHENA Have we now heard enough? Should I tell these
              judges
        to cast their votes where they think justice lies?

APOLLO Our quiver's empty, all our arrows shot.   790
        I'll wait to see which way the trial goes.

ATHENA

                              (*turning to the* CHORUS)

        And what must I do now to avoid your reproach?

CHORUS LEADER You've heard what you've heard, and as you vote, my
                    friends,
            with all your heart respect the oath you've sworn.

ATHENA Now hear my ordinance, you men of Athens,
        you who have been chosen to decide

this first trial ever for the shedding of blood.
Now and in future time, this court of judges
will continue to exist for the people of Aegeus,
here on this hill of Ares where the Amazons   800
pitched their tents when they invaded, armed,
and angry at King Theseus, raised up
against the city the towering walls of their
own battlements, and slit the throats of beasts
in sacrifice to Ares. This is why
we call this place the rock and hill of Ares.
Here the people's awe and innate fear
will hold injustice back by day, by night,
so long as the people leave the laws intact,
just as they are, and never alter them   810
with foul infusions: muddy the cleanest spring,
and all you'll have to drink is muddy water.
I urge my people to follow and revere
neither tyranny nor anarchy,
and to hold fear close, never to cast it out
entirely from the city. For what man
who feels no fear is able to be just?
And if you fear and justly revere this court,
then you will have a bulwark for your land,
the city's guardian, the like of which   820
nobody else on earth possesses, not even
the law-abiding Scythians, or Spartans.
This council I establish will be immune
from greed, majestic, poised for wrath, the country's
wakeful watchman over those who sleep.

I've given this long advice to all my people—
it's for the future. But now you must stand up,
take up your ballots and decide the case,
respecting your sacred oath. My speech is done.

> *During the following exchange, the jurors arise,*
> *proceed to the voting urns, deposit their ballots,*
> *and return to their seats.*

CHORUS LEADER I warn you all—if you dishonor us,   830
               we'll be a crushing burden on your land.

       APOLLO And I tell you to fear the oracles,
               Zeus's and mine. Don't keep them from bearing fruit.

CHORUS LEADER You honor bloody crimes that aren't your business.
               Your oracles will never now be pure.

       APOLLO So Zeus made a mistake when Ixion,
               the first to kill, appealed to him for help?

CHORUS LEADER You said it, I didn't. But if I don't get justice,
               I will come back to crush this land forever.

       APOLLO How so? You have no honor among gods,   840
               young or old. I will win this case.

CHORUS LEADER You did the same thing, too, in Pheres' house:
               you persuaded the Fates to let men hide from death.

       APOLLO Is it unjust to treat someone so kindly,
               someone that pious, in his time of need?

CHORUS LEADER You overturned the age-old covenant
               by duping those ancient goddesses with wine.

       APOLLO And when you lose this trial, you'll vomit all
               your venom at the ones you hate—quite harmlessly.

CHORUS LEADER Young one, since you would trample down your
                              elders,   850
               I'll have to wait to hear if the court will give me
               justice, or the city feel my wrath.

       ATHENA My office makes me last to judge this case.
               And I will cast my ballot for Orestes.
               No mother gave me birth, and in all things
               but marriage I wholeheartedly approve

the male—I am entirely my father's child.
And this is why the killing of a woman
who killed her husband, guardian of the house,
can have no overriding claim on me.   860
Orestes wins, even if the votes be equal.

(turning to the jurors)

You jurors who have this duty to fulfill,
quickly spill out the ballots from the urns.

Two jurors return to the urns and begin the count.
ATHENA *takes a place behind the urns.*

ORESTES   Phoebus Apollo, how will it be decided?

CHORUS LEADER   Black Night, our mother, are you watching this?

ORESTES   It's time now—to feel the noose, or see the light!

CHORUS LEADER   To be disgraced, or forever keep our honors!

APOLLO   Count up the spilled out votes precisely, friends,
make no mistake, be sure the sum is just.
Out of bad judgment comes catastrophe,   870
But when the judgment's sound, a single vote
can reestablish order in a house.

ATHENA   *(examining the ballots)*   This man's acquitted on the
                     charge of murder—
the number of votes for both sides is the same.

ORESTES   O Pallas Athena, you have saved my house!
When I was stripped bare of my homeland,
you gave it back to me. Now Greeks will say:
"The man is Argive once again; he lives
among his father's holdings by the grace
of Pallas and Apollo, and of the third,   880
the savior, he who brings all to fulfillment."

Yes he, himself, gave due weight to the way
my father died, and has delivered me
to safety from my mother's advocates.

And now before I leave for home, I swear
to your country and your people, now and forever,
up to the fullest ripening of time
that no helmsman of my realm, spear poised for
      battle,
will come against them. Even from my tomb,
I'll torture the transgressors of this oath   890
with failure and befuddlement. I'll sap
the spirit from their marches, and beset
their way with ominous wingbeats, so that they
regret they ever did what they have done.
But only if they keep an upright course,
and give enduring honor to the city
of Pallas with their loyal spears, will I
remain a blessing to them.
                    And so goodbye
to you, and to the people of your city.
May the hold you get on all your enemies   900
allow them no escape, and keep you safe,
and if war comes bring you the victory.

ORESTES *exits to the left, accompanied by* APOLLO.

CHORUS IOU! IOU! You young gods—you   *Refrain* 1
      have trampled down the age-old laws,
        ripped them out of my hands!
      My honor stripped away, enraged,
        aggrieved, now I
      will squeeze out all the poison in my heart
      against the land for all I've suffered,
      yes, poison now will ooze and drip   910
      unbearably into the soil.
        And out of it pale fungus
      blighting leaf and child (O justice!)
        will quicken across

the land to cover it and all the people
   in a miasmal fog of
killing illnesses. Sorrow!
What can I do? Mocked! Spit on
   by the citizens!
We suffer the insufferable,   920
   luckless daughters of Night
who have been wronged, stripped of our honor!

ATHENA Let me persuade you not to shoulder such
        a burden of grief—because you weren't defeated,
        the voting in the trial was truly equal;
        you haven't been disgraced, no. After all,
        the evidence from Zeus shown clear, and he
        who gave the oracle bore witness that
        Orestes should not be harmed for what he did.
        So don't be angry; no longer aim your out-   930
        rage on this land, or send out blight against it,
        the piercing vapors that eat up the seeds.
        I swear wholeheartedly to you, in justice,
        that you will have your seat in a vast cavern
        deep in this land of justice, and there you will sit
        on gleaming thrones beside your sacred altars,
        forever honored by my citizens.

CHORUS IOU! IOU! You young gods—you   *Refrain* 1
        have trampled down the age-old laws,
           ripped them out of my hands!   940
        My honor stripped away, enraged,
           aggrieved, now I
        will squeeze out all the poison in my heart
        against the land for all I've suffered,
        yes, poison now will ooze and drip
        unbearably into the soil.
           And out of it pale fungus
        blighting leaf and child (O justice!)
           will quicken across
        the land to cover it and all the people   950
           in a miasmal fog

of killing illnesses. Sorrow!
What can I do? Mocked! Spit on
   by the citizens!
We suffer the insufferable,
   luckless daughters of Night
who have been wronged, stripped of our honor!

ATHENA Not stripped of honor, no. You're goddesses,
don't in a rush of anger blast the land
of mortals. I have Zeus on my side and—   960
why even bring it up?—I'm the only one
among the gods who knows where he keeps the key
to the chamber in which the lightning bolt is sealed.
No, we won't have need of that. Please,
let me persuade you not to spew from foolish
lips such curses against the land as make
all things that bear fruit shrivel up and die.
Soothe into sleep the black wave of your rage,
its bitter surging: for you'll be honored here,
and worshipped, and share my home. And when   970
you receive the first fruits of this great land
offered up to you in hope of children
and for the fulfillment of the marriage rite,
you'll thank me for this advice I've given you.

CHORUS That they would do this to me!   *Refrain 2*
Force me, with all my age-old wisdom,
   under this earth
like some defiled contaminated thing!
I'm breathing rage, sheer rage.
   OTOTOTOI POPOI! DA!   980
What torture slides down over me
   and through my brain!
Hear me O mother Night—the gods'
sleight of hand has snatched
my ancient rights away and made me
   less than nothing.

ATHENA I'll put up with your anger, for you are much
       older than I am—and, therefore, so much wiser.
       But Zeus has given me a keen mind too,
       and if you leave here for a foreign country   990
       I warn you now you'll long just like a lover
       for this country you have left behind.
       For time as it flows forward will bring great
       and greater honors to the people here,
       And honorably seated near the house
       of Erechtheus, you'll receive from long
       processionals of men and women more gifts
       than any other place on earth could give.
       Don't set the inciting whetstone of bloodshed spinning
       throughout my land, sharpening the hearts of young   1000
       men till they're seized by a wildness not of wine.
       Don't make their hearts seethe like the seething hearts
       of fighting cocks, infusing in my people
       a war lust they'll turn inward on each other.
       May all their warfare be with foreigners,
       and may the wars be plentiful enough
       to sate their fiercest hunger for renown.
       There's nothing brave about a cock who fights
       inside the nest.
                       So it is your choice now
       to take what I am holding out to you: 1010
       to do well and receive well and, well honored,
       have your own share of this land the gods love well.

CHORUS That they would do this to me!   *Refrain 2*
       Force me, with all my age-old wisdom,
           under this earth
       like some defiled contaminated thing!
       I'm breathing rage, sheer rage.
           OTOTOTOI POPOI! DA!
       What torture slides down over me
           and through my brain!   1020
       Hear me O mother night—the gods'
       sleight of hand has snatched

my ancient rights away and made me
   less than nothing.

ATHENA I'll never tire of telling you the benefits
I'm offering, so you can never say
that you, an elder goddess, have been disgraced
and driven into exile from this country,
either by me, a younger goddess, or by
the mortal keepers of the city. No!   1030
But if you hold in awe Persuasion's glory,
the power of my tongue to soothe and enchant,
you might live here with us. Still, if you don't,
if you choose not to, it would not be right
to bring the riot of your raging hate
against the city, to harm the people. The way
is free for you to be a landholder here,
enjoying honor justly and forever.

CHORUS LEADER What kind of place would be mine, Queen Athena?

ATHENA One free of pain. Will you make it yours?   1040

CHORUS LEADER And if I do, what honor will I have?

ATHENA No house will ever grow without your blessing.

CHORUS LEADER You'd make me as powerful as that?

ATHENA We'll swell the fortunes of your followers.

CHORUS LEADER You promise me this power's mine forever?

ATHENA I wouldn't promise what I won't fulfill.

CHORUS LEADER You might persuade me; I feel my anger easing.

ATHENA Live with me here, and you'll have more friends, new
     friends.

CHORUS LEADER What blessings would you have my chant call forth?

ATHENA Blessings that bring victory without dishonor,   1050
blessings that come from earth, and from the water
of the sea, and from the sky that make the air
across the land breathe out in sunlit breezes;
blessings that make the earth's yield swell, and the
    thick
herds grow more bountiful as time goes on
and never fail my people. Their seed, too,
you'll bless and protect, and may you favor most
the purest among them, make them prosper most.
I'm like a gardener, caring for the stock
of these just men, keeping them safe from sorrow.   1060
These are the blessings that are yours to give
while I will shower glory on their battles,
and never fail to let the city's fame
for victory resound in every land.

CHORUS I will accept a home   *Strophe* 1
here in the house of Pallas,
and won't dishonor the city
ruled by Zeus all-mighty
and Ares as the fortress
of the gods, protector of   1070
the altars of the Greeks,
city that all rejoice in,
city for which I pray
and lovingly foretell
that the bright rays of the sun
will make the earth bring forth
in rich profusion all
the good things that foster life.

ATHENA Since my heart is filled with tenderness
    for all my people,   1080
I have ensconced these powerful,
demanding goddesses here among them,
goddesses whose task it is

183

to oversee the lives of men.
    And any man
they train their hate on doesn't know

from where the flurry of hard blows
    crashes against
his life. Ancestral crime pulls him down
before their judgment seat, and while   1090
he brags out loud, silently
their crushing hatred hits him, their
    implacable rage
grinds him completely down to dust.

CHORUS May no fierce wind blast the trees—   *Antistrophe 1*
these are my words of grace—
and may no heat that sears
the plants and kills their buds,
cross this land's boundary.
May no blight waste the crops.   1100
May Pan swell the swarming
flocks, double their yield
at the appointed time.
And may the land's children
find veins of wealth within
the soil and honor the gods
with sacrifice for the luck
of their discoveries.

ATHENA Jurors, bulwark of the city,
    do you hear what blessings   1110
she'll bring about? The power of the great
Erinyes awes the gods above
and those below, achieves their ends
for all to see, bringing bright
    joyous life
to some, life blind with tears to others.

CHORUS I ban, too, the untimely   *Strophe 2*
killing of young men;

and you gods who possess
the power to do so, let   1120
young girls find husbands—
especially you Fates,
our sisters from one mother,
goddesses whose share is just,
who have a hand in every
home, whose force weighs
heavily in every season,
whose reckoning, exact
in all ways is in all
ways honored by the gods.   1130

ATHENA They bless my land so lovingly
            that my heart swells.
        I'm glad Persuasion's eye watched over
        my lips and tongue when I first faced
        their brutal "No!" But Zeus who guides
        men's speech won out. Our rivalry
            in doing good
        gives victory to good forever.

CHORUS I pray that the crazed voice   *Antistrophe 2*
        of civil strife that feeds   1140
        on evil and is never full
        may never roar through this land.
        And may the earth not guzzle
        down the black blood of its people,
        and then, hot for revenge,
        welcome the city's ruin,
        murder paid back with murder.
        Instead let citizens
        give joy for joy,
        loving the common good,   1150
        hating a common foe:
        they'll cure most ills this way.

ATHENA These women, have they the wisdom to find
            a path of blessing?

Then I discern in their dread faces
great gain for all my people. Revere them,
be kindly to these kindly ones,
and you will keep the land and city
    on the straight path
of justice, and shine in everything.   1160

CHORUS Farewell! Rejoice amid   *Strophe 3*
the wealth you've earned! Goodbye,
you people of the city
dwelling near the throne
of Zeus, loving the goddess
who loves you well, wiser
with every passing day,
safe in the wings of Pallas
whose father honors you.

ATHENA Goodbye to you! I'll go before you   1170
    and show you to
your chambers by the sacred light
these escorts hold. Now go, and take
with you these holy offerings.
Hurry beneath the ground and hide
    down deep within it
whatever's harmful to the city;

whatever's to the city's gain
    send up, so she
may always be triumphant! You sons   1180
of Cranaus, keepers of the city,
lead the way for them, our new
inhabitants, and may the people
    receive with good
hearts all the goodness they are given.

CHORUS Farewell! Goodbye again   *Antistrophe 3*
I say, to everyone
within the city, gods
as well as mortals. Watch over

Athena's city well,   1190
revere my dwelling here
among you, and the lives
you lead will give you nothing
ever to complain of.

> *A group of women equal in number to*
> *the Chorus enters, carrying crimson robes, preceded*
> *by torchbearers, and followed by one or more sacrificial*
> *animals led by attendants.*

ATHENA I thank you for the blessings you have spoken.
I'll lead you by the dancing light of torches
to your deep chamber underneath the earth,
accompanied by my attendants, the women appointed
in justice to guard my image. I invite you
into the very heart of Theseus' land.   1200
And now, you honorable band of young
girls, women, aged ladies, dress them
as suits their dignity in purple robes,
and let the torches flare and dance, so that
they'll always show their kindness to the land
in blessings that bring glory to our men.

> *The* ESCORT, *made up of the jurors and*
> *the band of women and led by the torchbearers,*
> *accompanies the Erinyes to the right.*

ESCORT Go on to your new home, you awesome children
of Night, you aged children,
childless children, covetous of honor,
under a kind escort.   1210
Hush now, people, all of you, speak well,
only auspicious words.
Deep in earth's oldest caverns, you'll be graced
with worship and sacrifices—
Hush now, citizens, all of you, speak well,
only auspicious words.
Gracious and favoring the land that favors you,

come this way, venerable ones,
radiant in the torch-devouring flame,
    rejoicing as you go.   1220
Lift up a joyous cry in rhythm to our song.
    There will be peace forever
among the people of Pallas. All-seeing
    Zeus and Fate have helped
us make it so. Lift up a joyous cry
    together and crown our song!

NOTES ON THE TEXT

1–47 / 1–39 *Prologue* The prologue consists of a short speech, but one in which the tensions of the drama to come are foreshadowed. Indeed the shape of this speech sets the pattern that the play will display again and again, moving from hopeful anticipation to foreboding. If, as there is no real reason to doubt, the Watchman appeared on the roof as the play began, it will also have provided a striking and probably novel scenic effect. It is possible that a permanent wooden stage was first erected in the Theater of Dionysus shortly before the first performance of the *Oresteia,* and this may well be the first time that the roof of the scene building was used for an entrance. See Hammond, "Conditions of Dramatic Production."

6 / 6 *the unignorable bright potentates* The major stars or constellations whose movements through the heavens mark the changing seasons.

33–34 / 28 *a shout / of triumph* This cry, *ololugmos* in Greek, is heard again at strategic points in the trilogy. At 669/587, Clytemnestra says that she "cried in triumph" when she first had news of Agamemnon's reurn; and at 1413–14/1236, Cassandra foresees, as if it had already happened, how Clytemnestra "trumpeted / her triumph" at Agamemnon's slaughter. At *Libation Bearers* 441/387, the Chorus looks forward to sounding a "shrill triumphant cry" when Clytemnestra and Aegisthus are slain in turn, and at 1071–75/942–45 they call for a song of triumph for what they hope is the rescue of the house. Only at the end of *Eumenides* does the *ololugmos* become truly "a joyous cry" (**1221 and 1225**/1043 and 1047) of celebration.

39 / 33 *rolls a triple six* A winning cast of the dice in *petteia*, a kind of ancient backgammon.

48–296 / 40–257 *Parodos* This choral entrance song is the most extended, complex, and magnificent in surviving Greek drama. The first section (**48–123/ 40–103**) is a chant that accompanies the entrance proper; the following choral ode consists of a series of stanzas in varied rhythms, articulated in pairs of metrically equivalent stanzas known as "strophe" and "antistrophe." This pattern is characteristic also of act-dividing choral songs. In this parodos there is also one "nonresponding" (i.e., unpaired) stanza referred to as an "epode" (**159–78/140–59**). The Chorus sang its choral odes to the accompaniment of the *aulos*, a sort of ancient oboe, while dancing to the rhythm of each stanza. Each paired strophe and antistrophe ("turn" and "counterturn") presumably also featured closely matched dance steps.

48–123 / 40–103 The rhythm of these lines is called "marching anapests" because it is often associated, as here, with the entrance of the choruses in marching formation. It seems to have been chanted in a manner midway between the heightened speech of dialogue verse and the full singing mode of the choral ode.

71 / 59 *the Erinys* The ominous name (usually translated "Fury" and denoting a spirit of retribution sent by the dead against the living) is withheld in the Greek, as in our translation, until the very end of the sentence. Aeschylus thus introduces early on the figure of revenge that will play so central a part in the trilogy. The simile of birds lamenting the loss of their young has as its immediate referent the Greeks poised to seek retribution from the Trojans, but it suggests also the sacrifice of the young Iphigenia, to which the Chorus will return in their song. See further the Introduction, p. 8.

73 / 61–62 *Zeus, protector of host and guest* Zeus *xenios* (i.e., protector of the rights of *xenoi*, those who are in a reciprocal relation of guest-friendship) is invoked because the justice of the war against Troy lies in its punishment of Paris's violation of the Menelaus' hospitality by stealing Helen from him.

77 / 62 *one woman claimed by many men* Helen was abducted by Theseus, courted by all the Greek heroes, and won by Menelaus. Taken to Troy Paris, after his death she married his brother Deiphobus.

79–80 / 65 *the flickering rite / before the blazing sacrifice* The battles over Troy are imaged as *proteleia*, preliminary rites before the sacrifice that is the city's destruction. This use of *proteleia* is deeply ironic, since the word is associated primarily with a sacrifice offered before marriage and therefore has in its ordinary usage happy and propitious associations. It will be used again in contexts of bloodshed and violence at **260/226** and **821/720**, and see also on *Eumenides* **972–73/835**.

85–86 / 69 *tongue / of fire, or liquid* Burnt offerings or libations, the most common forms of propitiatory sacrifice. Once the struggle has reached its "destined end," such rituals will have no efficacy.

100–102 / 83–84 It is possible that Clytemnestra has appeared at the doors of the palace at this point, but since she will not be addressed again until **297/258**, it seems far likelier that the Chorus here summons her by way of motivating their appearance at the palace. They have observed the sacrifices that she has instituted throughout the city (**102–15/85–96**), and they hope to learn why she has done so.

124–296 / 104–257 The choral ode proper is exceedingly rich and complex. It is divided by rhythm as well as subject into three main divisions: **124–78/104–59** deals with the omen that greeted the assembled Greek fleet at Aulis; **179–221/160–90** is largely devoted to the "hymn to Zeus," in which the Chorus gropes to understand the meaning of the events that their song evokes, but also includes the beginning of the narrative of the sacrifice of Iphigenia that is developed at length and with extraordinary pathos in the third section, **222–96/191–57**.

139 / 121 *Sing sorrow, sorrow* This line becomes a refrain (cf. **158/139**, **178/159**) as the power of "persuasion" (another leading theme of the trilogy introduced early and in an equivocal fashion) leads them against their will, as it were, to sing the terrible story of Iphigenia. Notice how quickly the mood changes from the confident declaration of "mastery . . . to sing of the good omens" at **124/104** to this note of discomfiture as the omens turn against them.

140 / 122 *the good seer* Identified as Calchas at **175/156**.

148 / 130 *Fate* Greek *Moira*, literally "lot" or "portion," personified in the *Oresteia* to represent not a general notion of destiny but a specific divine enforcer of the connection between actions and their consequences, and thus a moral, or even quasi-legal, force. One godsent *moira* can conflict with another (see on 1166/1025–27), but at the end of *Eumenides* Zeus and Fate stand together (1224/1045–46) as guarantors of the new civic peace.

154–55 / 136 *her father's flying blood- / hounds* The eagles, birds identified with her father Zeus. The depiction of the hare as pregnant with "unripe young" (**156/137**) suggests that it is as goddess of childbirth that Artemis is angered, in which case the culmination of the prophecy in the slaughter of Iphigenia takes on a dark irony.

159–62 / 140–43 These lines emphasize Artemis' role as protector of wild beasts, but since the eagles in the omens represent the Atreidae, we can also interpret her revulsion at the birds (connected with her father in his role as enforcer of the laws of guest-friendship) as opposition to their expedition. In Homer's *Iliad*, Artemis is a supporter of the Trojans, and here she seems to be exacting her own retribution for the loss she will suffer there. It is worth noting that the saga tradition (known to us from Hesiod and the fragmentary remains of the *Cypria*, a post-Homeric epic of the Troy cycle, has Artemis punish Agamemnon for shooting one of her sacred deer and boasting that he was a better archer than she. Aeschylus prefers to leave her anger—and Agamemnon's responsibility—less clearly explained.

179–82 / 160–62 *Whoever Zeus may be* The "Hymn to Zeus," following the pained description of Calchas's interpretation of the omen, sounds as much like an attempt to achieve some peace of mind as like a declaration of faith. In this context, a prayer formula meant to assure that the desired god is addressed by the correct name takes on the overtones of a real question: who—what—is the overwhelming, incomprehensible power apparently at work everywhere the Chorus looks?

189–99 / 168–75 Uranus (Greek *Ouranos*, the sky), is "he who was once great," the first ruler of the universe. He was castrated and deposed by his son, Cronus, "he who threw him." Cronus and his siblings of the Titan generation were defeated and deposed in turn by Zeus. That they are nameless, as if they never existed, is an indication of Zeus's might and the completeness of his victory. The language of this victory is taken from the Greek wrestling match, in which the victor had to win three falls. See further the Introduction, p. 37–38.

211–21 / 83–90 The law of Zeus expounded in the preceding strophe is exemplified in its antistrophe by a specific dilemma, the winds that keep the fleet from sailing. The resulting example of violence and suffering—Agamemnon's decision to sacrifice his daughter—is one from which the Chorus implicitly hopes some grace can be shown to have come, some lesson to have been learned.

248–53 / 218–21 *the yoke-strap / of necessity . . . mere ruthlessness* Notice that although Agamemnon has clearly set out the dilemma and his possible responses to it, his decision is treated first as tantamount to acting under compulsion, then as yielding to an evil madness. Both reactions express deeply felt reactions to the horrible sequence of events. Their apparent incompatibility (at least from our point of view) demonstrates the utter insolubility of the dilemma.

260 / 226 *an early offering* This translates *proteleia*, the usual name for an offering made before a wedding, but which here ironically refers to the sacrifice of the still unmarried daughter. See further on 79–80/65.

261–84 / 228–47 For comments on some aspects of the representation of the sacrifice of Iphigenia, see the Introduction, p. 30. This is one of the most important of a series of perverted rites of sacrifice analyzed in detail by Zeitlin, "The Motif of Corrupted Sacrifice."

270 / 235–36 *he had her mouth gagged* This is the first of many instances of cloths used to bind, stifle, and ensnare; and these images are closely related to the motif of the yoke or bridle, as at **248**/218.

297–406 / 258–354 *First episode*

320–59 / 281–316 Clytemnestra's beacon speech. The leading image here is that of fire leaping from Mount Ida, above the plain of Troy, to Arachne's peak, a mountain close to Argos, from which it "swooped down on the royal house" (**352**/310). Symbolically, then, the movement of the beacon flame that ostensibly signals the end of a long and terrible war suggests instead the passage of the flames that have ravaged Priam's city to Agamemnon's, where they will wreak further destruction. Although not all the places mentioned are identifiable, the pattern of movement from east to west is clear and suggests at once Clytemnestra's careful planning for Agamemnon's return and the ineluctable approach of new deaths and suffering.

354–57 / 312–14 Clytemnestra likens the passing of the beacons to a torch-relay race, such as those held at Athens in honor of several deities, including Athena, at the great Panathenaic festival, and the god of fire himself, Hephaestus (cf. 320/281). In Clytemnestra's race, she says with heavy irony, there are only victors, but although the import of the beacons is decidedly mixed, this "flame descendant of the fire of Ida" will have as its final offspring the final torchlit procession of the Athenians who accompany the Eumenides to their new home (*Eumenides*, 1195ff./ 1021ff.).

386–98 / 338–47 Clytemnestra's warning of troubles to come for the Greeks is both prophetic and ironic. The original audience would have been aware of a number of atrocities and sacrileges attributed to the victors, such as Neoptolemus's slaughter of Priam at the altar of Zeus, where he was a suppliant, and the rape of Cassandra by Ajax, son of Oileus, in the temple of Athena, where she had sought refuge. They knew that as a consequence, the gods had sent a terrible storm that dispersed the returning fleet, in which many warriors were drowned and others set on long, difficult homecomings. The irony that comes from Clytem-nestra's murderous intentions is clearest in her final prayer, with its entirely equivocal wish that "the good / win out completely for all men to see" (399–400/349), but extends as well to her warning against wak-ening "the anger of the dead / for what was done to them" (396–97/ 346), which might surely include Iphigenia. Clytemnestra's admonition about the desecration of sacred places (386–89/338–40) is sometimes taken as an ugly pretense masking her real hopes, but its primary pur-pose is not to characterize her, but to invest with a sense of inevitable ruin the Greek Herald's announcement (598–99/527–28) that Troy's altars and shrines have been destroyed (see further the Introduction, pp. 10–11).

407–552 / 355–488 *First stasimon* (act-dividing choral song) The Chorus Leader ended the first episode on an hopeful note, and the Chorus proceeds to sing the song of thanks he promised to the gods. As in the parodos, however, the mood quickly changes to one of discontent and forebod-ing. becoming a lament for all who died in the struggle and a warning against striving for "excessive glory" (533/468). This song, like many others in tragedy, separates events—here, the announcement of Troy's fall by means of the beacons and the return of Agamemnon and his Argives—that are depicted as simply following one another but cannot (and need not) be regarded as contiguous in time.

411 / 358 *the smothering mesh* This net is another example of the trilogy's pervasive binding/bridling imagery (see on 270/235–36).

417 / 362 *Zeus, lord of host and guest* Zeus *xenios* (see on 73/61–62).

441 / 385 *miserable Persuasion* Persuasion is another central motif of the trilogy (for an overview, see the Introduction, pp. 21–22). The persuasion referred to here is the sort of temptation with which personified Destruction (Greek *Atê*) is said to lead people astray, and which can thus be personified as her daughter. Helen is one agent of such temptation (in her case erotic temptation, a form so well known that Persuasion is sometimes pictured as a minor goddess in Aphrodite's retinue), and her sister Clytemnestra will soon prove to be another.

447 / 390 *bad bronze blackening* Bronze adulterated with lead turns black with use.

500 / 438 *The war god, broker of bodies* Ares is compared to a gold-changer, who gives gold (or gold dust) in exchange for objects that would almost certainly be much heavier. Ares sets up his scales in the midst of battle, exchanging live warriors for the ashes that comes from the funeral pyre. This dust, however, is said to be heavy (*baru*, which can also mean "grievous") because it is freighted with the grief of loved ones.

548 / 483 *So like a woman's sharp spirit* At 403/351, the Chorus Leader spoke of Clytemnestra's account of the beacons and Troy's fall as spoken "like a wise man," but by the end of their song, the Chorus's mood is somber and they are less ready to give credence to what they construe as a woman's credulous hope.

553–773 / 489–680 *Second episode* The pattern of movement from hope to foreboding, good news to bad, continues in the speeches of the Argive Herald, who announces Agamemnon's imminent arrival.

553–67 / 489–500 The manuscripts give these lines to Clytemnestra, but we follow most recent editors in giving them to the Chorus Leader, and believe that Clytemnestra does not return to the stage until 669. The grounds for these positions are given by Taplin, *Stagecraft of Aeschylus* 294–302.

577 / 510 *your shafts no longer raining down* Apollo, although addressed by a cult name—king of Pytho—that derives from his oracular role at Delphi, is invoked specifically as archer god. The Greek audience would think of the plague Apollo sent against the Greeks with his arrows in Book 1 of Homer's *Iliad*, especially because the god is asked to be "once again our healer" (580/512), another of his traditional roles.

588 / 519 *deities that greet the sun* The reference is uncertain, but we are apparently to imagine that images of gods revered in Argos are standing before the palace; that they "greet the sun" may mean no more than that the palace faces east.

597 / 525–26 *avenging Zeus* Zeus *dikêphoros*, literally "vengeance bearer" or "bringer of justice."

598–99 / 527–28 *The altars . . . are leveled* See on 386–98/338–47.

600 / 529 *the yoke* For the image, see on 248–53/218–21 and 270/325–26.

667–68 / 585–86 The Chorus Leader's final couplet may accompany Clytemnestra's entrance, but is even more effective (as Taplin, *Stagecraft of Aeschylus* 299–300, points out) if it is spoken before she appears, and is in effect an invitation to the Herald to enter the palace and give Clytemnestra his news. In that case, Clytemnestra's abrupt entrance, before he can even knock on the door, will confer an almost uncanny sense that she is in control of the situation. She will leave with similar abruptness after making her speech, but without involving anyone else in dialogue. As she says (681/598), she has no need of the Herald's message.

669 / 587 *I cried in triumph* See on 33–34/28. The *ololugmos* is repeated at 678/595.

688 / 604 *take to my lord this message* Clytemnestra boldly tests in the presence of the Chorus the hypocritical professions of fidelity with which she will later greet Agamemnon.

695 / 609 *the marriage seal* The Greek simply has "seal" and might refer to the normal practice of sealing treasures in storerooms during a king's absence, but we have preferred to make clear that the word in this context connotes "seal of chastity," as indicated by the lines immediately following.

698 / 612 *how to dye bronze* The phrase might refer to the tempering of metal—in which a woman would presumably be untrained—but Greek *baphas*

can equally denote dyeing of fabrics (as at 1100/960), and here suggests the coloring of a sword with blood—something that Clytemnestra will soon show Agamemnon she knows how to do.

703 / 617 *tell me now of Menelaus* The wanderings of Menelaus, recounted in Book 4 of Homer's *Odyssey*, formed the subject of *Proteus*, the lost satyr play that followed the three tragedies of the *Oresteia* (see the Introduction, footnote 1). Here, the Chorus Leader's questioning leads the Herald, against his will (722–23/636–37), even further into words of ill omen.

730–31 / 642–43 *double-pointed . . . two-tipped . . . twins* The image here derives from the two points of the Greek whip or scourge, the repetition presumably emphasizing the doubling of disasters, public and private, of which the Herald is speaking.

735 / 645 *to sing in tribute to the Erinyes* The Herald proposes, in a shocking oxymoron, to offer the *paean*, a song of thanksgiving or triumph associated above all with Apollo, in honor of the Erinyes. The music that befits them is "the dirge the lyre shuns" (1135/990–92, and cf. *Eumenides*, 390/332–33).

741 / 651 *fire and sea* The fire is Zeus' lightning; the phrasing is designed to evoke the proverbial emnity of fire and water to suggest a world in which even the elemental forces of nature conspire to destroy the returning Greeks.

774–891 / 681–809 *Second stasimon* This song turns back to the beginning of the Trojan calamity through the figure of Helen, who becomes the starting point for a meditation on the more general truths that no evil action is without its consequences.

782 / 687 *Helen: destroyer* In the Greek, there is a bitter pun, in which the root *hel-* (seize, destroy) is treated as if it were the source of Helen's name, so that she can be called *helenas, helandros, heleptolis* (ship-destroying, man-destroying, city-destroying). An aspect of the power of words in ancient thought is the belief that names contain clues to one's nature or destiny (the *nomen-omen* principle). Thus, for example, in Sophocles' *Ajax*, the hero's name (Greek *Aias*) is said to foretell his woe by its similarity to the cry *aiai*, and in Euripides' *Bacchae*, Pentheus's name is used to predict his grief (*penthos*).

799 / 699 *a marriage whose name is mourning* This translates the Greek word *kedos*, which can mean both "connection by marriage" and "mourning."

805–6 / 707–8 *fell then to the bride- / groom's kin to sing* Since the bride's kin are perforce absent, the wedding song they would normally sing must be sung by her husband's family.

818–43 / 717–36 An extended and complicated parable, applying in the first instance to Helen, but with far wider applicability. The lion cub raised in the house grows up, and "in return for all / the kindness it received" (831–32/728–29) turns to horrible destruction. This apparent injustice, however, both accords with its true nature as a lion ("the color of its bloodlines," 830/726–27), and reveals its role as agent of destruction, "priest of death / and ruin, ordained by god" (841–42/735–36). The wider applicability of the parable resides in its model of nurturing within the house a wrong that becomes its own vengeance. The "house foul / with blood" (836–37/732) is Troy ravaged by ineluctable vengeance, but also the house of Atreus, with its crimes still to be avenged.

821 / 720 *in the beginning* The Greek here refers literally to "the preliminary offerings of life," using a word, *proteleia*, usually used to refer to offerings made before a marriage. As in the earlier uses of this word (see on 79–80/65 and 260/226), there is an ironic contrast between the usual happy associations of such sacrifices and the violence that is to follow when the lion cub grows up to be a "priest of death / and ruin" (841–42/735–36).

854–56 / 748 *Zeus, / protector of host / and guest* Zeus *xenios* (see on 73/61–62).

881–91 / 773–82 The final antistrophe, with its image of Justice turning her back on wealth and power, sounds an ominous note to accompany Agamemnon's entrance.

892–1118 / 783–974 *Third episode* The unwitting Agamemnon is met by Clytemnestra with all her wiles.

892–928 / 783–809 The stasimon ends as Agamemnon comes on stage, probably riding with Cassandra in a single carriage, but without other attendants. The Chorus greets him with a chant in marching anapests (see on 48–123/40–257), whose main function seems to be to deliver a veiled warning against the hypocritical expressions of loyalty they expect he will hear from Clytemnestra. They make it clear enough that Agamemnon will meet dissatisfaction and opposition at home, but give no clue that the real threat will come from his wife. Agamemnon's response to their concerns (954–77/829–50) shows that he has heard what they said, but not guessed their meaning.

935 / 815 *urn of blood* Agamemnon's language offers an ironic foreshadowing of the trial scene with which the fate of his avenger, Orestes, will be decided in *Eumenides*. This "trial" is held to decide the fate of Troy; the pleas come "not from any mouth but from force of arms" and the jurors are the gods, who cast their ballots "into the urn of blood" in a unanimous death sentence for the city.

967 / 841 *who dragged his feet at first* This alludes to a well-known story that Odysseus feigned insanity to avoid going to Troy until another Greek hero, Palamedes, unmasked his deception by putting Telemachus, Odysseus' infant son, in harm's way (sources and further details in Gantz, *Early Greek Myth*, 580). There may be irony in Agamemnon's mention of Odysseus as the sole example of true loyalty, since Odysseus was famous for his wily pursuit of self-interest.

980 / 854 As if in ominous answer to Agamemnon's prayer for continued victory, Clytemnestra enters, blocking the exit into the palace that he has just announced and giving further evidence of her control of the situation (cf. on 667–68/585–86). The king's exit comes more than a hundred lines later, by which time its manner and meaning have been fully orchestrated by his wife.

981–1007 / 855–76 It is remarkable that Clytemnestra does not speak directly to the husband she has not seen for ten years until she turns to him to explain the absence of their son Orestes in line 1008/877. Instead, she addresses the Chorus with a second brazen assertion of her fidelity to her husband (cf. 688–700/604–14), almost as if she is daring them to disagree. This culminates with the most far-fetched conceit of all, that Clytemnestra repeatedly attempted suicide in her despair at the rumors of Agamemnon's death.

1027–35 / 895–902 Speaking again of Agamemnon in the third person, Clytemnestra produces a string of hyperbolic comparisons that show her blatant use of flattery.

1036–37 / 904 *Let Envy / not begrudge me* The prayer to Envy (*Phthonos*) is ironic, for it is followed immediately by Clytemnestra's invitation to tread on the sacred purple tapestries, thus ensuring that *phthonos* (the gods' jealousy) will pursue Agamemnon—as he himself recognizes (1056/921).

1043–49 / 910–13 A passage steeped in irony, since its every word can be understood to refer to Clytemnestra's plan for killing Agamemnon.

1050–67 / 914–30 Agamemnon's reply is frosty, for he understands perfectly well that Clytemnestra has just proposed an unseemly and dangerous honor, suited to gods not men (1058–61/922–24). He recoils instinctively at Clytemnestra's pampering him with luxury, as if he were a woman, and at the oriental excess of her language and gestures, as if he were a barbarian (1054–56/918–20). Agamemnon hopes to behave with appropriate moderation (1066–67/930), but he will succumb to Clytemnestra's shrewd temptation almost immediately.

1076 / 939 A *life unenvied is an unenviable life* Clytemnestra inverts the motif of envy as a danger (cf. on 1036–37/904) by pointing out that only a great man arouses it in others.

1089 / 950–51 *Now bring this stranger in* This is the first reference to Cassandra, whose identity, however, the audience will already have known. Some disposition for her on Agamemnon's part seems to be required, but by placing the command for good treatment of his concubine between his decision to yield and his actual treading on the embroideries, Aeschylus creates the impression of a futile attempt on Agamemnon's part to reassert control, while at the same time drawing attention to another cause of his downfall. Agamemnon's mention of the involuntary "yoke" of Cassandra's slavery (1091–92/953), which recalls Agamemon's own "yoke-strap of necessity" (248–49/218), further links the two, who are destined to die together.

1097–1118 / 958–74 This heady speech continues Clytemnestra's persuasion and flattery, but its opulent language gives it a note of barely suppressed triumph. At some point during the speech, Agamemnon reaches the door of the palace, and by line 1116/973 he has made his exit.

1115–18 / 972–94 *sovereign . . . sovereign accomplisher, / accomplish* This translates the Greek words *andros teleiou . . . teleie . . . telei.* Clytemnestra ironically calls Agamemnon *teleios* as the man who has final authority in the house, then prays to Zeus *teleios*, who truly has final authority, to fulfill her prayer—to preside at the rite of Agamemnon's sacrifice. In the Greek, "to do" (1118/974) is again expressed with the verb *telein*.

1119–73 / 975–1034 *Third stasimon* The return of Agamemnon brings only more intense fear to the Argive elders. They express their apprehension only in vague terms, but their tone confirms the audience's expectation that the moment of Agamemnon's death is approaching.

1135 / 990–92 *the dirge the lyre shuns* See on 735/645.

1146 / 1001 *well-being at its utmost* The Chorus expresses the ideal of moderation in a way that may seem paradoxical, but the point is that too much of a good thing is dangerous: even health pursued to excess can turn to disease.

1157–58 / 1014–5 *the great gift of Zeus springs / abundant* The gift of new life to the fields as a remedy for famine is introduced here to contrast with the lack of remedy once a man's blood has been spilled (1160–62/1019–21).

1163–65 / 1022–24 Aeschylus follows the tradition that regarded Asclepius as a mortal son of Apollo and a healer so great that he was able to restore the dead to life. (For sources and variants, see Gantz, *Early Greek Myth*, 91–2). Zeus, who at the end of the previous stanza presided over the renewal of life in the fields, here kills Asclepius with a lightning bolt for renewing life that was never meant to be renewed.

1166 / 1025–27 *And if one fate didn't block another* An enigmatic phrase, which can be more literally translated, "And had not one appointed portion prevented another portion from getting more than its share." Following directly as it does the example of Asclepius's breaching of bounds, this can perhaps best be understood as a way of suggesting the impossibility of putting into words (the "portion" of the tongue) that which wells up inside the Elders' breasts (the "portion" of the heart).

1174–1517 / 1035–1330 *Fourth episode* The audience has now been fully prepared for an announcement of Agamemnon's murder, presumably from the lips of a messenger, but that is not what what happens. Cassandra is still sitting silent and motionless in the carriage, and Clytemnestra now emerges from the palace to bring her inside. The scene thus mirrors Clytemnestra's encounter with Agamemnon, but with a diametrically opposed result. Clytemnestra fails to persuade Cassandra, or even to elicit a response from her, and withdraws in defeat. When she has left, however, Cassandra unburdens herself in a long, unexpected, and harrowing dialogue with the Chorus. In the end, she takes the same brief walk that Agamenon took from the carriage into the palace, but she does it under her own control, in her own time, and her own way. Unlike Agamemnon, Cassandra goes to her death knowingly and prophesying vengeance to come. And along her path, she reveals much about the past, present, and future that clarifies what still remained unspoken or obscure.

1178 / 1038 *Zeus who guards the house's wealth* The Greek gives only the cult name *ktêsios*, god of possessions. The cult was a modest one, with a simple household shrine usually located in a storeroom. Clytemnestra emphasizes Cassandra's new status as a possession of the house who will stand among the other slaves.

1180 / 1040 *even Heracles, they say* Heracles was sold into slavery, in most accounts as a punishment from Zeus for the treacherous slaying of Iphitus, the son of Heracles' guest-friend, Eurytus of Oechalia. Heracles was enslaved to a woman, Omphale, the queen of Lydia. There is evidence for numerous divergent versions of the story (see Gantz, *Early Greek Myth*, 434–42), the best known being that in Sophocles' *Women of Trachis*, 248–80.

1193 / 1050 *twittering like a swallow, barbarian-style* "To twitter like a swallow" seems to have been proverbial for the sound of foreign tongues. Indeed, the term "barbarian" derives from the Greeks' contemptuous view of foreigner's speech as sounding like a series of incoherent grunts: *bar, bar, bar.*

1208 / 1063 *She's like a captured beast* This is the first indication that Cassandra is no longer sitting impassive, but is now agitated. The violence of her spasms is suggested at 1212–14/1066–67, where Clytemnestra compares her to a horse who has not yet been broken in.

1219 / 1071 *this new yoke* See on 1089/953.

1220–1348 / 1072–1177 *Kommos* This is the first of several formal exchanges in the *Oresteia* between an actor or actors and the chorus in which sung verse is used by at least one of the parties. The *kommos* is a powerful vehicle for the expression of strong emotions.

1220 / 1072 *OTOTOI POPOI DA* Greek is rich in interjections of grief, alarm, horror, and the like; English on the other hand is poor. We have kept some of the Greek interjections as a way of conveying the heightened emotional register of this scene. Emotional intensification is also achieved in this scene by virtue of the contrast between sung lyric verse and spoken dialogue verse. Cassandra is the only actor (other than the members of the Chorus) to be given lyrics in this play. During the first part of the scene, the Chorus Leader answers her in spoken verse, but from **1274/1119** onward, the Chorus as a whole takes up Cassandra's mood of foreboding and leaps, after two spoken verses, into agitated song. Cassandra turns to spoken dialogue meter at **1349/1178** (see note), and the remainder of the scene is spoken.

1223 / 1075 *no god to come to with a dirge* The Olympian gods shun everything connected with mourning and lament, and just as the *paean* is inappropriate for the Erinyes (see on **735/645**), so mournful song is entirely unsuited to Apollo, god of the *paean*.

1229 / 1081 *God of the roadside* Cassandra addresses a symbol of *Apollo agyieus*, "guardian of the street," whose function seems to have been to protect the entrance to houses. The symbol, a conical pillar that stood outside the Greek house, was apparently a regular feature of the stage set, since several surviving tragedies and comedies make reference to it.
my destroyer There is a pun in the Greek that cannot be reproduced in English. By the same "nomen-omen" principle with which the chorus equated Helen with destruction (see on **782/687ff.**), Cassandra expresses the god's true meaning (at least for her) by connecting his name to the verb *apollumi*. Thus she can equate the Greek name for Apollo, *Apollôn* with the participle *apollôn*, "destroying." The pun continues in **1231/1082** with *apôlesas* ("destroyed").

1246 / 1095 *Yes, there they are* Cassandra, on the scent of blood, as the chorus has just said, sees a vision of slaughtered children that confirms her premonitions. These are the children of Thyestes, killed when his estranged brother Atreus invited him to a feast of reconciliation, secretly killed and cooked the children, and served them to Thyestes to eat. The vision returns at **1391–98/1217–22**, and Aegisthus, Thyestes' sole surviving son, who takes part in the killing of Atreus' son Agamemnon, tells the story in in greater detail at **1830–40/159–97**.

1257 / 1105 *These prophecies I can't quite follow* Every time Cassandra's visions reach the present and immediate future, the Chorus finds itself lost. This is not a sign of their lack of insight, but (as Aeschylus' audience would have known) a reflection of Cassandra's curse, to see the future clearly but never to be believed (see **1382–87/1208–13**). It is true that Cassandra's agitated song is disjointed and allusive, but later, when she speaks less emotionally and more directly, the chorus will equally be at a loss (e.g., **1422–23/1245, 1431–32/1252–53**).

1305 / 1142 *the tawny nightingale would grieve* The Chorus compares Cassandra in her unceasing lament to the emblematic mourner of Greek mythology, Procne. Procne's husband Tereus, a Thracian king, raped Procne's sister Philomela and then cut out her tongue so she could not tell anyone. But Philomela managed to communicate the crime to her sister by embroidering the story on a cloth. Procne in her anger killed Itys, the son she had born to Tereus, and served him up to his father to eat. When Tereus discovered what had happened, he tried to kill both sisters with his sword, but the gods changed Procne into a nightingale, ever crying the name of Itys, Philomela to a nonsensically chattering swallow (see on **1193/1050**), and Tereus into the sharp-beaked hoopoe. The story has a glancing similarity to that of Atreus and the children of Thyestes, but Cassandra reminds the Chorus that she is not another Procne, whom the gods rescued and freed from further suffering, while she faces only a violent death. (**1310–14/1147–49**).

1349–50 / 1178–79 *my prophecies won't peek again / like some shy newlywed* In response to the Chorus's protestation that they still do not understand the meaning of Cassandra's prophecies, she now turns to spoken verse and a more coherent, although still largely allusive, account of her visions. The metaphor she chooses for this change to more direct speech is particularly poignant in light of what she will soon say about how she gained her prophetic power from Apollo, then broke her word and rejected his suit (**1376–86/1202–12**).

1360–61 / 1189–90 *a home-brewed, / rioting band of Erinyes* The Erinyes that beset the house of Atreus are pictured as a *kômos*, a Dionysiac rout or revel, but instead of going out to sing and dance in the streets after a drinking party, these revelers are drunk on blood and sing their song of destruction within the house that gave them birth.

1364 / 1192 *that ancestral sin* Cassandra is alluding to an earlier stage in the strife of Atreus and Thyestes. The Erinyes spit on Thyestes' bed because he defiled it by seducing Aerope, Atreus' wife, the act that led to his terrible punishment at Atreus' banquet.

1399 / 1224 *a skulking lion* Aegisthus. The choice of metaphor is unexpected, especially in light of **1438–39/1258–59**, where Clytemnestra is depicted as a two-footed lioness bedding with a wolf (Aegisthus) in the absence of the noble lion (Agamemnon). Here, however, the emphasis is on the un-lionlike skulking of this cowardly lion.

1409–10 / 1233 *two-headed serpent, or / a Scylla* The two-headed serpent is an amphisbaena, a mythical monster with a head at both ends. Scylla is the many-headed, man-eating monster that dwells opposite the whirlpool Charybdis; in Book 12 of the *Odyssey*, she devours six of Odysseus' crew.

1440–43 / 1260–63 The point of these lines is the complete intertwining of Cassandra's death with that of Agamemnon. The image of poisoning is figurative and means that Clytemnestra will regard her death as suitable payment ("my quittance") for her association with Agamemnon; the picture of Clytemnestra wielding a sword is literal (at least as regards the means of death) and makes clear that Clytemnestra will equally be exacting payment from Agamemnon for bringing Cassandra home at his side.

1445–46 / 1265 *this staff, these fillets, these trappings / of prophecy* Cassandra, in a gesture that must have shocked the original audience, strips herself of the insignias of the prophetic office conferred on her by Apollo, but which because of his curse have been only a mockery (**1444/1264**). Preparing to die, she has nothing more to fear from the god, and she now exacts her own form of payment (**1449/1267**) as she destroys and tramples the symbols of her vocation and her misery, addressing them as if they were living enemies. As with Agamemnon, so with Cassandra an act of sacrilege precedes her exit into the palace, but this one cast as a grand, if ineffectual, act of vengeance and self-assertion. The stage directions that we have added here are more than usually conjectural, but — unusual for Greek tragedy — something of the sort is necessary to make the action clear.

1454–55 / 1272 *friends / turned enemies* Cassandra's own family and countrymen, who scorned her because of Apollo's curse — but in vain, because her prophecies have proved true to their destruction.

1460 / 1277 *not my father's altar* The primary reference is presumably to the death of Priam, who was killed by Achilles' son Neoptolemus at the altar of Zeus where he had taken refuge as a suppliant during the sack of Troy. Might there also be a glance at the sacrifice of Iphgenia at another father's altar? The image of sacrificial death at any rate links the two women's fates.

1463 / 1279 *Yet my death, too, will not go unavenged* Cassandra's final prophecy goes beyond her own death to foretell in specific terms the son's murder of his mother that will avenge his father's death—and her own. This prophecy will be fulfilled, of course, in *Libation Bearers*, but in saying that the deed will "put / a capstone on this killing of his kin" (1468–69/1283) she points toward the resolution only achieved in *Eumenides*.

1475 / 1290 *I will dare to go* Cassandra will hesitate twice before she finally, and resolutely, enters "the door of Hades." She recoils in horror at the "stench of slaughter" (1494/1309) as she approaches the door and turns away once more to ask the Chorus to "be my witnesses" (1503/1371), perhaps a reflection of the requirement in Athenian law that deeds of violence can be brought to trial only if a cry of distress has been heard.

1483 / 1293–94 *more calmly than a cow the god escorts* It was part of sacrificial ideology that the animal to be slaughtered should go willingly to its death.

1490 / 1305 *Alas for you, father, and for your high-born children* This perfectly clear but disconnected phrase is oddly enigmatic. Does she ignore the Chorus, absorbed in her own troubled thoughts, or is this her answer to the Chorus's attempt to console her with the notion of a glorious death: What good has glory done them?

1518–33 / 1331–42 *Choral interlude* Rather than the full-fledged choral ode we would expect to separate the Cassandra scene from the news of Agamemnon's death, Aeschylus gives the Chorus a brief interlude in marching anapests (see on 48–123/40–103) in which they meditate on what they have learned from Cassandra about the fate of Agamemnon. The next episode begins with the murder itself, as the Chorus hears and responds to Agamemnon's death cries.

1534–1813 / 1343–1577 *Fifth episode* After the startling death scene itself, Clytemnestra enters and the bodies of her victims are revealed. The Chorus's shock at her boastful vaunts leads to an elaborate exchange that takes up the remainder of the episode from which a degree of mutual understanding appears to be emerging when it is cut short by the arrival of Aegisthus. See further the Introduction, pp. 13–15.

1534–62 / 1343–71 Agamemnon's death cries are heard from offstage, and assuming that the wooden scene building had newly been added to the theater (see further the note on **1–47/1–39**), this may have come as a startling innovation. At any rate, there are no such voices from offstage in the earlier surviving dramas of Aeschylus. The Chorus responds with indecisive dithering that may seem comic or even embarrassing to many modern readers and spectators. Of course the Chorus cannot really stop the slaughter, nor can they very well stand silent, much less simply leave the orchestra. But neither was Aeschylus obliged to write such an extended scene of confusion and indecision. The effect should be considered in relation to the triumphant Clytemnestra who enters just as the Chorus has concluded that it can do nothing. The contrast suggests that he wanted to underline the triumph of a dominant, self-assured woman who emerges to boast of her deeds over the leaderless and demoralized men of Argos.

In any case, this is emphatically not naturalistic theater. It is worth noting that Agamemnon's "cries" are complete and properly formed lines of verse, and the "debate" among the Elders is a symmetrical exchange of paired verses. After the initial call for discussion (**1537–38/ 1348–49**), which we have given to the chorus leader, there are twelve such pairs. The simplest explanation of this arrangement is the usual supposition that the chorus numbered twelve (later in the century, it was certainly fifteen), and that each member spoke one pair of lines. This is by no means certain, however. For other possibilities, see Taplin, *Stagecraft of Aeschylus*, 323–24.

1561 / 1370 *All my votes go for this course* This translates an enigmatic Greek phrase whose literal meaning seems to be, "I am filled from all sides to approve this." The best available explanation seems to be that the last Elder sums up the impression he has got from the others by comparing himself to a voting urn that has been filled with votes for the course he recommends.

1563 / 1372 Clytemnestra appears in the midst of a tableau, with the bodies of Agamemnon and Cassandra. Several passages strongly suggest that Agamemnon is still enveloped in the "net" of robes that Clytemnestra describes (**1575–76/1382–83**; see **1715/1492** = **1745/1516, 1819/1580**) and still in the bathtub in which he was killed (see **1717/1494** = **1747/1519, 1773–74/1539–40**). The most likely way to stage this scene would have been to roll it out form the central door of the stage building on the *ekkyklêma*, a wheeled platform that could bring the entire tableau into full view of the audience. In **1571–72/1379**, Clytemnestra says, "here I stand / here where I cut him down," which suggests that the tableau is still to be thought of as inside the palace, but the precise location is not insisted on and will hardly have been in the forefront of the spectators' minds. It is of course possible that the elements of the tableau were brought in by silent extras, although that would miss the effect of seeing the scene appear all at once with Clytemnestra looming over it. In any case, the tableau must be in place before Clytemnestra launches into her speech of triumph.

1563–95/1372–98 Clytemnestra's first speech displays breathtaking daring and shocking perversion of religious and social norms; it is all the more horrifying for the ecstatic pleasure she takes in what she has accomplished. Her role as the sole killer of Agamemnon (emphasized again in the Aegisthus scene, 1886–88/1633–35 and 1897–1900/1643–46) is probably an innovation of Aeschylus. In the *Odyssey* 4, 524–37, Aegisthus is depicted as planning and executing the asssassination, although elsewhere in the epic, Clytemnestra's role as Aegisthus' lover and helper is emphasized, and it is she who kills Cassandra (11, 405–39).

1579 / 1386 *the third stroke fell* For the perversion of the rite of the three libations and the inversion of its accepted meaning, see the Introduction, p. 31.

1584 / 1390 *he drenched me in the dark red showering gore* Clytemnestra perversely turns her blood-pollution into a symbol of rebirth by likening the blood spurting from Agamemnon's wounds to a rain shower that Zeus, the weather god, sends to give new life to the fields in spring. This image powerfully conveys the elemental joy of her revenge, while its perversity reminds us that blood begets no new life, only more death.

1604–11 / 1407–11 The Chorus, horrified by Clytemnestra's acts and words, responds in agitated lyrics. In this stanza, they suggest that Clytemnestra must be suffering the effects of poison, in the next (1630–35/1426–30), they claim to see symptoms of her madness. At the same time, each of these stanzas raises the beginning of an argument to which she must respond. Here they say that her act will cause her to be driven from the city, in the next they remind her of the vengeance that awaits her. To each of these points she responds firmly, and in the calmer tones of spoken dialogue.

1625 / 1422 *threaten me all you want* Threatened with exile, Clytemnestra makes it clear that she will fight to retain her power.

1636 / 1431 *hear my solemn oath* Clytemnestra invokes a second, sinister triad that culminates with the Erinys (see the Introduction, pp. 31–32) to swear that she is immune from fear so long as "the fire on my hearth is kindled / and kept bright by Aegisthus" (1641–42/1435–36). In so doing, she introduces the name of Aegisthus for the first time and assigns him the role of her legitimate consort and lord of the house.

1652 / 1444 *like a swan* Clytemnestra associates Cassandra with a bird sacred to Apollo, which, moreover, was believed to sing most beautifully when near death. This is the first mention in Greek literature of that belief, found memorably in Plato's *Phaedo* 84E.

1655–1812 / 1448–1576 The episode ends with a long *kommos* (exchange between actor and chorus in which sung verse is used by one or both parties). In this case, the Chorus expresses itself in sung lyric meters and Clytemnestra responds in chanted anapests. The choral lyrics add an extra stanza between each strophe and antistrophe. Some editors turn all three of these stanzas into refrains by repeating them after the the antistrophe, but we have followed the manuscript tradition by keeping the first and last as *mesodes* ("mid-odes," so called because of their position in the midst of a strophic pair) and repeating only the second of the stanzas as a refrain.

1662–63 / 1453 *who in a woman's name / suffered so much* The woman is Helen, and in the following stanza the Chorus says that she, who caused all the deaths at Troy, now has put on the "last, perfect garland" of victory in the death of Agamemnon by means of "blood not washed away" (1670–71/1459–60). The precise significance of these lines is elusive. Perhaps the Chorus refers to the sacrifice of Iphigenia, regarded as the means by which the events that Helen began came to pass, or perhaps to the unexpiated murders of Thyestes' children. On the other hand, a precise reference is hardly necessary, since all the unavenged bloodshed of the house could be understood as the medium for Helen's destructive work.

1681–82 / 1468–69 *the two / heirs of Tantalus* Agamemnon and Menelaus. Tantalus was their great-grandfather. See the Glossary for the story of his notorious transgression and punishment.

1692–93 / 1476–77 *the triple-glutted / Spirit of this race* Although compounds in *tri-* in Greek can have an intensive rather than numerical force, Clytemnestra's vivid picture suggests that the spirit of the house has sated himself on blood through three generations. This "spirit" (*daimôn*) is the Erinys or curse that dwells within the house and ensures that each violent deed is requited with yet more violence. Clytemnestra had urged the Chorus to think not only of Helen as the cause of all grief they have endured (1675–79/1464–67), and she approves their invocation of the spirit of the house (1680/1468). Although they protest that she is praising "sheer evil / that fills its maw with misfortune" (1700–1/1483–4), they also recognize that all the spirit does has been willed by Zeus, the final cause of everything (1704–10/1487–88). Clytemnestra then urges them to see her not as Agamemnon's wife but as "the old and / pitiless avenger of Atreus (1725–26/1501–2), an embodiment of the Spirit of the house. Although the chorus seems no more reconciled than before to Clytemnestra's deed, the terms in which they understand it are beginning to change (see especially 1730–40/1505–12).

1751–52 / 1521–22 *There's nothing slavish, I think, in this / man's death* "Slavish" (*aneleutheron*, literally "unfree," i.e., shameful or base) picks up the Chorus lament that Agamemnon's died "on a slavish bed" (trapped and helpless in the bathtub). Clytemnestra argues that there is nothing shameful in a death that avenges an unjust death.

1798 / 1564 *he who does will suffer* The long exchange with Clytemnestra leads the Chorus to restate the central law of retributive justice. Responding to the Chorus's outrage at the murder of their king, Clytemnestra has argued that Agamemnon suffered justly for what he did (1754–58/1525–57). "Charge answers charge" (1793/1560), but as the Chorus sees, there is no obvious end point to the cycle. They sense that a new "blade of justice" (1769/1535) is already being honed for Clytemnestra, but they take no pleasure in the continuation of the violence, for they know that unstopped it will lead only to ruin (1794–1800/1560–66).

1806 / 1571–72 *If only he will go from the house* Clytemnestra recognizes that the Chorus has "found a true prophecy," and she tries to circumvent it by making a bargain with the Spirit of the house, an ironic echo of the "foresight" recommended at 1152–6/1008–13. She offers to part with as much of her wealth as is necessary to seal the agreement (1809–13/1574–76). No such bargain can be struck, but it is remarkable how far Clytemnestra has come toward understanding the reality of her situation in the course of this *kommos*. There is no evidence that she regrets or repents the deed that she has taken such pains to defend—and

210

whose part in the dialectic of retributive justice the Chorus has come to admit. But she has begun to recognize its larger meaning and its implications for her future and the future of her house.

1814–1934 / 1577–1673 *Exodus* The final scene of the play is not separated from the preceding episode by a choral ode, but the singing of the *kommos* that occupies the second half of the episode makes further choral lyrics superfluous. Furthermore, the sudden and unannounced entry of Aegisthus comes as a surprise. Although he had been alluded to earlier in the play, and finally named by Clytemnestra (**1641/1436**) as her partner in revenge and rule, his appearance lacks any preparation and is anomalous. From a formal point of view, it is unusual to have a new character (making exception for the deus ex machina, not found in Aeschylus) arrive on the scene at the very end of the play. (Aegisthus, in Sophocles' *Electra*, is the only case that comes to mind, and his arrival is expected and prepared for.) From the perspective of the play's inner movement Aegisthus' entry disrupts what felt like a conclusion— not harmonious, certainly not final, but expressive of fundamental insights drawn from the action of the drama. The Aegisthus scene undoes all that, and prepares for the next stage of confrontation in *Libation Bearers*.

1814 / 1577 *O kind light of the day of final justice* Aegisthus' speech begins with a triumphant claim of vengeance on Agamemnon for the crimes that his father, Atreus, committed against Aegisthus' father, Thyestes, and his other children, which he describes in lurid detail, although with none of the harrowing intensity of Cassandra's account. Aegisthus uses the word *dikêphoros* ("bringing justice") applied to Zeus himself at **597/ 525**.

1825 / 1585 *who challenged his right to rule alone* Unlike Casssandra (see **1364–66/ 1192–93**), Aegisthus makes no allusion to Thyestes' adultery as a cause of the dispute.

1864 / 1615 *when justice is meted out* A nice illustration of the symmetrical claims of retributive justice. To Aegisthus' assertion that his plan to kill Agamemnon was inspired by justice (**1852–57/1607–11**), the Chorus replies that justice demands he be killed for that plan by public stoning.

1866–68 / 1617–18 The image comes from the trireme, a ship with three rows of oars, and plays on the poetic metaphor of the "ship of state," well known from Greek archaic poetry.

1876 / 1625 *You woman!* Aegisthus, the "skulking lion" (**1399/1224**), is described as a womanish man, just as Cassandra is a mannish woman. He did not join the men at Troy, but betrayed Agamemon and plotted his death in the safety of Agamemnon's own house. And when Agamemnon returned, he would not do the deed himself, but instead entrusted it to Clytemnestra (**1888/1635**, **1897–1900/1643–46**).

1881 / 1629 *The tongue of Orpheus* Aegisthus can only answer with threats of violence. Here, with rather brittle irony, he contrasts the charm of Orpheus' voice with the unpleasant "barking" of the Elders, and Orpheus' gift of leading of all who heard him with the Elders' coming fate of being led to their punishment.

1891–92 / 1638–39 *But with his wealth now I will try / to rule the citizens* Aegisthus reverses Clytemnestra's offer to part with her wealth (**1809–13/1574–76**), which he will use as a political tool for the control and suppression of his opponents. Aegisthus' threats have led the Chorus to charge him with plotting to become tyrant (**1886/1633**). Although the Greek term *tyrannos* does not necessarily imply more than ruler (who is not in the royal line of succession), the remainder of the play makes it clear that what Aegisthus intends to institute is precisely the kind of repressive regime that we call tyranny.

1901 / 1646 *does Orestes see the light* The Chorus's thoughts turn to Orestes, the true heir of Agamemnon, whose fate they do not know. At **1928/1667** they say they will escape Aegisthus' vengeance, "if the Spirit brings Orestes home." Spirit (*daimôn*) might mean "fate" or "a divine power," but in the context of its use in this play (most recently **1920/1660**, and see on **1692–93/1476–77**), it can only refer to the Spirit of the house, the Erinys who presides over retribution.

1906–34 / 1650–1673 The Chorus, old and feeble and armed only with their staffs, respond to Aegisthus' threats by preparing to fight his armed guard. Aegisthus welcomes the fray and the two sides face off. Clytemnestra's decisive intervention prevents a battle, but the acrimony continues until she again intervenes to take Aegisthus inside. Their exit into the palace at once symbolizes his accession to the role of *tyrannos* in place of the fallen king, and his dependence on the queen. Unusually, the Chorus exits in silence. The play comes to an end, but not to a conclusion.

LIBATION BEARERS

1–25 / 1–21 *Prologue* As if in fulfillment of Cassandra's prophecy (*Agamemnon* 1463–70/1279–85) and the Chorus's last hope (*Agamemnon* 1901–3/1646–48, 1928/1667), *Libation Bearers* opens with the return of Orestes to Argos to avenge his father's murder (22–23/18–19). The first part of the play will reunite him with his sister Electra at their father's tomb, the place where the power of his spirit can most directly inspire them and strengthen their resolve.

1–11 / 1–9 These lines are not transmitted in the manuscript tradition of the *Oresteia*. 1–6/1–5 have been restored from Aristophanes' *Frogs*, and 7–11/6–9 from scholia (later annotations included in our manuscript tradition) to other authors. This is by no means the complete opening of the prologue, but we cannot say how much has been lost. No information essential for the audience's understanding of the situation is missing, however, and only a few lines may be lost.

1 / 1 *Hermes of the dark earth* This is Hermes the escorter of souls to the underworld. The god appears in many of his main functions in the course of the trilogy, for example, as the patron god of heralds (*Agamemnon* 582–83/514–15), as the god of stratagems and deception (934–40/811–18), and as protector of travelers (*Eumenides*, 105–6/89–90). Orestes calls him "overseer of my father's power" (2/1) because he hopes to enlist him as a god associated with the realm of the dead, Hermes, in his own cause. The meaning of this phrase was already debated by the shades of Euripides and Aeschylus himself, in Aristophanes *Frogs* 1138–49. Euripides sustains quite improbably that it means "who looked upon my father's murder," Aeschylus that it refers to Hermes as "watching over his father's [i.e., Zeus's] realm" (at least possible, since the Greek does not specify whose father is meant). Both appear to be wrong, which may be part of Aristophanes' joke.

14 / 12 *What bad luck could it mean?* Despite the hopefulness of Orestes' return, the beginning of the play is shadowed by uncertainty and foreboding. Orestes' first reaction on seeing the libation bearers is that their mourning garb is ill-omened. He and his companion Pylades hide in order to discover their purpose in visiting the tomb. The Chorus's dirge and Electra's mourning continue the atmosphere of gloom—"sheer sunlessness" (58/51)—into which the reappearance of Orestes will come like a ray of light.

213

27–104 / 22–83 *Parodos* The Chorus, a band of slave-women, are led on by Electra, who remains silent until the parodos has been completed. Despite having been captured (at an unspecified time and place) by the Argive army and brought as slaves to Argos (92–96/75–78), the women are loyal to their dead master, Agamemnon. Their song emphasizes the fear and misery that beset Argos, and their own helplessness; but they predict that Justice will still find "way to right the balance" (69/61).

27–37 / 22–31 The Chorus describes (and their dance presumably mimes) all the traditional behaviors of female mourners—blows to the head, raking of the cheeks with fingernails, rending of garments, beating of the breast. Thus, as they bring Clytemnestra's libation to Agamemnon's tomb, they enact a belated dirge for Agamemnon, the tribute that the Elders were sure he would not receive from Clytemnestra (*Agamemnon* 1775–82/ 1541–50).

38 / 32 *terror, dream-seer of the house* The Chorus has been sent from the palace with libations (27–28/22–23); now we learn that the cause was a terrifying dream, attributed by expert interpreters to the anger of the dead who lie still unavenged (45–47/39–41). Nowhere is Clytemnestra, whose dream it was and who instigated the libations, named. She figures in the second strophe simply as "the godless woman" (51/46).

50 / 44 *O mother Earth!* She is invoked here as an averter of evils (as at Aeschylus' *Suppliants* 890–91 = 900–1) and because the libations are to be poured into the earth. How will she receive such "ill-favored favors"?

71–74 / 62–65 *bright day . . . twilit shadows . . . black night* A formulation of the idea, expressed again and again in the trilogy, that justice may come soon or late, but it will inevitably arrive.

85–90 / 71–74 An implicit comparison is to be understood in this expression: *just as* there is no remedy for the violation of a virgin, *so* there is no cleansing of the blood stain from a murderer's hand.

105–668 / 84–584 *First episode* The first half of the play is one long act, set at Agamemnon's tomb. At its center is the enormous *kommos* (see on *Agamemnon*, 1220–1348/1072–1177) that honors the slain king and calls on his aid from the world below (352–552/306–478); otherwise, the action is limited to the reunion of brother and sister and, following the *kommos*, the forging of Orestes' plan. Following this expansive, highly ritualized first half, the second part of the play will move swiftly and with a sense of inevitability to enact Orestes' vengeance on Clytemnestra and Aegisthus and to show its consequences for him.

129 / 106 *like an altar to me* Cf. 383/336, where Electra says that Agamemnon's tomb "welcomed us as suppliants," although one would ordinarily take refuge at the altar of a god, not at a tomb. The force of equating Agamemnon's tomb with an altar is to stress his character as a hero who still exercises power from his grave. In Euripides' *Helen*, Helen is a suppliant at the tomb of the dead king of Egypt, Proteus, who receives heroic honors; and in Sophocles' *Ajax*, the young Eurysaces is placed as a suppliant at the body of the fallen Ajax, as if to show that his father has already become a sacred hero.

143 / 120 Electra asks, in effect, whether she is to pray for a "judge" (*dikastês*, the regular Athenian term for a juror) or an "executioner" (*dikêphoros*, literally, a bringer of justice; the term Aegisthus used at *Agamemnon* 1814/1577 of the day that has brought Agamemnon's death). The first alternative is unreal in the sense that judicial remedies do not yet exist, but it is the clearest indication so far in the *Oresteia* of the possibility of a legal decision replacing an act of reciprocal vengeance.

145–46 / 122–23 Electra's question implies a surprising distance from the standard Greek morality of "good to my friends, harm to my enemies" that the Chorus embraces in its answer. The explanation may be, as is often said, that Electra is thinking of the murder of Clytemnestra—an enemy, indeed, but also her own mother. But since Clytemnestra is not specifically mentioned here, some have concluded that Electra is depicted as one—unlike Clytemnestra—to whom desire for vengeance does not come naturally, and who still needs instruction. At 164–76/138–148, Electra scrupulously places her prayer for evil in the midst of prayers for good. Certainly, the tone of Electra's religious scruples could hardly be more different from that of Clytemnestra's delight in *Agamemnon* at shedding her enemies' blood.

147 / 124 *Greatest herald* For Hermes as chthonian escort of souls from this world to the world below, see on line 1. Here, however, it is not Hermes but "nether spirits" (*daimones*) who are said to "oversee my father's house" (149–50/125–26), the Erinyes or Curses who come from the realm of the dead.

156–76 / 130–48 Having decided on the appropriate form of prayer and invoked Hermes as conveyor of the message, Electra turns in these lines to the prayer itself that accompanies her libation. We have put the entire passage in quotation marks to reflect that these are the ritual words that preface her libation.

157 / 131 *a saving light* The imagery of light, so pervasive in the trilogy as a whole, is focused in *Libation Bearers* on the figure of Orestes. As he takes vengeance on Aegisthus and Clytemnestra, Orestes is repeatedly hailed as the bringer of the light of salvation and freedom (**932–33**/808–10, **988–91**/863–65, **1087**/961). When his task is completed, the light appears to be extinguished by the Erinyes, and Orestes himself sets out to seek salvation at Apollo's shrine at Delphi, with its eternally burning fire (**1174–75**/1035).

182–84 / 154–55 *this earthwork of the good / that turns back / evil* A description of the power of the hero's tomb to protect his friends by defending them from his enemies.

190 / 159 *let him come soon* The unspoken subject is Orestes, depicted as a spearman, an archer, or wielding a sword, like Ares himself—a more or less exhaustive list of the weapons the "savior of the house" might use.

192 / 161–62 *the Scythian bow* A kind of bow with a double curve made famous by the skilled archers of Scythia.

198–351 / 164–314 As the ritual in commemoration and exhortation of Agamemnon ends, the recognition scene begins. The recognition tokens in this scene were parodied by Euripides in his *Electra*, 518–44, for his own purposes, but they are not as naive as the judgment of many critics of the nineteenth and earlier twentieth centuries might suggest. Since the audience already knows the truth, they will have no inclination to be skeptical. In any case, the scene is staged as the answer to prayers that Electra herself can hardly believe to have been fulfilled at last—a finely judged play of hope and doubt that leads with dramatic and emotional conviction to the joyous reunion.

198 / 165 *What's this?* Electra sees a lock of hair left on the tomb, and the fact that this is a characteristic offering made by a close relative of the dead renders Electra's insistence on the similarity of this hair to her own less implausible.

237 / 205 *Wait! Look!* The token of the matching footprints is to be understood as an additional piece of evidence that revives Electra's hopes after her realization that she cannot know with certainty who sent the offering of hair. But then, paradoxically, her lack of confidence in her own judgment returns, and it is only when Orestes shows her the certain token of her own childhood weaving (**263**/231)that she accepts that he is truly her long-lost brother.

265–66 / 233–34 These lines serve as a sort of stage direction: this is the point at which Electra's joyous recognition becomes manifest, and Orestes must restrain her from the shout that might betray his return to his enemies.

270–77 / 238–44 A reminiscence of the memorable lines of the *Iliad* 6, 429–30, in which Andromache calls Hector in her father, mother, brother, and husband. Ironically, Andromache is pleading for Hector to stay out of battle, Electra is urging him to do battle against their enemies.

274–75 / 242 *the sister, too, / so cruelly slaughtered* The only direct reference to Iphigenia in *Libation Bearers* (but see on **287–88**/255–56), a momentary reminder that Agamemnon, the great king foully slain, was not himself free of blood-guilt.

277–78 / 244–45 *Power and Justice / and Zeus the third, supreme* Another idiosyncratic version of the three libations, but with Zeus in his rightful place; see further the Introduction, p. 32.

280 / 247 *orphans of a father eagle* The father eagle is of course Agamemnon, and the viper who killed him, Clytemnestra. Since the eagle is Zeus's bird, the comparison is likely to elicit Zeus's favor in guiding the avengers. Snakes and eagles are traditional enemies in Greek literature, but here a viper is specified because of the belief that the female of that species killed the male while copulating and was killed in turn by her children, who chewed their way out of her womb (see, e.g., Herodotus, *Histories* 3, 109). Orestes himself becomes the snake that draws his mother's blood (**603–11**/526–34, **627–28**/549–50, **1057**/928).

287–88 / 255–56 *nestlings of a father who never failed / to sacrifice to you* In the context of the metaphorical connection of Agamemnon with the eagle, there may be an indirect reminder of the sacrifice of Iphigenia here. The Greek word for sacrificer [*thutêr*] is used elsewhere in the *Oresteia* only of Agamemnon's role in the killing of his daughter. In *Agamemnon*, the omen of the eagles destroying the pregnant hare (**132–56**/114–38) is what leads to the sacrifice of Iphigenia.

290 / 257 *holy banquets opulent as his* The underlying principle here is that of *do ut des*, the idea that suitable homage must be given to the gods to obtain their favor—and that a god's failure to reward the homage will threaten its continuation. The same principle is applied in the appeal to Agamemnon's ghost at 557–62/483–88.

302 / 268 *their bodies hissing as the black pitch burns* This might refer to burning on the funeral pyre, but might also be understood as a wish that the victims be covered in pitch and burnt alive, a punishment at least known to the Greeks (e.g., Plato, *Gorgias* 473c).

303 / 269 *Apollo's great oracle* Orestes makes clear that Apollo, through his oracle at Delphi, has explicitly charged him with avenging Agamemnon's death, and has ordered him to kill the killers in the same way they killed his father—by *dolos*, craft or trickery.

311–38 / 76–96 Orestes gives a long and vivid account of the terrors that await him if he does not follow Apollo's instructions. The description fluctuates between what anyone unable or unwilling to avenge kinfolk must expect to suffer and particulars that reflect his own circumstances. Apollo tells him what will happen if he does not kill Aegisthus and Clytemnestra; but the audience, familiar with the outline of the story, will recognize that the speech also describes what awaits him for killing them: to be driven from his city maddened by the pursuit of his mother's Erinyes. The threat of punishment by his *father's* Erinyes (320–38/283–96) thus makes it unmistakably clear that there will be no easy escape for Orestes.

340–41 / 298 *I'd still be driven / to carry out the work* At the end of the speech, Orestes insists that even without the threats of punishment, his own desires determine his decision to avenge his father. Though Orestes will understandably hesitate before striking down his mother (1027–31/899–904), indecisiveness and moral qualms have no place in Aeschylus' characterization. Orestes has made up his mind before the play begins.

350 / 305 *he has a woman's heart* See on *Agamemnon* 1876/1625.

352–552 / 306–478 *Kommos* This is the longest and formally most complex of all such lyric structures in extant tragedy, and the one that most fully integrates Chorus and actors as equal partners. It has four distinct parts of varying size and formal makeup (following the schema set out in

A. F. Garvie's commentary, 124–25). The first and longest section (352–82/306–422) is a great dirge of highly symmetrical structure: six strophic pairs (i.e., metrically equivalent strophe and antistrophe; see on *Agamemnon*, 48–296/40–257) arranged in four triads, with each triad introduced by marching anapests (see on *Agamemnon*, 48–123/40–103) chanted by the Chorus, and the stanzas of each triad sung in alternation by Orestes, the Chorus, and Electra. The second section (483–524/423–55) is a lyric narrative of the events since Agamemnon's murder in three strophic pairs asymmetrically arranged and distributed among the participants. In this section, Orestes announces his determination to kill his mother (499–503/435–38). The third section (525–36/456–65) is a brief direct appeal to Agamemnon single contained in a strophic pair in which both stanzas are symmetrically divided among the three participants. This appeal will be continued by Orestes and Electra in the spoken iambics of 553–83/466–609). The final section (537–52/466–78) consists of a single strophic pair sung, in the manner of a brief stasimon, by the Chorus. It sums up the dire situation of the house and posits its children, Orestes and Electra, as the only hope for a "bloody healing" (546/472).

361 / 314 *the story three times old* Here as at *Agamemnon* 1692–93/1476–77 we have the sort of Greek compound in *tri–* that often has an intensive rather than numerical force. Here both senses seem to be at work. The "story" of retributive justice is very old and important, and it corresponds to the curse on the house that is repeatedly imagined in the trilogy as extending over three generations (see further on 1204–17/1065–76).

370 / 322 *here before the palace door* The first half of the play is set at the tomb of Agamemnon, and the scene building, which will later represent the palace, has no designation or function. At what point does it become the palace? With certainty only when, after the first stasimon, Orestes knocks on the door (750/652). However, the reference here to burial *prosthdomois*, "before the house," and the reference at 666/583 to "the god who stands there at the door" (see the note there) suggest that Aeschylus is preparing the scene building's later function. We have used this clue to stage Electra's exit "inside" at 668/584—and her disappearance from the play—through the door of the stage building.

386 / 339 *wrestle Ruin to a third fall* In a Greek wrestling match, the victor had to win three falls. Thus "third" here has the sense of "third and last," "final." See further the Introduction, pp. 36–37.

396 / 346 *a Lycian spear* The Lycians were the Trojans' principal allies in the *Iliad*; here the name is practically a synonymous with Trojan.

418 / 368 *killed in the same way* Orestes, in the corresponding strophe, has said it would have been better if his father had died fighting at Troy (395–98/345–48). Electra answers with an equally unreal wish—his killers are the ones who should have died in battle at Troy.

425–26 / 373 *the blessed race that lives / beyond the North Wind's lair* These are the Hyperboreans, "those beyond Boreas," a mythical tribe that lived in the distant north in a state of bliss. They were associated with Apollo, who had visited their land before he went to claim Delphi as his seat, and returned for three months each winter.

429–30 / 375–76 *the sharp snap of this / double lash* the sound of the laments of Orestes and Electra; for the double lash, cf. on *Agamemnon*, 730–31/642–43.

441 / 387 *the shrill triumphant cry* See on *Agamemnon* 33–34/28.

459–61 / 402–4 The end of *Libation Bearers* will show that this principle applies as much to Orestes as to any of his predecessors in revenge.

483–85 / 423–24 *the way a Mede would do . . . a wailing woman from Susa* The Greeks associated passionate and violent lament with Oriental, and especially Persian cultures. The Greek text refers to "the Arian manner" and "a Cissian wailing-woman"; since "Arian" was an alternate name for the Medes, and Cissia was the region of Persia surrounding the ancient capital city of Susa, we have used those more familiar names.

504 / 439 *he was mutilated* Agamemnon's corpse is said to have undergone *maschalismos*, literally "armpitting," in which a murder victim's hands and feet were cut off and strung on a rope that was then drawn under the corpse's armpits and tied around the neck. The purpose of such a rite was presumably to disable the corpse and so prevent the victim from taking revenge on the murderers. Here, however, it seems to be mentioned chiefly as a further aggravating factor in the crimes against Agamemnon.

531 / 461 *Now force will battle force, and justice justice* Not only a violent struggle, then, but a conflict of one *dike* against another. We are reminded for the first time in *Libation Bearers* of Clytemnestra's and Aegisthus'

claims to have accomplished justice by killing Agamemnon (e.g., *Agamemnon*, 1637/1432, 1754–58/1525–27, 1814/1577, 1848–52/1604–7).

557–62 / 483–88 For this appeal to the self-interest of Agamemnon's ghost, see on 290/257.

584–87 / 510–13 The Chorus Leader marks the end of the long prayer sequence at Agamemnon's tomb by turning Orestes' thoughts to the planning of the deed he has vowed to do. Orestes' questioning of why Clytemnestra sent libations to Agamemnon's tomb (588–98/513–22), will provide the key to that plan.

619 / 542 *Look how I read it* Orestes in effect makes the dream his own by the act of interpreting it in a way that gives him at once an omen of victory and the means to shape his plan. At 629–30/551–53, the Chorus adopts his interpretation and adds a prayer for its realization.

634–35 / 556–58 *the ones who killed . . . / by treachery, will by treachery be killed* This is the form of vengeance Apollo enjoined at 309–10/273–74.

642 / 563 *we'll both speak with a Parnassian accent* This is the accent spoken in the region of Phocis, around Mount Parnassus, to which Orestes was sent as a child (cf. *Agamemnon* 1008–13/877–81). Nothing in the language Orestes uses in his role as the Phocian stranger (750–810/653–706) deviates from standard Attic Greek of tragic dialogue. It is possible that his delivery had a flavoring of Phocian pronunciation, but perhaps more likely, within the non-naturalistic conventions of tragic performance, that the audience found it sufficient that he said he would do so.

644–57 / 565–76 Orestes' plan contains provisions for situations that do not arise (the possibilities that he and Pylades are not admitted to the palace and that Aegisthus is found at home and sitting on Agamemnon's throne). Aeschylus may be using versions of the story known to his audience (Aegisthus is shown being murdered as he sits on his throne on a number of red-figure vases from earlier in the fifth century) to create uncertainty about just how the plot will develop. It is significant that, apart from the plural in the promise of revenge against "the ones who killed an honored lord" (634/556), Orestes avoids any mention of the killing of Clytemnestra, the act that will be so fraught with emotion and laden with consequences for him. Instead, he breaks off with the successful completion of the plot against Aegisthus. Orestes will only confront the human meaning of matricide when the moment has come to commit it.

657–60 / 577–78 Orestes refers to the murder of Aegisthus as yet another third libation, reminiscent of Clytemnestra's libation of blood (*Agamemnon* **1577–81/1384–87**), but dedicated to the Erinys that cries out for vengeance. We should recall that Orestes is the snake that drinks his mother's blood (**627–28/549–50**), the embodiment of the Erinys. See further the Introduction, pp. 32–33.

660 / 579 *You, Electra* Orestes' reiteration of his instructions to Electra with which the speech began signals the end of her role in the play. She will not appear or even be mentioned again.

666 / 583 *the god who stands there by the door* Our translation is more explicit than the Greek text, which says simply "this one here." Who is meant? Pylades has been suggested, but the verb translated "watch over" (*epopteusai*) elsewhere in Aeschylus is used to invoke divine oversight of human affairs. Agamemnon would be possible, and the verb is appropriate enough for a sacred hero such as he has become. We join most editors, however, in assuming that Orestes points to the statue or symbol of a divinity placed near the door of the stage building. The pillar of Apollo agyieus that Cassandra addressed in *Agamemnon*, apparently a regular feature of the stage set (see on *Agamemnon* **1229/1081**), is the most likely candidate and would be apt given Orestes' reliance on Apollo's oracle. A statue or herm of Hermes, who was invoked as "overseer" of Agamemnon's power at the beginning of the play, and will be called on again to "oversee / and guide the contest" (**837–38/728–29**), be equally, or perhaps even more, appropriate. If the reference here is in fact to a deity represented near the door of the stage building, Aeschylus is here shifting our focus from the tomb to coming role to the palace (see on **370/322**).

669–749 / 585–652 *First stasimon* This choral ode is the first surviving example of a type that becomes common in the works of Sophocles and Euripides: a situation within the play is illuminated by examples drawn primarily from mythology. In this case, natural terrors as well as terrifying stories from myth set off the enormity of Agamemnon's murder. The mythical examples all illustrate violent and destructive deeds of women, shifting attention from Aegisthus (cf. on **644–57/565–76**) to Clytemnestra, who will soon appear on stage. The Chorus emphasizes "passion . . . that . . . perverts / the yoke of wedlock" (**683–86/599–601**) and results in the killing of children (Althaea), fathers (Scylla), and—even worse—husbands (Clytemnestra and the Lemnian women).

701 / 613 *the bloody Scylla* This is the first surviving evidence of a story that must nevertheless have been well known to Aeschylus' audience, since it is treated allusively here. Scylla's name is not given in the Greek text, which merely refers to a "bloody maiden." Nisus, however, was the brother of Aegeus, who was king of Athens, and father of Theseus, so the story is part of Athenian lore. We cannot trace it again until it reappears in works by the Roman poets Vergil and Ovid. The Romans tend to conflate this Scylla with the sea-monster of the *Odyssey* (cf. on *Agamemnon* 1409–10/1233), but there is no reason to connect them.

708–9 / 619 *his lock / of immortality* A life-token, like Meleager's brand (692–99/ 604–11), and also akin to the hair that gave the biblical Samson his strength.

711–37 / 623–38 We print the third strophe and antistrophe in the order transmitted by the manuscript tradition. It implies the following sequence of thought: Clytemnestra's outrageous murder of Agamemnon (strophe) *is worse than the crimes of Althaea and Scylla, so horrible that it calls to mind* the most terrible crime of all, the Lemnian women's massacre of their husbands (antistrophe). That this order is correct is perhaps confirmed by the Chorus's statement that the Lemnian crime is worst (*presbeuetai*, "takes pride of place") among all such tales. Many scholars, however, have preferred to reverse strophe and antistrophe, making Clytemnestra's crime the climactic element, and providing an easier transition to the consideration in the final strophic pair of vengeance still to come.

725–26 / 631 *the crime / of Lemnos* Apparently already a byword for any horrifying deed (730–31/633–34), the transgression of the women of the island of Lemnos was so well known to Aeschylus' audience that he could merely allude to it as something that caused them to be despised by gods and men. The women had failed to pay due honors to Aphrodite, and she therefore caused their husbands to spurn them in favor of Thracian women captured on raids. The women retaliated by slaying all the men of the island. Aeschylus emphasizes that their collective folly wipes out an entire people (733/636).

746–48 / 649–51 *a child / is brought to the house . . . / by the far famed Erinyes* The child is both a new crime to requite the old crimes that are its parents (cf., e.g., 928–29/805, *Agamemnon*, 874–80/763–71) and the literal son, Orestes, who returns as the Erinyes' agent to avenge his father's murder.

750–902 / 652–782 *Second episode* This episode consists of two short, self-contained scenes separated by a brief passage in anapests chanted by the chorus (829–35/719–29). After a relatively static first half, centered around the rituals at Agamemnon's tomb, Orestes' revenge will move forward with headlong speed.

750 / 652 *Boy! Boy!* Orestes calls to the slave who would be expected to open the door to visitors. The theatrical technique of knocking on the door is widely taken up in comedy, but seen only rarely in later tragedy. As Taplin points out *(Stagecraft of Aeschylus*, 340), Orestes' return as an ordinary traveler makes a marked contrast to Agamemnon's homecoming in the preceding play. His entrance into the palace to exact revenge will also be utterly unlike Agamemnon's as unwitting victim.

756–65 / 658–67 The deception that is an essential feature of Orestes' revenge begins with the assumption of a persona established by the elaborate imagery and somewhat supercilious tone of his instructions. There is a slightly comic atmosphere here, but of course in the service of grim ends; and some of Orestes' ironies are quite pointed. Speaking of the mistress of the house as the one "who runs the place" (762/664), for example, has a special application to Clytemnestra, and Orestes' suggestion that he would "frankly say whatever's on his mind" (765/666–67) if he could speak to the master has a particular edge considering the elaborate plot now under way.

766 / 668 Until the palace door opens, we do not know who will receive the false report of Orestes' death. That his mother now enters heightens the dramatic tension considerably. In her welcome there is once again irony, but of a different kind from that of Orestes. The offer of "warm baths" (768/670) cannot help but have a sinister ring in light of Agamemnon's fate, and there is irony, too, in her mention of "the attention of judicious [*dikaiôn*, literally "just"] eyes" (769/671). Clytemnestra's deferral to men when it comes to "graver business" (770/672) is something we know to be mere pretense.

791 / 690 *His parent, though, should know* The Greek word translated "parent" is a masculine participle; it might conceivably mean "mother or father," but even then presupposes at least the possiblity that there is a living father. Orestes ironically pretends ignorance of Agamemnon's death.

793–802 / 691–99 There has been much dispute about whether Clytemnestra is sincere in her lament for Orestes. The Nurse will assert catagorically that Clytemnestra's tears were feigned (848–54/737–41), and her capacity for blatant hypocrisy was made amply clear in *Agamemnon* (e.g., 683–700/600–12, 981–1007/855–73; cf. 1563–65/1372–73). On the other hand, there is nothing in Clytemnestra's words themselves that brands them as hypocritical. If they do not reflect a close human bond, that may be a sign that they are not feigned, for indeed there has been no such bond between Clytemnestra and her son. What she laments is the way in which the curse on the house destroys even at a distance the son she thought was safe, and we know that what is still to come will only confirm her fear of its "hideous carousing" (802/698). What is less clear is the meaning of the hope she apparently invested in Orestes while he was still alive. The Greek text here has been much disputed and emended without any fully satisfactory understanding being reached. The apparent idea is that Orestes might somehow, at some later time, have put a stop destruction of the Argive royal house by agreeing to some compromise satisfactory to all concerned.

825–39 / 719–29 *Choral interlude* The Chorus, left alone on stage, prays for Orestes' success in marching anapests (see on *Agamemnon* 48–123/40–103) Because the passage is preceded by an exit and followed by the entrance of a new character, it meets Taplin's criteria (*Stagecraft of Aeschylus*, 51–56) for an act-dividing song, a function usually filled by a full-fledged choral ode. From another perspective, however, two scenes are joined by this brief stanza into a single unit: the intrigue launched by Orestes' dialogue with Clytemnestra in the previous scene will be unexpectedly extended by the Chorus's timely intercession with his old Nurse.

831–39 / 726–29 The Chorus's invocation of Persuasion and Hermes as Orestes' helpers in the coming battle emphasizes the all-important role of deception in achieving victory. Hermes plays a double role, with his chthonic character aligning him with the prayer to earth and Agamemnon's tomb (828–29/722–23) and reminding us of a long series of prayers in the first half of the play. But as "lord / of stealthy night" (836–37/728), Hermes is also the god of shady dealing, stealth, and guile.

840–902 / 730–82 The Chorus intercepts the Nurse, whom Clytemnestra has dispatched to fetch Aegisthus. They have just prayed to Persuasion and stealthy Hermes to help Orestes; now the Chorus Leader helps by using persuasion to bring about Aegisthus' death by stealth. The intervention of the Chorus in the action is unusual, but in emphasizing the role of deceit in Orestes' revenge, it also draws attention to the fact that Aegisthus will enter the palace like Agamemnon, unsuspecting and defenseless. The Nurse is an almost comic character, with her prattling about babies' bowels and other subjects that normally have no place in tragedy, but she is not here for comic relief, like the Porter in *Macbeth*. She brings the perspective of a person who loves Orestes for himself, as a mother should, but his own mother does not and cannot; and her reaction to his supposed death is touchingly immediate and intense.

841 / 732 *Cilissa* An ethnic name, "the Cilician woman," presumably indicating that the Nurse was captured or bought in Cilicia, a region of southeastern Asia Minor (present-day Turkey). Slaves in tragedy, unlike those in comedy, are rarely given names.

844 / 734–35 *The mistress orders me* Once again Clytemnestra sends someone out to do her bidding, and again the result will be the opposite of what she intended.

848–54 / 737–41 Whether the Nurse's depiction of Clytemnestra's hypocrisy is taken at face value or not (cf. on **793–802/691–99**), it certainly makes clear that she is no ally of her mistress, and lends force to the contrast of her own very maternal lament with the far less intimate one of Orestes' natural mother.

871 / 753 *like a dumb beast* There is an implicit comparison between the beast-like baby Orestes the nurse once nurtured and Clytemnestra's recent dream of the snake who suckled at her breast—the now grown and no longer helpless Orestes who will kill her (cf. **627–28/549–50**).

903–59 / 783–837 *Second stasimon* An extended prayer for the success of Orestes' mission, articulated in three triads, each consisting of a strophic pair separated by a single stanza in a different meter ("mesode"). The first triad is directed to Zeus, the second to a different god or gods in each of its stanzas, and the third anticipates Orestes' struggle and victory.

912–14 / 791–93 Another appeal to the god's self-interest (see on **290/257**), although this time with no threat of withholding favor for noncompliance.

915–21 / An extended metaphor in which the Chorus asks Zeus to help Orestes, the colt of Agamemnon, win the race in which he is now engaged, his quest for vengeance. Orestes "yoked to the chariot of struggle" recalls a series of figures yoked in *Agamemnon*, among them Agamemnon yoked to horrible necessity (248–49/218), Troy yoked to its destruction (600–601/529), and Cassandra yoked to slavery (1091–92/953, 1219/1071). Here, however, the metaphor serves the hopeful meaning of a prayer for victory.

922 / 800–803 *you gods within* These are gods like Zeus *ktêsios* (see on *Agamemnon* 1178/1038) and Hestia, goddess of the hearth, who received simple domestic forms of worship, and were regarded as guardians of the family's possessions.

926–27 / 803–4 *wash clean the blood . . . with / a fresh-kill act of justice* The Chorus appears to hope that a new deed of blood can cancel out all those that came before and bring an end to the cycle of crime and retribution. By the end of the play, they will see that this "solution" is far more equivocal and uncertain (1212–17/1073–76).

929–30 / 807–8 *the magnificent / great cave* Apollo was thought of in antiquity as communicating with his prophetess at Delphi from a chasm beneath the temple. Since modern archeology has shown that there was no such geological feature, one can only speculate what might have given the impression of a cavern entrance within the temple's inner chamber.

934–40 / 812–18 Hermes is invoked, as before, both as chthonic power and as god of stealth (cf. on 831–39/726–29), but in addition as god of voyage, whose favoring breeze can keep the ship on course. The Chorus makes that image their omen in the following strophe (943–45/821–24). The imagery surrounding Hermes in this stanza, however, is largely associated with darkness. Hermes does his work in the dark, through trickery, and Orestes must do the same. This emphasis on darkness has an ominous ring, particularly after the prayer in the preceding stanza that Orestes be allowed to bring light from darkness.

939–40 / 811–18 The image of Hermes as "the dark before our eyes" by day as well as night suggests his ability to mystify at will, with deceptive messages or disturbing dreams. The image may allude to the "cap of Hades," which grants invisibility, and which Hermes obtained for Perseus, to whom Orestes is compared at 954–59/831–37.

958 / 835–36 *run red with Gorgon gore* The comparison of Orestes and Perseus is continued in the analogy between Clytemnestra and Perseus' victim,

the Gorgon Medusa. While this is apt in itself, it may also foreshadow the next stage of the drama. Perseus was pursued by the other Gorgons for his killing of their sister, and Orestes will be pursued by Clytemnestra's Erinyes, who he says are "like / Gorgons" (1187–88/1048; cf. *Eumenides* 59–60/48–49). Here, he is also urged to kill "the man whose hands are red from killing" (Aegisthus), but in doing so he will become just such a man himself, and the target of the Erinyes' murderous intentions.

960–1064 / 838–934 *Third episode* The central action of the play moves forward at a headlong pace and with corresponding intensity of focus. Aegisthus enters and exits again after an extraordinarily brief dialogue with the Chorus. After a short interlude marking his death, the Slave enters to give what amounts to the scantiest, most agitated messenger speech in Greek drama, followed almost immediately by Clytemnestra, and a few lines later by Orestes and Pylades. The result of all this commotion is a confrontation of mother and son — the climactic moment of the drama — that lasts a mere forty lines.

960–79 / 838–54 Aegisthus appears alone, in accordance with the Nurse's instructions, thus demonstrating the success of the intrigue in the previous scene and preparing for his immanent murder. One senses again the formal care with which Aeschylus connects the scenes in this part of the play (cf. on 825–39/719–29). This scene is like a mirror of the preceding scene, also a self-contained and employing a single actor. There, the Nurse exited from the palace and was engaged in dialogue by the Chorus Leader before exiting through the orchestra. Here, Aegisthus enters through the orchestra, briefly engages the Chorus Leader in dialogue, and exits into the palace.

965 / 842 *would make its deep wounds ooze and drip again* The obvious irony emphasizes Aegisthus' cluelessness: not Orestes' death, but his own and Clytemnestra's, will open the wounds of the house. There is similarly blatant irony in Aegisthus' final statement that the stranger who reported Orestes' death "can't deceive a mind that's open-eyed" (979/854).

980–95 / 855–68 *Choral interlude* Again, marching anapests (see on *Agamemnon*, 48–123/40–103) fill the interval between Aegisthus' exit and his death, marked immediately afterwards by a single outcry (996/869). As at 825–39/719–29), the passage seems to connect the preceding scene to what follows, rather than to mark a full act-division.

992 / 866 *all by himself* The next round of the wrestling match will pit Orestes as *ephedros* (the wrestler who waits "on the bench" to meet the victor of the previous contest) against not one victor, but two.

1004 / 877 *Open up* The staging here is in doubt: what doors are to be opened up? The most obvious solution is to suppose that there is a second door at one side of the stage building that is to be imagined as leading to the women's quarters, and that the Slave calls to other servants expected to be at that door. However, no other tragedy seems to require a second door, and a good case for requiring such a door can only be made for comedies of the 420s and later. The alternative is to suppose that the Slave refers to an inside door and calls back into the house; it is highly unlikely that, as has sometimes been proposed, lines 1002–7/875–80 are spoken from inside before the Slave appears.

1014 / 886 *the dead are killing off the living* This "riddle," as Clytemnestra calls it (1015/887), refers to the story that Orestes was dead, but its phraseology is designed to reveal a larger truth about what is happening, and in this sense it confirms the Slave's insight that his mistress will soon "fall to the blade of just revenge" (1012/884).

1016 / 888 *We killed by treachery* Cf. 634–35/556–58.

1017 / 889 *an axe to kill a man* Clytemnestra's resistance comes too late, but with her old daring and "manly" decisiveness, effectively putting the lie to the image she earlier cultivated of a woman who defers to men when it comes to "graver business" (770/672).

1020–59 / 892–930 Orestes and Clytemnestra meet at last in a brief but terrible scene, which has been repeatedly promised, but whose human implications Orestes has not yet fully confronted (cf. on 644–57/565–76). Now he cannot avoid them.

1024 / 896–97 *take pity on this breast* It is usually assumed that Clytemnestra bares her breast at this point, as Hecuba did to her son Hector in a vain attempt to keep him from fighting Achilles (*Iliad*, 22, 79–81). On the Athenian stage, however, women's parts were played by men, and it may have been difficult to present breast-baring to the right effect; at any rate, it is not presented on stage in any other extant tragedy. Perhaps the idea was conveyed here simply by a gesture.

1027 / 899 *What do I do, Pylades?* Orestes' resolution falters, and he turns to his companion for help. Pylades, who until now has merely shadowed Orestes as a mute extra, will hardly have been expected to speak, and the surprise makes his words all the more effective. Speaking in effect for Apollo, Pylades confirms Orestes' decision to do the deed he has long known awaits him.

1041 / 912 *a mother's curse* Orestes will feel its effects before the play is over, but here he tries to deflect it by pointing out that Clytemnestra was not a proper mother to him. At 1053–54/924–25, he answers the more explicit threat of pursuit by the "mad dogs" of her curse, if he kills her, by referring to the threat of his father's curse, if he fails to do so (see on 311–38/276–96).

1044 / 915 *I was sold* Electra made the same allegation at 158–60/132–34. In both cases the notion is that Clytemnestra's "price" for the sale of her children is her relationship with Aegisthus.

1053 / 924–25 *mad dogs of a mother's curse* These are the Erinyes, often pictured as hounds (cf. 1193/1054 and *Eumenides* 143–45/131–32 and 276–78/246–47) because they pursue their victims by the scent of blood.

1055 / 926 *a deaf tomb* Clytemnestra means Orestes, but in the next line Orestes transfers the words to Agamemnon's grave, to which as his murderer she cries in vain.

1057 / 928 *you are the snake* Clytemnestra's dream has not been mentioned since Orestes made precisely this claim for himself (627–28/549–50; see on 619/542). Acknowledging the meaning of her dream, Clytemnestra admits defeat. We will not hear her death cry—her life is over when she leaves the stage.

1060–64 / 931–34 The Chorus Leader caps the scene and introduces the choral ode with a note of pity for Aegisthus and Clytemnestra that yields immediately to the thought that Orestes has saved the house. He is its "eye" both as its most precious part and its guardian.

1065–96 / 935–72 *Third stasimon* This song of triumph, which the Chorus had prayed to sing at 441–43/386–89 (and cf. 941–47/819–26), sums up their view of Orestes' vengeance as the liberation of the house from its curse, presided over by Justice and guided by Apollo. The joyful mood provides an effective contrast to the final scene.

1068 / 938 *a double lion* Most commentators take this to refer to Orestes and Pylades, but since in the following lines, the Chorus comments that Orestes "drove the whole / course by himself," they appear to be calling him a double lion, i.e., the one responsible for the double slaughter of Aegisthus and Clytemnestra.

1071 / 942 *Shout out in triumph* See on *Agamemnon* 33–34/28.

1079 / 949–50 *we speak truth when we name her Justice* Another example of the *nomen-omen* principle (cf. on *Agamemnon* 782/687). In the Doric Greek of this choral lyric, *Dika* (Justice) is derived from the words that immediately precede it, **Dios kora**, "daughter of Zeus."

1081 / 953–54 *the great cave of Parnassus* See on 929–30/807–8.

1087 / 961 *the light has come* See on 157/131.

1093 / 967 *when all pollution is expelled* The notion that a house can be purified from pollution is common; such a rite is described already in the *Odyssey*, 22, 480–94. Here, however, the Chorus's assumption that the house can so easily be cleansed will prove deluded, and by 1198–99/ 1059–60, the Chorus will realize that Orestes must go to Apollo's shrine at Delphi to seek purification.

1096 / 971 *the alien tenants* The Erinyes, who have so long lived in it as "resident aliens" (*metoikoi*). Ironically, they will only leave the house to pursue Orestes (1200–1201/1061–62), ending their journey in Athens, where they will agree to stay, this time as honored *metoikoi* (see on *Eumenides* 1182–83/1011).

1097–1217 / 973–1076 *Exodus* The concluding dialogue of Orestes and the Chorus leads quickly from triumph to anguish to something like desperation, as Orestes departs into a new and uncertain exile. The reversal is more sudden and far more complete than that in the encounter between the Chorus and Clytemnestra in *Agamemnon* (1563–1813/1372–1577). Instead of light, darkness descends again in Orestes' vision of the black-robed Erinyes; instead of victory, there is madness, pollution, and pursuit.

The exodus begins with a version of the tableau seen in *Agamemnon*, where Clytemnestra appeared along with the bodies of her victims (see on *Agamemnon*, 1563/1372). As in that scene, the most likely way to stage Orestes' appearance here with the corpses of Clytemnnestra and Aegisthus would have been to roll out the tableau on the wheeled platform called the *ekkyklêma*, although it is possible that the elements of the tableau were brought in by extras. The two tableaux are further linked by Orestes' display of the bloody robes in which his father was slain, and, however it was managed, we may be sure that both were staged in the same way.

1102 / 977 *their oath, too, has been faithful to its pledges* A mild personification equivalent to saying that they abided by the terms of their oath. The word translated "pledges" (*pistômasin*) is often used of marriage vows (see on *Eumenides*, 238/214).

1108 / 983 *Here, spread it out* Perhaps the robe is spread out in the same place as the embroideries on which Agamemnon walked to his death (see Whallon, *Problem and Spectacle*, 87), which would add a second parallel to *Agamemnon* and a second illustration of the retributive "fit" of Orestes' murders.

1110–12 / 984–86 *my father . . . the Sun* It is common in Greek literature to appeal to the sun as a witness, since he sees everything as he crosses above the earth. At *Agamemnon*, 718–19/632–33, the Herald says that only the sun can know who survived the shipwreck of the Greek fleet, and at *Agamemnon*, 1509/1323–24, Cassandra, departing for death, prays to the "sun's last shining" that her death will be avenged. The notion of the Sun as father is encountered less frequently, though it is a natural enough reflection of the role of Sun and Earth in the genesis of life in Greek thought. Here it is used to fine pathetic effect, as Orestes' invocation of his father is interrupted to remind us that he has no living father but the Sun. It may be significant that Orestes invokes the Sun as *martus en dikê*, a phrase that might be translated "witness in a trial," but if it constitutes a hint of what still awaits him, it is nothing more than a hint.

1118 / 990 *the law's the law* Athenian law allowed for an adulterer to be killed with impunity by the husband or other family member. Aegisthus' murder needs no further defense; it is the matricide that brings pollution and needs justification. There is, however, an irony built into this and the many other references to law and legal procedures in the trilogy, for the premise of private retribution is that no legal avenues yet exist for those wronged to get satisfaction.

1123 / 994 *If she had been an eel, or viper* This returns the metaphor of the snake to Clytemnestra (as at 281/248–49), after its association with Orestes through Clytemnestra's dream.

1139–42 / 1007–9 and **1147–51/1018–20** Symmetrical outbursts in marching anapests (see on *Agamemnon*, 48–123/40–103) expressing the Chorus's dawning recognition of the misery that still faces Orestes.

1144 / 1011 *Aegisthus' sword* Aegisthus, in Aeschylus' version, has been excluded from any part in the actual murder of Agamemnon, but one need not confect elaborate scenarios to explain this reference to him. Clytemnestra would be using his sword simply because, as a woman, she had none of her own; and Orestes' mention of the detail reminds us of the adultery that for him is at the root of her crime (1099–1104/975–79).

1157–59 / 1022–24 The first indication of Orestes' madness, presented in a striking metaphor. Earlier, the Chorus pictured Orestes as a colt striving to win a chariot race (915–21/794–99); now he sees himself as a charioteer losing control of his team, i.e., his mind.

1169 / 1031 *guiltlessly* At 303/269, Orestes said simply that "Apollo's great oracle will never betray me." Here he specifies for the first time that Apollo has promised that he will be freed of any guilt, but how that is to happen will be made clear only in *Eumenides*.

1172 / 1034–35 *armed with this branch and wreath* An olive branch wreathed with tufts of wool is the suppliant's usual emblem, and when we next hear of Orestes as a suppliant in Delphi, he will still be carrying it, along with his sword (*Eumenides*, 50–56/40–45). Orestes will not have been holding the branch when he entered at 1097/972, but one of his attendants presumably brought it on, so that he can take it now. Orestes is presumably still carrying the bloody sword, and the contrast of the two implements makes for a striking visual oxymoron that continues until he leaves the stage.

1174–75 / 1037 *called / Forever Burning* The famous eternal flame that blazed in the hearth of Apollo, beside the earth's navel stone within the temple at Delphi.

1180 / 1041 *when Menelaus comes* Menelaus is said in Book 4 of the *Odyssey* still to be wandering at the time of Agamemnon's death; Proteus urges him to hurry home, foretelling that either he will find Aegisthus still alive, or Orestes will just have killed him (*Odyssey*, 4, 544–47). Menelaus' adventures on his way home were the subject of the lost satyr play *Proteus*, which followed the three tragedies of the *Oresteia* (see the Introduction, footnote 1).

1198 / 1059 *There's only one way* See on **1093/967**.

1204–17 / 1065–76 The final marching anapests (see on *Agamemnon* **48–123/40–103**) bring not just *Libation Bearers*, but also *Agamemnon* (which ended without a closing choral "tag") to an end—but no conclusion—by asking what the future will bring. They recall two earlier visitations of the curse on the house, the slaughter of Thyestes' children and the murder of Agamemnon; then they try without success to divine the meaning of the third, the murder of Clytemnestra that was meant to put a stop to the cycle of violence but seems to have brought only more ruin.

1214 / 1073–74 *a savior, or should I say a death* The Chorus momentarily identifies Orestes with Zeus Savior of the third libation, still hoping he may prove to be the salvation of his house, but fearing that he should instead be called its downfall. See the Introduction, p. 33.

1217 / 1076 *destruction* The final word in this translation represents the ominous final words of the Greek text (*menos atês*, "the might of ruin"). Hope is not lost, but ruin is still undefeated. We await the third fall, the final play of the trilogy.

EUMENIDES

1–156 / 1–139 *Prologue* Substantially longer than the prologues (defined simply as the portion of the play before the Chorus makes its entrance) of the first two plays of the trilogy, this is really a sequence of separate scenes with a remarkable cumulative impact. First, there is a scene-setting speech by the Pythia (**1–40/1–33**), who exits only to return with a kind of messenger speech, an agitated report of the presence in the temple of Orestes and the Erinyes (**41–76/34–63**). In the next scene, Apollo promises Orestes his continues protection and prescribes the journey to Athens through which Orestes will win release from his troubles (**77–108/64–93**) He has put the Erinyes to sleep, and Orestes is able to make his escape. In the final scene of the Prologue, the ghost of Clytemnestra awakens her Erinyes and stir them into pursuit of Orestes

(109–156/94–139). Taken as a whole, this sequence presents the essential outlines of the coming struggle clearly and with dramatic force.

1–76 / 1–63 Structurally, the Pythia's speech resembles the two preceding prologues in that all three are intersected by a startling sight that changes the speaker's mood. In this case, the initial mood is markedly different from that which prevailed in the final scene of *Libation Bearers*, since the Pythia's prayers emphasize the order and peace of the shrine at Delphi, and the harmony among the gods associated with it (see on 6/5) The Pythia's report of what she has seen in the temple, on the other hand, directly continues the situation and tenor at the end of the preceding play.

2 / 2 *the first prophet, Earth* There was a shrine to Earth in the sanctuary at Delphi through its active history, and her importance to the site is presumably reflected in the story that Delphi was found to be the center of the earth when the two eagles Zeus sent out from either side of the earth met there.

6 / 5 *by her own choice and not by force* Aeschylus explicitly rejects the standard account, in which Apollo used force to capture Delphi from a chthonic predecessor, usually the monstrous serpent Pytho, occasionally Earth or Themis. See further the Introduction, pp. 22–23. This picture of peaceful succession helps bridge the gap between the violence of the past (the succession of crimes in the house of Atreus; the violent overthrow of Zeus's predecessors, leaving them unnamed and without honor [*Agamemnon*, 189–99/168–75]) and the more pacific order to come (Orestes' acquittal and the end of the curse on the house; the reconciliation of Olympian and chthonic deities, with continued powers and honors given to the latter).

7 / 7 *Phoebe* Not otherwise associated with Delphi, Phoebe is apparently given her place here to make the picture of harmonious relations among the generations and orders of divinity more complete. In addition to being Themis' sister in the Titan generation, Phoebe was Leto's mother (Hesiod, *Theogony* 404–6), and thus Apollo's grandmother. Aeschylus also establishes an etymological connection between the cult name Phoebus ("bright one") and Delphi, since he has Apollo adopt it in gratitude for Phoebe's gift.

12 / 10 *the ship-hive coast of Pallas* I.e., the coast of Attica, whose patron god is Pallas Athena. This version of Apollo's journey seems designed to honor Athens (cf. on **14**/13); a number of other sources have him landing in Boeotia, to the north.

14 / 13 *The children of Hephaestus* A reference to the Athenians, who regarded themselves as descended from Hephaestus through their early king Erichthonius, born of seed that fell to earth when Hephaestus attempted to rape Athena. The reference to the Athenians as road builders is explicated by a fragment of the fourth-century historian Ephorus, who says that Apollo first traveled to Delphi along the road that the Athenians still use to send their delegation to the Pythian Festival (a quadrennial Panhellenic competition like the Olympics, but featuring musical and poetic as well as athletic contests). Aeschylus is here alluding to (or perhaps even inventing) the story of how that road came to be built.

21 / 19 *spokesman for his father Zeus* The implication of this statement is that Zeus, the great ruler of the gods, stands behind Apollo's oracles, including the demand that Orestes kill his mother and the promise of protection when the deed is done.

23–34 / 21–28 The Pythia's prayer concludes with mention of a rather disparate group of gods, major Olympians and local nature deities, in no apparent order, except for reserving the final place for Zeus "who brings all to fulfillment" (see on **33–34**/28). All the gods, however, have connections to Delphi: Athena's shrine that "stands there, apart" (**24**/21) gives her cult at Delphi the name *pronaia*, "before the temple," because it is some distance from the temple of Apollo, and would be reached by the approaching traveler before they entered his precinct. The Corycian cave (**25**/22), sacred like many others to the Nymphs, lies on the slopes of Parnassus above Delphi. Bromius (**27**/24) is a cult name of Dionysus, who was thought to take up residence at Delphi during the three winter months when Apollo visited the Hyperboreans (see on *Libation Bearers*, **425–26**/373). Pleistus (**32**/27), god of the river that flows below Delphi, was the father of the Corycian Nymphs. Poseidon (**33**/27) was the father of Delphus, the eponymous king at the time of Apollo's arrival (**18**/16), and had an altar within Apollo's temple, indicating a long-standing association with the shrine (in one tradition, he originally shared the shrine with Earth).

29–30 / 25–26 *led his troop of women* / ... *to hunt down Pentheus* This story, best known to us from Euripides' *Bacchae*, was also enacted in a lost Aeschylean trilogy. Dionysus, who was born in Thebes, wished to establish his cult there when he returned to Greece after a long absence. King Pentheus tried to ban this new form of worship, but Dionysus drove a group of his maenads, led by Pentheus' own mother, to tear him to pieces on Mount Cithaeron, near Thebes. Here, the tale serves to explain when worship of Dionysus began at Greece—when he returned to Thebes and established his cult in Greece—but it sits uncomfortably in an otherwise peaceful prayer. The effect seems willed: the detail that Pentheus was snared like a hare (31/26) reminds us of the omen of a hare torn apart by eagles that led to the sacrifice of Iphigenia (*Agamemnon*, 129–57/108–38), and his "net of death" evokes the slaughter of Agamemnon.

33–34 / 28 *Zeus, / who brings all to fulfillment* This is Zeus *teleios* (see on *Agamemnon* 1115–18/972–74), he who fulfills prayers, and who may or may not show the way to fulfillment and finality here. (Like others before them in the trilogy, the Erinyes in this play will see themselves as *teleoi* [see on 370–73/ and 463/382].)

39 / 32 *in order of the lots they drew* Ordinarily, after purification and sacrifice, those admitted to consult the oracle drew lots to determine the order in which they would approach and put their questions.

40 / 33 The Pythia now enters the temple to perform her duties, and the audience awaits the arrival of another character or the entrance song of the Chorus. Exits such as this that leave the stage completely empty are rare, but there is no parallel at all in tragedy for the disappearance and reappearance of the same character. The shock is increased by the manner of her reentry, so terrified by what she has seen that she can only crawl on all fours (44–47/36–38).

51 / 41 *sitting the way a suppliant would sit* A suppliant must be in physical contact with a sacred object, of which he becomes in effect an extension, i.e., the inviolable property of the god to whom the object belongs. Here, that object is the "navel stone" (52/40), the sacred stone that stood in the inner chamber of the temple to mark the center of the earth. He may be sitting on it (as we have translated the phrase) or beside it— the Greek can indicate either, and vase paintings show both—but he must be touching it with his hand or a suppliant branch such as he was carrying when he left Argos (*Libation Bearers*, 1172/1035).

57 / 47 *sleeps* Why this ferocious gang has fallen asleep around their prey remains a mystery until Apollo tells us the answer at 80–81/67–68.

61–62 / 50–51 *flying female- / creatures* These are the Harpies, represented in fifth-century vase painting as winged women. The Pythia, having compared the Erinyes to Gorgons (as did Orestes, at *Libation Bearers*, 1187–89/1048–50), finds the likeness inadequate, and tries again by recalling an image she has seen of the hideous creatures who persecuted Phineus, King of Thrace. The Harpies ("Snatchers") swooped down and snatched his food whenever a table had been set for him. (Aeschylus wrote a *Phineus*, performed in 472 along with his *Persians*.)

66 / 55 *Their dark rags* The Erinyes, as daughters of Night and dwellers in darkness, dress in the color of mourning, inappropriate and inauspicious for wearing in a temple. The Pythia, as a priestess of Apollo, will be wearing white.

77–108 / 64–93 Apollo assures Orestes of his continued support and sends him on his way to Athens, guided by Hermes. For possible ways of staging this scene, see on 109–56/94–139.

77 / 64 *I won't betray you* Cf. *Libation Bearers*, 303/269, "Apollo's great oracle will never betray me," and 1169/1030–32, [Apollo] "told me I could do this guiltlessly." Apollo here makes his promise more explicit, offering his protection "to the end" (*dia telous*, i.e., until the goal is reached).

95 / 80 *holding her age-old image in your arms* The venerable and venerated olive wood statue of Athena Polias, which was ceremonially given a new embroidered robe at the Great Panathenaea, the major Athenian festival in honor of Athena. Again, the suppliant is to maintain physical contact with the sacred object (see on 51/41).

96 / 81 *we'll have judges for your case* The first inkling that resolution will come in the form of a trial, although there is no indication that the judges will be mortals rather than gods. But the promised resolution will be worked by persuasion ("words / that spellbind," 96–97/81–82; cf. on 1032/886), and it will bring Orestes permanent release from his troubles.

105 / 90 *be your own namesake* Hermes is given his title "the escorter" (*pompaios*) and asked to be true to its meaning. Although it is often supposed that Hermes must be present on stage there is no need to assume that Hermes appears in this scene, and no reason to think he reappears with Orestes in Athens. Apollo calls his brother, who can hear him even from afar (cf. 342/297) and asks him to protect and guide Orestes, again something he can do without appearing on the scene.

109–56 / 94–139 Clytemnestra's ghost appears and exhorts the sleeping Erinyes to rouse themselves and pursue their escaping prey. Ghosts were far from common on the Greek stage; among extant tragedies, we find only the ghosts of the Persian king Darius, in Aeschylus' *Persians*, and of Hecuba's treacherously slain son, Polydorus, in Euripides' *Hecuba*. Clytemnestra's ghost has the additional oddity of coming to her intended audience, the Erinyes, as a dream (156/139), whereas the theater audience witnesses her appearance as a real event. The scene completes preparations for the great confrontation to come. Apollo has seen to Orestes' escape and provided protection and instruction; now Clytemnestra charges her agents of retribution to follow Orestes and give him no quarter.

Regarding staging, although it is impossible to know precisely how Clytemnestra's entrance was handled, several satisfactory ways can be imagined. The real problem is to decide at what point the audience sees the sleeping Erinyes. The main choices seem to be these: (1) Before 77/64, the temple door opens, and the *ekkyklêma* (see on *Agamemnon*, 1563/1372) rolls out, with Orestes seated among at least a small group of sleeping Erinyes. Apollo then appears from behind the *ekkyklêma*, eventually guiding Orestes out into the orchestra, sending him on his way and reentering the temple after 109/93. Clytemnestra then appears from one of the side entrances, or through a subterranean entrance (if the theater had one: see Taplin, *Stagecraft of Aeschylus*, 447–48), or perhaps most appropriately and effectively, since she is a dream-apparition, on the roof of the stage building. (2) Apollo and Orestes exit from the temple in the usual way, and play their scene, with Orestes departing to the side at the end and Apollo reentering the temple. The door then opens again, and a tableau with Clytemnestra's ghost among a group of sleeping Erinyes rolls into view on the *ekkyklêma*. At the end of the scene, Clytemenestra exits to the side and the Erinyes on the *ekkyklêma*, urged on by the Chorus Leader, enter the orchestra, joined, as the parodos begins, by others who had been out of sight inside the stage building. (3) Apollo and Orestes perform their scene as in 2; Clytemnestra appears in any of the ways listed in 1 and performs her scene with no Erinyes to be seen, although they begin to be heard after 133/116. Clytemnestra exits in the same way she entered, the temple door opens, and the Erinyes enter the orchestra at the urging of the Chorus leader as the parodos begins. Each of these stagings has advantages and disadvantages, but we are persuaded to opt for 3 by the considerations suggested in Taplin, *Stagecraft of Aeschylus*, 369–74. Withholding the actual sight of the Erinyes until Clytemnestra has departed prevents visual distractions in the prologue scenes and builds expectations for the moment when they take over the orchestra, heightening the dramatic effect of their appearance when the doors are opened at last.

110–17 / 95–102 Clytemnestra has two separate complaints: she suffers dishonor in the world below because her Erinyes have not yet exacted vengeance for her death, and in addition she has to endure the constant reproaches of her own victims. The implied connection between these complaints is that the lack of any show of divine anger for the wrongs she suffered makes her vulnerable to their attacks. Giving and receiving due honors will be an important theme of *Eumenides*. The Erinyes in particular are incensed that the younger generations gods want to deny them their honors and, after Orestes' acquittal, they will have to weigh the honors they have lost against the new ones that Athena offers them instead.

120–25 / 106–9 For the notion that offerings are made in the understanding that they will be reciprocated with favor, see on *Libation Bearers* 290/257. Although wine was the regular medium of drink offering, the Erinys were among the deities honored with libations of water and honey. The burnt offerings might be cakes or animal sacrifices.

127 / 110 *my offerings trampled* A phrase reminiscent of other images of trampling down what ought to be sacred, and of the image's enactment when Agamemnon treads on the sacred embroideries (*Agamemnon* 1038–96/ 905–57. The Erinyes in turn will complain that their ancient rights are being trampled by the younger gods (165–66/149–50, 850/731, 903–5/ 808–9).

129 / 112 *out from the middle of your net* Aeschylus again uses one of the leading images of the trilogy. Zeus's net was cast over Troy so that no one could escape (*Agamemnon* 410–15/357–61), and Clytemnestra set hers "so high no one can over- / leap them" (*Agamemnon* 1568–69/1376); only Orestes, the leaping fawn, has leapt free from the hunting net the Erinyes set. The Chorus takes up the metaphor at 163–64/147–48.

134 / 118 Preceding this line and 136/121, the manuscripts carry the onomatopoeic expression for whining, *mugmos*. Before 138/124 and 140/127, we have a similar expression for moaning, *ôgmos*, and before 142/130, "high, repeated *mugmos*." These are among the few "stage directions" that come down in ancient dramatic texts. Whether or not they stem from Aeschylus himself, they represent the needed response of the Erinyes.

It is perhaps significant that the response starts as soon as Clytemnestra says her name.

141 / 128 *the poison from the dread snake's tooth* The image of the serpent, applied to the trilogy's stealthy murderers Clytemnestra (*Libation Bearers*, 281/248–49 and 1123–25/994–95; cf. 1186/1047) and Orestes (*Libation Bearers*, 603–11/526–34 and 627–28/549–50; cf. 1057/928), is especially appropriate to the Erinyes. In art, they were often represented as serpents, and when Orestes first saw them, he described "snakes swarming all over them, / braiding and unbraiding" (*Libation Bearers*, 1188–89/1049–50).

157 / 142 *let's see if this dream is a truthful prelude* Did the dream give, like the introductory section of a musical performance, a foretaste of what is to come? The Chorus Leader is asking whether the dream truly predicts that Orestes has escaped.

158–99 / 143–78 *Parodos* The chorus express their horror at having let Orestes escape and their passionate condemnation of Apollo for aiding a murderer whose very presence has polluted his shrine. It is not clear whether the entire Chorus is already in the orchestra when the parodos begins. A scholiast (an ancient or medieval commentator whose annotations are included in our manuscript tradition) suggests that the first strophe is divided among individual members of the Chorus, and this is all the more likely if, as it seems, the Chorus enters from the stage building by ones and twos, and may hold for the antistrophe as well.

158 / 143 *IOU! IOU! POPAX* An expression of horror at the recognition that Orestes is nowhere to be found. (It seems likely that the Chorus Leader and those who immediately follow him into the orchestra briefly mime a search before the song itself begins.)

165–71 / 149–54 These lines contain the essential elements of the Erinyes' quarrel with Apollo: he is a young upstart who has no respect for their seniority and has denied them their rights; although he is a god, he protects as a suppliant a mortal who has violated the gods' laws; and he has not acted in accord with justice (*dikaiôs*). The disrespect of the younger (male) gods will only be set right by Athena's persistence in showing the ancient female deities due deference (987–88/848–49, 1025–30/881–84). Supplication will be vindicated, but (like purification, its partner in eliminating blood-guilt) it will be shown to be inadequate in this difficult case (see on 266/237). Indeed, it will only be a new way of working *dikê*—the establishment of a court of law—that will at last allow the quarrel to come to an end.

176–78 / 160–61 The Erinyes liken their pain to that of a criminal submitting to a public flogging.

181–92 / 164–73 The Chorus's charge that Apollo has polluted his own sanctuary is a pendant to their objection to his receiving suppliants guilty of murder. Their picture of Apollo's throne and earth's navel stone dripping with blood gains effectiveness from the notion of blood pollution as a kind of contagion that spreads by contact (cf. 219/195). But, as Orestes will point out (531–38/448–52), it is only by undergoing rites of purification that a suppliant guilty of shedding blood can be freed from pollution. Apollo's answer is that the Erinyes themselves are the ones polluting his sanctuary by their presence (206/185, 231/207).

192 / 172 *the age-old power of the fates* the Erinyes are referring to the ancient dispensation (one meaning of *moira*) that gives them their function. But they are half-sisters of the divine *Moirai*, the Fates, by their mother Night (1122–23/961–62); and they are closely associated with them as agents of the retributive justice over which the Fates preside. The Fates might be thought of in this context as the bookkeepers of justice, making sure that in the end the accounts are brought into balance; cf. the invocation of the Fates as accomplishers of justice, along with Zeus, at *Libation Bearers* 352–61/306–14.

199 / 177 *a new avenger* When Orestes goes to the world below, his punishment will continue. See 305–18/267–75, where the Chorus threatens to drag Orestes to the underworld still living, and it is explicit that the "new avenger" who holds transgressors to a strict accounting is Hades himself.

200–263 / 179–234 *First episode.*

202 / 181 *a flying snake* Apollo's arrow is given an image used of the Erinyes themselves, and of the trilogy's chief murderers (see on 141/128).

207 / 186 *your jurisdiction* Apollo describes a set of customs involving mutilation, torture, and killing, all of which would be regarded by Greeks as abhorrent cruelties practiced by barbarians. Almost all can be paralleled by descriptions of Persian customs in Herodotus's *Histories*. The one exception is stoning, which was used by Greeks as a form of execution

in which a whole community could participate, and was therefore reserved for those who had injured the whole community. Public stoning is the punishment foretold by the Chorus of *Agamemnon* for Aegisthus (1864–65/1615–16). Perhaps it is included here simply as an example of mob violence.

217 / 194 *blood-lapping lions* The lion has appeared in the trilogy as a symbol of fierce strength, as a ruthless killer, and even (in Cassandra's sardonic description of Aegisthus, *Agamemnon*, 1399/1224) as a coward skulking in the bedroom. In its final appearance, the lion is reduced to a monstrous creature, dwelling in darkness like the Erinyes—who will make the imagery of bloodsucking their own at 300–4/264–66.

221 / 197 *No god* Somewhat hyperbolic, since this "herd" is itself divine, but Apollo is clearly talking about respectable Olympians, like himself. See further on 413–15/350–52.

222 / 198 *It's your turn to listen* Thus, appropriately, begins a debate that suggests how disputes can be pursued without bloodshed. The Chorus accuses Apollo of responsibility both for Orestes' crime and of shielding him from punishment (223–28/199–204). Apollo challenges their exclusive concern for mother-killers, which he regards as doing dishonor to Hera, Aphrodite, and the bonds of marriage (234–42/210–16). Although the debate unsurprisingly leads to no agreement, Apollo sets out the means, if not the content, of a peaceful settlement: Athena will "oversee the issue of this case" (253/224; in Greek, Apollo uses a plural form of *dikê*, *dikas*, which can mean "legal proceedings").

230 / 206 *And you malign us for serving as his escort?* The irony of this defense lies in the use of a word (*propompoi*) that suggests a ceremonial procession—the Chorus uses it of "marching" to Agamemnon's grave (*Libation Bearers*, 27/23)—or a guard of honor—the Athenian citizens who escort the Erinyes-Eumenides to their new home are called *propompoi* in a scholion (later annotation included in our manuscript tradition)—rather than the pursuit of fleeing prey by relentless hunters.

235–36 / 211–12 Apollo's question is reminiscent of Clytemnestra's objection at *Agamemnon*, 1612–21/1412–18 that the Elders should have condemned Agamemnon for his slaughter of Iphigenia. Orestes will raise Apollo's question again, and receive the same answer, at 702–3/604–5. Here, Apollo accuses the Erinyes of insufficient regard for another sacred

bond, the sexual union of a man and a woman. There, he will inter-
vene to argue the case that mother and son are not in fact related by
blood at all.

238 / 214 *the solemn vows of Hera the fulfiller* Marriage vows (*pistomata*, pledges of
trust) sacred to Hera *teleia*, who both alone and in the company of her
consort Zeus *teleios* is the patron deity of marriage. This cult name
derives from the use of *telos* to designate religious rites in general, and
Zeus *teleios* is "the fulfiller" in a broader sense as well (see on *Agamemnon* 1115–18/972–74).

243–49 / 217–21 Apollo emphasizes the sacredness of marriage and its claim on justice
to show the injustice of the Erinyes' pursuit only of killers within the
bloodline.

24 / 218 *greater than any oath* An oath would ordinarily be the strongest form of
pledge or promise, but Apollo argues that marriage vows are even
stronger. He will later say the same thing of the will of Zeus (**722/621**),
which perhaps suggests how bold Apollo's claim here is. Apollo makes
his case for the special sacrality of marriage in part simply by calling
it "a thing of destiny," which does not imply what we mean by "a
match made in heaven" (Agamemnon's and Clytemnestra's clearly was
not), but rather that it is the allotted portion of men and women to
unite in marriage.

258–63 / 229–34 The Chorus Leader and Apollo cap the scene with three lines each
in which they state the equally intransigent positions from which the
trial will begin. The effect is clearest if the Chorus depart immediately
as soon as their Leader has spoken, and Apollo, who cannot stop them
but is resolved to defeat their plans, delivers his lines after they leave
the orchestra.

260 / 230–31 *get our justice* The Erinyes use the same word, *dikas*, that Apollo used
at **253/224** to indicate that Athena would oversee Orestes' trial. In their
mouths, however, *dikas* still means the old retributive justice of blood
for blood.

262–63 / 233 *a dreadful thing for gods / and men alike* This is one of several passages
in *Eumenides* that suggest the gods' respect for mortals and sense of
responsibility to them (see on **882–84/760–61, 1169/1002**). There is also
the implication here that the gods seek to avoid the anger or displeasure

of mortals by shirking their responsibilities (see further on 558–61/470–72).

264–352 / 235–306 Second episode No choral ode separates the second episode from the first. None is possible because the Chorus has left the orchestra, which makes possible the change of scene that now occurs. Instead of an act-dividing stasimon, there is a momentary pause before Orestes enters, alone. There need be little change to the playing space — simply the removal of props (if there were any) that identified the setting as Delphi and their replacement by a wooden statue of Athena (cf. on 95/80, and see 290–92/258–59). From Orestes' first words we understand that he has reached Athens, as Apollo ordered. This sort of change of scene is rare in Greek drama. (The closest parallel, Sophocles' *Ajax*, 815, also involves the Chorus disappearing from view.) The Erinyes reappear, apparently again by ones and twos, miming bloodhounds following a scent, and sing what is usually referred to as an "epiparodos," or second entry song (285–318/254–75). The remainder of the episode is a pair of speeches (not an exchange — see 349/303; Orestes will not address the Erinyes until his trial) for Orestes and the Chorus Leader.

266 / 237 but one no longer stained Orestes has been purified from blood-guilt and his hands are no longer stained. In this passage, the cleansing appears to have happened in the course of his journey, but at 326–27/282–83, Orestes explicitly states that he was purified by Apollo at Delphi; apparently we are to understand that both the Delphic rite and the trials of his wanderings were necessary for his cleansing. Orestes mentions multiple purifications again at 535–37/451–52. Most important, however, although Orestes repeatedly insists that his formal purity has freed him to have normal contact with others (268–69/238–39, 329–30/285, 528–30/445–46), it does nothing to placate the Erinyes or make them abandon their pursuit.

273 / 243 waiting for justice to be fulfilled literally, "guarding the final outcome of justice." Two of the trilogy's most powerful words, *telos* (finality, fulfillment) and *dikê* (justice, judgment) are combined in this phrase. Orestes is praying for Athena's intervention, but it will not come until after the Erinyes have found him and we have witnessed their attempt to get him in their power.

275 / 245 the voiceless snitch a riddle in the form of a kenning, whose answer is given as "blood drops" at 278/247.

284 / 253 *the warm smile of an old friend* In Greek, the verb *prosgelai*, "smiles on," can simply mean "greets me," but the Erinyes' delight in blood gives the image its grotesque charge.

285–318 / 254–75 *Epiparodos* (second entry song) The Erinyes sing and mime their hound-like pursuit of Orestes and threaten terrible violence, their own and that in the world below. This passage is in lyric verse reminiscent of the Chorus's first entry song (parodos, 158–99/143–78), but without the usual strophic responsion, presumably indicating a freer and perhaps less elaborate choreography.

290–91 / 258 *once again / protected* As at Delphi, so in Athena's shrine, Orestes is safe in the deity for protection. The Erinyes can threaten, but they cannot attack.

296 / 262 *it can't return again, not ever* This phrase resonates with a series of statements and images throughout the trilogy, in some of which the blood disappears (e.g., *Agamemnon* 1160–62/1017–21), and in others remains as a source of disease and suffering (e.g., *Libation Bearers* 54–55/48 and 76–79/66–67). Here, the emphasis is on the debt of blood that Orestes owes for the mother's blood he has shed, but Apollo will later use the same argument in defense of Orestes' actions (756–58/647–48), and the Eriynes-Eumenides will repeat it in a political context in their prayer against violent civil strife (1143–45/979–80).

305–6 / 267 *drag you, still alive / into the underworld* The Chorus has already said that Orestes' punishment will continue among the dead (195–99/175–8); now, the terrible threat to suck his blood and shrivel him (300–305/264–67) is figured as a preliminary for the tortures of the underworld. The repeated notion of payment (300/264, 307/268), however, reminds us that this is also the Erinyes' exaction of justice for Orestes' murder of his mother (see on 313/272).

311–12 / 270–71 *honor owed to gods, guests, / or loving parents* This corresponds to the three "ordinances of Justice" set out in Aeschylus' *Suppliants* 701–9 and expresses basic precepts of Greek popular morality. The Erinyes do not here claim that they themselves enforce all three, and elsewhere they systematically ignore the claims of Orestes' other parent and of Apollo, but traditionally Erinyes are associated with punishing infractions on all these counts. The Erinyes' recognition here of the larger values of which they see their own "appointed task" (232/208) in part prepares for the new role they agree to undertake at the end of the play. See also on 639–41/545–49.

313 / 272 *you'll see them get the justice they deserve* The Chorus in effect answers Apollo's proposal of a court overseen by Athena (252–53/224) with just punishment meted out in a strict accounting by Hades himself.

320 / 277 *the many ways of being purged* Cf. on 266/237.

327 / 283 *by sacrificing swine* This was a standard form of purification, involving a kind of homeopathy or sympathetic magic. A young pig's throat was cut over the head of the person to be purified, so that its blood flowed down his body and carried off blood-guilt with it. Swine were sacrificed particularly to chthonic powers, and there is evidence of swine-purification at the great sanctuary of Demeter at Eleusis, the Attic deme that was home to Aeschylus' family.

336 / 291 *as her true allies* The offer of an alliance with Athena in return for his safety (for this kind of bargain with the gods, see on *Libation Bearers*, 290/257) is in effect an offer of alliance between his city, Argos, and hers, Athens. This is the first of three references to such a pact, reflecting one recently concluded between the two cities: see 782–87/669–73 and 885–98/762–74 (with note).

337 / 292 *wherever she is* This is a standard prayer formula, no doubt reflecting the widespread influence of the divinity, but, more important, assuring that the prayer will reach the right destination. In this case, Aeschylus is also preparing us for the lack of an immediate response that permits the Erinyes' attempt to get Orestes in their power. We learn at 480–81/397–98 that Athena was at Troy when she heard Orestes' prayer, thus confirming Orestes' belief that "a god can hear even from far away" (342/297).

Libya A natural place to mention in this context because of the tradition of Athena's birth there, but perhaps made more pointed because of an Athenian military expedition still ongoing in Libya at the time the *Oresteia* was produced. Thucydides reports in his *History of the Peloponnesian War*, 1, 104, that the Athenians had, a year or two before Aeschylus wrote the trilogy, sent an expedition of some two hundred ships to Egypt to help King Inarus of Libya free Egypt from Persian domination. This expedition eventually met with disaster, but only several years later. An Athenian audience in 458, hearing of

Athena in Libya "on the march to help her friends," would surely think of this ambitious and dangerous undertaking.

341 / 295 *the Phlegrean plain* The site of the great battle between the Olympian gods and the giants, in which Athena played a major part. There does not seem to be a contemporary allusion in this reference, but it is appropriate in a number of other ways: it expresses the wide extent of Athena's influence, taking her far to the north as Libya took her far to the south. It shows her once again in her military aspect, aiding her allies in struggle. And this battle between Olympians and dangerous and primitive children of Earth is emblematic in much Greek art and literature for the struggle between the forces of civilization and those of brutalitiy and barabarism.

350–51 / 304–5 A shocking perversion of sacrificial rite. Orestes is a choice animal, fattened for sacrifice, who will be eaten before the sacrifice can take place.

352 / 306 *the spell we sing to bind you fast* Orestes has just asked Athena to set him free. The Chorus Leader replies that, on the contrary, the Erinyes will cast a spell over him to hold him fast. The choral song that follows, then, is more closely integrated than usual into the action of the drama. Binding spells were part of ancient magical practice, and a large number of these have been found, inscribed for the most part on lead curse tablets. Faraone, "Aeschylus' *hymnos desmios*," suggests that the Erinyes' song shares some motifs with a class of such tablets designed to provide magical superiority over one's opponent in a trial.

353–479 / 307–96 *First stasimon,* The Erinyes' "Binding Song" The Chorus sings and dances, hoping to bind and madden Orestes in their spell. He continues to clasp the image of Athena and remain impassive (as he evidently did at **349/303**), knowing as he does when silence is proper (**321/277–78**). The earlier choruses of this play began unconventionally with the Chorus entering in small groups, miming their pursuit of Orestes. This song, on the other hand, displays a high level of formality within which to display its images of horror and madness. As at *Agamemnon*, **407–22/355–66**, there is a chanted prologue (**353–74/307–20**) in marching anapests (see on *Agamemnon*, **48–123/40–103**), even though the Chorus is already in the orchestra. The ode that follows uses repeated refrains, a formal feature that befits its ritual character. The manuscript tradition repeats only the first of these refrains (**385–**

92 = 404–11/328–33 = 341–46), but we have followed many editors in repeating the two other nonresponding stanzas (416–24 = 429–37/354–59 and 442–49 = 454–56/372–76).

370–73 / 318–20 The language here uses terms familiar from the Athenian judicial system to describe the Erinyes' pre-legal justice. They invoke the notion of finality, associated elsewhere in the trilogy with the dispensation of Zeus, by appropriating the adverb *teleôs* (here rendered by the adjectives "last" and "final") to describe their authority. For the Erinyes' further appropriation of this language, see on 463/382.

374 / 321 *Mother, O mother Night* These enforcers of a mother's rights begin their song with the invocation of their own mother, and will refer to her again several strategic points in the course of the play (499/416, 865/745, 921/791–92 = 956/821–22, 983/844–45 = 1021/876–77; and cf. 1123/962 and 1207–9/1033). They never mention their father, given by Sophocles as Skotos (Darkness), and elsewhere as Cronus or Acheron, a river of the underworld. In this sense, they are the complete opposite of Athena, who has a father, but no mother (see on 855/736).

382 / 325–26 *this trembling hare* The memorable image of the trembling victim from the omen at Aulis ("her father's flying blood- / hounds eating in sacrifice / the trembling hare," *Agamemnon*, 154–56/136–37) now attaches itself to Orestes.

390 / 332–33 *the lyre-shunning song* See on *Agamemnon*, 735/645.

393 / 335 *Fate* Once again, the notion of a fixed dispensation (*moira*) that gives the Erinyes their function is combined with a personification of their half-sisters by mother Night, the *Moirai* (see on 192/172).

413–15 / 350–52 The Erinyes express the mutual aversion between them and the Olympian gods (see also 427–28/365–66, and cf. the scorn expressed by Apollo at 221/197). Black is the color of the gods whose home below ground, white that of the gods of Olympus (see on 66/55).

418–19 / 355–56 *the spirit of Ares, reared / . . . in the home* The war god's name can be used to refer to violence even if it is not military. The image of violence "reared / . . . in the home" recalls the story of the lion cub that was raised as a pet but grew up to reveal its true nature (*Agamemnon*, 818–43/717–36).

438 / 368 *self-preening conceits* Literally, "awesome (self-) regard," a phrase made almost sarcastic by the transfer of the Erinyes' Attic cult name *Semnai*, "the Awesome Ones," to mortals who feel that they can escape punishment for their transgressions. The Erinyes will shortly reclaim their title by describing themselves as "awful (*semnai*) to men" (**465/383**).

441 / 370–71 *the quick kicks of our raging dance* This phrase and the following stanza, which has been read as a grim perversion of normal dance patterns, may give some clue to the wildness of the choreography here.

463 / 382 *unmatched* In the Greek, the Erinyes call themselves *teleioi* (**370–73/318–20**), fully accomplished, but also accomplishers of finality, of the definitive requiting of wrongs. The epithet picks up the assertion of authority in *teleôs* ("last . . . final") at **372/320** and looks forward to the assertion of power that "the gods made final (*teleon*)," **474/393**.

478 / 395 *beneath the ground* The Erinyes will be offered a very different home beneath the ground in Athens, and will finally accept it when they understand that it, too, will bring them honor.

480–578 / 397–489 *Third episode* Athena enters in answer to Orestes' prayer and asks first the Erinyes, then Orestes to explain their presence at her shrine. Both ask her to decide their dispute, but she prefers to have it tried by a jury of Athenian citizens, whom she goes off to select. The manner of Athena's entry has been a source of much discussion. We agree with most modern commentators in deleting a line (**405** in the Greek, following on our **488a**) that suggests that she arrives in the orchestra in a horse-drawn chariot. This is an alternative that probably found its way into the text when the producer of a revival of the trilogy decided to give Athena an entrance to match that of Agamemnon in the first play. Athena's description of her journey (**486–88/403–4**) suggests wingless flight, so it is possible that she entered on the stage crane (*mêchanê*), a device that permitted actors to be swung through the air and onto the stage or the roof of the stage building. There is nothing in the text, however, that necessitates her entering in anything other than the usual way, though presumably at a faster than usual clip.

480–85 / 397–402 Athena has been at Troy, taking possession of land awarded to her, i.e., to "Theseus' sons." the Athenians. Her temporary absence made possible the Erinyes' binding song, but why this particular journey? Aeschylus uses it to underline (once more; see on **336/291**) the easy identification of Athena with her city and its people, who are never far from her mind. He also brings the Trojan War into the ambit of successful Athenian undertakings rewarded by grateful allies, i.e., into a kind of model for the role Athens had chosen for herself since taking the lead in opposing Persian expansion in the early part of the fifth century. There may, however, be a more specific allusion here. We know that there was conflict between Athens and Mytilene in the sixth century over the town of Sigeum in the Troad, and that it ended with Sigeum in Athens' possession (see Herodotus, *Histories*, 5, 94–95). Herodotus also tells us (5, 63) that Sigeum fell into the hands of the Peisistratid family when their tyranny was overthrown and they were driven from Athens in 510, and must have been in the orbit of Persia for some time thereafter. By 465/64 Athenians were involved in fighting there, and an inscription of 451/50 makes it clear that Sigeum is by then a member of the Athenian alliance. In short, this was a place in which Athens had a special interest, and the suggestion that it was part of a grant by the Achaeans that made it "completely and forever" a dependency of Athens might well allude to whatever events had recently led or were then leading to Sigeum's absorption into the Athenian sphere of influence.

488 / 404 *my aegis* A regular attribute of Athena, a goatskin garment, often depicted with a fringe of snakes around it and the head of the Gorgon that Perseus killed at its center.

500 / 417 *"Curses"* The curse launched on a wrongdoer from the grave sends the Erinyes out to seek vengeance, and in this sense they are indeed embodied curses.

512 / 429 *He won't swear he's innocent, or yield if I swear to his guilt* In Athenian legal practice, if the parties agreed to employ the so-called "evidentiary oath," the trial opened with the accuser taking an oath that the defendant had committed the deed, and the defendant that he had not. Orestes here will not agree, since of course he did kill his mother, but the critical issue is not the deed, but whether it was justified. Athena recognizes this, distinguishing between seeming to be just by relying on an oath and doing justice by examining the merits of the case (513–15/430–32).

517 / 434 *the final one* the Greek phrase *aitias telos*, literally, the "endpoint of guilt" or the "completion of the case," is reminiscent in its use of the lan-

guage of fulfillment and finality of Orestes' "waiting for justice to be fulfilled" (*telos dikês*); see on 273/243.

518 / 435 The Erinyes here, and Orestes at 555–57/468–69, both accept Athena as sole judge of the case, making her decision not to do so but to appoint a jury of Athenians all the more remarkable.

524 / 441 *Ixion* See Glossary for details, and cf. on 835–36/717–18.

528–38 / 445–53 This is Orestes' most elaborate statement of his ritual purity, and Athena acknowledges its importance in her response (562–64/473–74). For the claim, see on 266/237.

558–61 / 470–72 Despite the agreement of both parties to accept her decision, Athena demurs. She explains her reluctance in terms of the burden, too great even for her, to judge a case that will produce so much anger however it is decided. She does indeed face a genuine dilemma, since her verdict must either damage her suppliant Orestes (see further on 563/474) or expose her beloved city to the poisonous wrath of the Erinyes (see on 566–69/477–79). The dilemma is very like that of King Pelasgus in an earlier play of Aeschylus, the *Suppliants*. Pelasgus must decide whether to accept the supplication of the Danaids, who are fleeing unwanted marriage to their cousins, the sons of Aegyptus, and risk a terrible war, or reject it and risk the wrath of Zeus, who protects the rights of suppliants. He, too, refuses to decide by himself and brings the issue before his people to gain their support. One difference here, of course, is that Athena is a great deity herself. The comparison thus underlines the fact that, notwithstanding the enormous disparity in power, gods seek to avoid the anger or displeasure of mortals by failing to meet their responsibilities to those to whom they have bonds of obligation or friendship.

563 / 474 *a proper suppliant* Athena explicitly acknowledge that Orestes' status as a suppliant who is ritually pure and brings no harm makes it grievous for her to reject his plea of innocence (cf. 262–63/233–34), and legitimate for him to feel wronged if she should do so.

566–69 / 477–79 To reject the Erinyes is dangerous for Athens, dearest of all places to Athena's heart (see on 480–85/397–402), and therefore a threat to her, too. These lines foreshadow threats that the Erinyes will make as soon as Orestes is acquitted (906–17 = 941–52/780–87 = 810–17).

570–71 / 483–84 *I'll choose / a panel of judges* Athena, having decided that judgment in this case cannot be rendered by a mortal or by herself alone, decides to judge it together with a chosen body of Athenians, establishing a tribunal for the purpose over which she will preside and in which she will, as it turns out, have the deciding vote. Here, however, she mentions only her role to choosing the jurors and emphasizes she is founding "a court to last forever" (573/484). Thus, this exceptional case leads not only to the first murder trial (797/682), but to an institution Aeschylus' audience still knows.

577 / 487 *my ablest citizens* This translates a phrase, *astôn emôn ta beltista*, that does not necessarily imply high social standing. Like the members of the Areopagus Council in Aeschylus' day, however, Athena's jury was not chosen democratically by election or lot. (See Wallace, *The Areopagos Council*, 94–97.

579–659 / 490–565 *Second stasimon* The Chorus presents itself, and its case, in a new and surprising light. Orestes' fate was at the center of the previous song, as the Chorus sang and danced its binding web around him. Here, his crime is only the starting point for a reflection that moves outward to encompass the importance of fear for the well-being of society, and the role of justice—the retributive justice of the Erinyes, needless to say—in the lives of individuals and communities. The Erinyes no longer present themselves as relentless bloodhounds or bloodsucking monsters; they are agents of a stern morality that makes them sound in places like the Elders of *Agamemnon* (see below on 614/520–21, 626–27/533, 633–35/539–42, 646–59/553–65), and will later be echoed by Athena (see on 610–20/517–28). The ode reminds us, just before the trial begins, that the Erinyes' case cannot easily be dismissed, despite their own repulsiveness. It is perilous in the extreme to leave the demands of justice unmet.

593–94 / 502 *We'll / let any murder pass* The Erinyes depict the spread of violent crime as their own refusal, should they be dishonored by Orestes' acquittal, to continue to fulfill their function. They identify their work so completely with that of justice (604–5/511–12), that for them the survival of justice in human society hangs in the balance at Orestes' trial.

609 / 516 *the house of Justice falls* In the previous ode, the Erinyes identified their task as "the destruction of houses" (417/354–55) in which injustice has held sway; here, they imagine a world in which they no longer do their work as one in which the house of Justice itself is destroyed.

610–20 / 517–28 These ideas will be repeated in very similar terms by Athena at 813–17/696–99.

614 / 520–21 *Wisdom comes from wailing* Literally, "prudence from duress," but our version makes use of the homophony of *stenos* "straits" and *steno*, "groan." The idea is very similar to *Agamemnon*, 200–10/176–83.

626–27 / 533 *sacrilege / gives birth to recklessness* Cf. *Agamemnon*, 868–70/758–59. Lines 626–30/533–37 as a whole echo *Agamemnon* 860–91/750–81, where the Elders are at pains to show that reckless behavior (*hybris*) is the result of wickedness, and that prosperity depends on respect for justice and the containing of ambitions and desires within sane boundaries. This view explains the seemingly paradoxical embrace of the "middle way" (622/530) by a band of "wild revelers" (590/500), whose attitude until now has hardly seemed moderate.

633–35 / 539–42 *the altar / of Justice, / don't kick it over* Cf. *Agamemnon*, 437–40/ 381–84.

639–41 / 545–49 These are two of the three prime ordinances set forth at 311–12/270–11. The third, honor the gods, is represented by the injunction to "revere / . . . the altar / of Justice" (632–34/539).

646–59 / 553–65 An extended parable, like the story of the lion cub (*Agamemnon*, 818–43/717–36), using nautical images familiar from *Agamemnon*, e.g., destruction by storm (745–49/653–57), jettisoning cargo (1152–56/1008–13), striking a hidden reef (1151/1006–7).

660–902 / 566–777 *Fourth episode* There is another change of scene at this point, but it resembles the refocusing of attention from orchestra to stage building that marks the shift from Agamemnon's tomb to the palace in *Libation Bearers*, rather than the marked change of locale from Delphi to Athens earlier this play. As at 264/235, little change to the playing space is needed for the move from Athena's temple to the Areopagus, the hill of Ares where Orestes trial will take place — the removal of the wooden statue of Athena, perhaps, and the placement on stage of a table with voting urns, and probably of benches for the jurors (who are instructed to stand up to cast their votes, 827/708).

This episode can be regarded as the turning point of the entire trilogy, since it enacts the institution of a new civic form of justice, replacing the old uncontrolled and unbounded pursuit of vengeance by a legal procedure whose verdict is binding on all parties, and therefore final. The long succession of crimes in the house of Atreus is brought to an end at last in Athens, and in the process the first trial by jury and the first court of law come into being there.

660 / 566 *Herald* No proclamation of the beginning of the trial appears in our text, and it may well be that no Herald appeared on stage. Taplin, *Stagecraft of Aeschylus*, 393, assumes that the trumpet call (661–62/567–68) is heard and amounts in effect to the Herald's summons, but it could equally well be that Athena's mention of proclamation and trumpet suffice to evoke them, so that their enactment is not required.

662 / 567–68 *Etruscan trumpet* Greek lore attributed the invention of this instrument to the "Tyrrhenians," whom we know as Etruscans, or alternatively considered it a gift to them from Athena.

665–66 / 572–73 *both / the city and these jurors* The treatment of jurors and city as separate groups has suggested to some commentators that at least a few extras, representing those who gather to see and hear the trial, have entered along with Athena and the jury. It seems likely, however, that Athena refers, with a sweeping gesture of her arms, to the spectators in the theater who do, in fact, represent the city.

669 / 574 *My lord Apollo* Apollo apparently enters silently and without announcement just before he is addressed, a procedure that is anomalous. The Chorus's greeting cuts short Athena's announced intention of expounding her laws (666/571) and changes the direction of the proceedings. Athena does not return to the establishment of her new ordinance until 795/681. Instead, the trial itself begins, and the inconclusive debate between Apollo and the Erinyes can only be settled when the jury votes. Athena's formal founding-speech for the new court is postponed until that moment is at hand.

680 / 583 *the pursuer* The Greek word *diôkôn* is the standard legal term for "plaintiff," but it literally denotes one who pursues, and thus describes as well the role that the Erinyes have been playing, and that is now being transformed from physical persecution to legal prosecution.

687 / 589 *Two more to go* There were three falls in a Greek wrestling match; see on *Libation Bearers* 386/339. Orestes replies that the Erinyes haven't

thrown him at all, because he never denied that he did the deed, only that he has any guilt from it.

702–6 / 604–8 Orestes' first question and the Chorus Leader's answer correspond closely to the exchange at **235–36/211–12**, but the subsequent dialogue moves in a new direction as Orestes' challenges the commonsense assumption that mother and son are blood relatives. He seems to have backed into a position he himself does not fully understand. He had earlier called the killing of his mother "blood- / shed that's my own," i.e., the shedding of blood he shared with her (*Libation Bearers*, **1175–76/1028**), and his only answer to the Chorus Leader's indignant objection is to turn to Apollo for help. Apollo will make the argument for him at **769–74/658–61**.

722 / 621 *No oath is stronger than almighty Zeus* This is the culmination of an argument designed to make Orestes' deed tantamount to following the command of Zeus and thus obligate the jurors to acquit him if they are not themselves to flout Zeus's will. Apollo's statement is couched in general terms, as at **243–44/217–18**, where marriage vows are said to be "greater than any oath," but it very generality disturbingly incorporates the oath the jurors took (**572/483**), and which Athena will enjoin them to respect when reaching their verdict (**829/710**).

731–32 / 627–28 *not even by the far-shot arrow of / some Amazon* To die in close combat brought glory (see, e.g., *Libation Bearers*, **395–98/345–48**); to be killed from afar by an arrow was less glorious; to be killed by a woman, even in battle, would be inglorious; to be killed by a woman's arrow would be an even greater indignity. And, says Apollo, Agamemnon's death was far worse even than that. For the Amazons' battle against Athens, see on **800–6/685–90**.

750 / 641 *chain up his ancient father, Cronus* For the myth of Zeus shackling Cronus and the Titans under ground after defeating them, alluded to already at *Agamemnon*, **189–96/168–72**, see Hesiod, *Theogony*, **664–735**. Such treatment of a father by a child would be reprehensible by human standards, although of course the Chorus Leader neglects to mention Cronus' habit of swallowing his children the minute they were born (*Theogony*, **453–67**). The Chorus Leader, however, is simply disputing Apollo's claim that Zeus ordained the priority of the father's rights over all others.

756–58 / 647–48 Apollo insists that the finality of death makes it entirely different from the imposition of chains; but his argument that "nothing can ever raise again" the man who has blood has been "sucked dry" by the ground is turned against him by the Chorus Leader's reminder that Orestes has spilled his own mother's blood on the ground (762–64/652–53). They insist, as they have all along, that such a pollution derived from kindred blood can never be purified (764–67/654–56). Now Apollo has no alternative but to present the argument that mothers do not share kindred blood with their children.

769–70 / 658–59 *the so-called mother of the child / isn't the child's begetter* This view, later supported by Aristotle (who ascribes it to the philosopher Anaxagoras, a younger contemporary of Aeschylus), cannot be regarded as the sole, or even the dominant, Greek view on the subject in Aeschylus' day. See further the Introduction, pp. 24–25. It is the conclusive argument not because we can be sure that Aeschylus' audience would have found it convincing, but because the Erinyes have no answer to offer. As for the play's "internal audience," Athena accepts Apollo's view as grounds for Orestes' acquittal (855–57/736–38), but the human jurors are evenly divided as to his guilt, and thus half of them appear to regard Apollo's argument as fallacious or inconclusive.

776 / 663–64 *And here before us is our witness* Apollo's proof is the exceptional case of Athena, born (in the version of the myth given here) entirely without a mother, although in Hesiod's account (*Theogony*, 886–900), she has a mother, Metis, who conceives her in the usual way, only to be swallowed by Zeus. In both versions, however, Zeus brings Athena to birth himself.

785 / 671 *a friend and ally* The second of three references to an alliance between Argos and Athens; the first was at 335–36/289–91; see further on 885–98/762–74.

795 / 681 *Now hear my ordinance* This is the speech that Athena seemed about to give when Apollo entered at 669/574. In this position, it introduces and solemnizes the moment of the jurors' decision.

797 / 682 *this first trial ever for the shedding of blood* Aeschylus is departing from a well-known tradition that explained the name Aereopagus ("hill of Ares," 800/685) by making it the site of an earlier trial of Ares for murder before a jury of his fellow gods. See further the Introduction, pp. 19–20. The trial of Orestes in Athens may or may not have been Aes-

chylus' invention; that Orestes visited Athens after his matricide certainly was not. There is evidence for non-Aeschylean versions of the story in which relatives of Clytemnestra or Aegisthus were the plaintiffs and a jury made up only of gods or only of men decided the case. This evidence postdates the *Oresteia*, but it is likely that the variant versions predate it, since it is hard to see how they would arise once Aeschylus had given the story so definitive a form. In any case, we can be reasonably certain that it was Aeschylus who connected Orestes' trial with the founding of the Areopagus Council, and who made the first act of that body the first murder trial in history.

800–806 / 685–90 In line with his change in the foundation myth for murder trials on the Areopagus from a trial of Ares by gods to a trial of Orestes by what would become the Areopagus Council, Aeschylus substitutes a new explanation for the name "Hill of Ares." This he does by making the future site of Orestes' trial the encampment of the invading Amazons, a tribe of barbarian women warriors, who sacrificed to the war god. The Areopagus would in fact be the best place from which to attack the Acropolis, and was the Persians' base when they sacked it in 490. The tradition that the Amazons used it for their attack may well predate Aeschylus. For the possible significance of this allusion to the Amazons, see the Introduction, p. 24.

802 / 686 *angry at King Theseus* This may refer to the story that Theseus had attacked their territory and carried their queen, Antiope, back to Greece, but the phrase (which could also be translated "jealous of King Theseus") is vague enough to be compatible with the tradition that the invasion was unprovoked by any prior hostilities.

807–17 / 690–99 Athena emphatically endorses ideas expressed by the Erinyes at 610–20/517–28. Lines 807–12/690–95 have generated enormous controversy because they are capable of being interpreted as representing Aeschylus' opinion of the recent reform of the Areopagus Council (see the Introduction, pp. 19–20). The very variety of interpretations, however, suggests that Aeschylus is making no such direct political statement. The text leaves it open to scholars to argue that the laws Athena instructs the people to "leave intact" and "never alter . . . with foul infusions" are the laws of Athens as a whole, or the laws concerning homicide, or the laws that governed the Areopagus Council itself. Similarly, some have argued that Aeschylus is condemning Ephialtes' reform of 462, and others that he is supporting the reform by suggesting that the state of affairs Ephialtes confronted, in which the Areopagus had assumed broad political authority, represents what happens when ill-considered changes "muddy the clearest stream." Nothing in Athena's words here, and nothing elsewhere in the trilogy, compels such choices.

822 / 703 *Scythians, or Spartans* Both peoples, one barbarian but "naturally" law-abiding, the other a Greek community whose long history of stable laws and good government helped them fend off tyranny, were considered models of successful self-government.

828 / 709 *take up your ballots and decide the case* The voting takes place during the following exchange. Assuming ten jurors, we can imagine that one juror reaches the urns and casts his ballot during each of the ten couplets at 830–49/711–30. (For other assumptions, see on 854/735.) The Chorus Leader's lines at 850–52/731–33 then mark the end of the voting, and during them Athena would proceed to a place behind the table with the urns. The "ballots" are tokens, usually pebbles (which is what the Greek word *psêphos*, used here, literally means). In this instance, the jurors cast their ballots into one of two urns to vote for conviction or acquittal.

835–36 / 717–18 Apollo adduces the case of Ixion, the first murderer (and already mentioned as a suppliant at 524/441) as the precedent set by Zeus himself for the purification of blood-guilt. Apollo's rhetorical question as to whether Zeus made a mistake would raise eyebrows among those who remembered the whole story, in which Ixion went on to betray Zeus by attempting to seduce Hera (see Glossary for details). The Chorus Leader, however, answers with a noncommittal "You said it, not I" (837/719) and returns to threats of destruction if the Erinyes should lose.

842–47 / 723–28 The Erinyes supply their own mythological example to illustrate Apollo's devious tampering with fate. This is the story, familiar from Euripides *Alcestis*, that Apollo tricked the Fates into allowing Admetus, the son of King Pheres of Thessaly, to live beyond his allotted time if he could find someone else to die in his place. The Chorus leader says that Apollo got the "ancient goddesses" drunk to secure their agreement (a detail not found in Euripides), thus connecting this episode to the charge that "you would trample down your elders" (850/731).

854 / 735 *I will cast my ballot for Orestes* Precisely what role Athena has in the voting has been the subject of vigorous debate. The most important question is this: Were the jurors' votes tied (implying an even number of jurors), with the tie then broken by Athena; or was there an uneven number of votes (implying a majority of one to convict), with the tie, and thus acquittal, being achieved only by counting Athena's vote? Unfortunately, the evidence of our text yields no easy answer. The original audience would have seen a voting procedure that clarified the text, so that every solution makes assumptions about how the scene was staged. E.g., those who favor an uneven number of jurors generally assume that an eleventh juror votes during the first two of the Chorus Leader's final three lines (850–52/731–33), leaving the final line for Athena's approach to the voting urns. Most important for our purposes, the result of the vote was regarded as decisive and final by all parties, however it was reached, and there is no suggestion of any irregularity or impropriety, even on the part of the Erinyes.

We have adopted the view that the jurors cast an even number of votes, so that the vote of Athena (a term that becomes proverbial for just this situation) is actually a tiebreaker. This approach has the notable advantage of avoiding Athena's overturn of a majority vote by the human jurors. If one takes the view that Athena creates the tie with her vote, one must either deal with that anomaly as part of Aeschylus' plan, or else assume that for the purpose of the vote, at least, the audience will accept Athena as simply another member of the jury, with no distinction between her vote and that of her mortal colleagues, even though it is she who set up the court and will shortly make the rule that a tie acquits (861/741). On the other hand, the greatest impediment to the view we have adopted is that Athena says she will cast her vote for Orestes before the votes are counted and a tie declared. A possible solution is that Athena does not actually put a voting token in the urn, so that her vote is notional and contingent on the tie that emerges from the counting completed between 864/744 and 873/752. This staging would in effect provide a sort of instantiation, in the foundation legend of the judicial system, of the Athenian practice that allowed a tie to result automatically in acquittal by invoking the purely notional "vote of Athena." Another, perhaps less persuasive, possibility is that she adds her vote only after she has announced the tie at 874/753.

855 / 736 *No mother gave me birth* Athena confirms what Apollo said about her (776–78/663–66), although without any indication that she subscribes to his general view about procreation. What she does assert is her predisposition to value the male, which constitutes the decisive reason for her vote. As a virgin goddess, Athena rejects the role of wife, but she does not share the antipathy for males felt by others who shun marriage

bonds, such as the Amazons or the Erinyes. She does, however, share a strain of androgyny with them, and with Clytemnestra. And yet, since she is "entirely my father's child" (857/738), she also abhors Clytemnestra's overturning of patriarchal order, and she will not condemn her killing. Her inclinations are thus entirely opposed to those of the Erinyes, who have a mother but no father (cf. on 374/321).

862 / 743 *You jurors who have this duty to fulfill* We know that in the fourth century B.C.E., four jurors were chosen by lot to count the votes. This passage is evidence for a similar practice before the middle of the fifth century.

880–81 / 759–61 The final appearance in the trilogy of the motif of the third libation to Zeus Savior, with the Savior restored to his proper place of honor. Now, at last, he has shown himself to be both savior and *teleios* (the one who "brings all to fulfillment;" see on *Agamemnon*, 1115–18/972–74) for the house of Atreus. See further the Introduction, p. 34.

882–84 / 760–61 One of the passages in *Eumenides* (cf. on 262–63/233) that suggest the gods can feel respect and responsibility for mortals.

885–98 / 762–74 An alliance between Argos and Athens has been mentioned twice before in *Eumenides* (335–36/289–91 and 782–87/669–73). Now, as Orestes leaves for Argos, he solemnizes the alliance with an oath to maintain friendship between his land and Athens both in his lifetime, and thereafter from the grave. Aeschylus thus gives a patina of great antiquity to an alliance made very recently between Athens and Argos. In 462, at about the same time as the reforms to the Areopagus were being undertaken, Athens abandoned an alliance with Sparta that was dear to the more conservative elements of the city in favor of a thirty-year treaty with Sparta's enemy in the Peloponnese, Argos. To the extent that this alliance is part of the ascendancy of more democratic policies in Athens, as has often been suggested, Orestes' warm offer of friendship between Argos and Athens may provide a clue to Aeschylus' political sympathies.

889 / 767 *Even from my tomb* The long-standing belief that a hero continues to exercise power from his grave was an important element of the first half of *Libation Bearers*, set at Agamemnon's tomb. Here, Orestes takes a solemn oath to use that power after his death to protect his friends, the Athenians. Similar promises are made to Athens by Oedipus in Sophocles' *Oedipus at Colonus* and by Eurystheus in Euripides' *Children of Heracles*. That such beliefs were not confined to tragic poetry

can be gauged from Herodotus' account of the importance that Sparta attributed to recovering the bones of Orestes from Tegea, where they had been buried and forgotten (*Histories*, 1, 67–8).

893 / 770 *with ominous wingbeats* The Greek *parornithas* literally means "contrary to bird [signs]," i.e., visited by bad omens.

900 / 776 *the hold you get on all your enemies* A final use of the wrestling metaphor. Orestes the wrestler (see 687–88/589–90 and *Libation Bearers*, 992–95/866–68) has in effect linked his victory with future victories for Athens.

902 / 777 With Orestes' exit, the great story of crime and retribution in the house of Atreus is over at last, and the curse that lasted through generations is finally lifted. Orestes is mentioned only once more in the remainder of the play (929/799). Apollo's part in the story is over as well, but his exit is far more problematic, since it is entirely unmarked, which is irregular in Greek tragedy even for a minor character—much less for a major deity. Furthermore, Orestes hardly mentions Apollo in his final speech, despite the crucial part Apollo played, as purifier and defense attorney, in winning his freedom. Nevertheless, the least jarring way for Apollo to exit seems to be in the company of Orestes.

903–1226 / 778–1047 The last third of the play is an extended scene for the Erinyes and Athena, capped by a short choral exodus sung by a group of Athenians as they escort the ancient goddesses to their new home below the Acropolis. Orestes' acquittal and disappearance leaves the Erinyes, who have repeatedly threatened to wreak terrible damage should their prosecution fail, ready to turn their full wrath against Athens. Athena uses her powers of persuasion to transform anger into benevolence and vengeance into blessing, and the Erinyes at last accept a new role in Athens as Eumenides ("kindly ones," see on 1158/992).

This scene is formally varied through alternation of song and speech, but its structure does not readily lend itself to the traditional divisions into episode and stasimon. The sequence begins with the strong act division of a choral song, which, however, turns out not to be the usual stasimon but the beginning of a kind of *kommos* (see on *Agamemnon* 1220–1348/1072–1177) in which the Chorus expresses its outrage in two stanzas, each repeated as a refrain between conciliatory speeches in dialogue verse by Athena (903–1024/778–880). There follows a short episode, again in spoken dialogue, in which Athena's persuasion works its magic as she explains the benefits she can offer the Erinyes in return for their blessings on the land and people of her city (1025–64/881–

915). The process continues in a *kommos* (the Chorus singing, Athena responding in anapests, 1065–1194/916–1020) in which the Erinyes agree to accept new honors, new functions, and a new home in Athens, and then sing songs of blessing that in effect cancel and replace the songs of wrath with which the scene began. Athena then leads the Erinyes-Eumenides on their way to new dwellings in the Attic earth, accompanied by their Athenian escort (1195–1226/1021–47).

903–22 / 778–93 Repeated verbatim (and presumably with identical music and dance) at 938–57/808–23, as is 975–86/837–47 at 1013–24/870–80. This is an effective way of showing the stubborn intransigence that Athena's persistence in persuasion has to overcome.

906 / 780 *my honor stripped away* Concern for the loss of honor has been a recurrent theme of the Erinyes' complaints (see on 110–17/95–102), and has previously been expressed, as it is here, by the metaphor of young gods trampling down their elders (see on 127/110). The Erinyes emphasize this fear obsessively in their refrains, and Athena keeps attempting to reassure them that they will continue to be held in the highest honor (926/796, 937/807, 958/824, 969–70/833, 995–96/854–55, 1011–12/868–69, 1025–28/881–84).

910 / 782–83 *poison will now ooze and drip* Apollo alluded to the Erinyes' spewing of venom, only to dismiss it as harmless (848–49/729–30), but their threat of blighting the land is a real and terrible danger for Athens. Averting it will test Athena's powers of persuasion.

934 / 805 *your seat in a vast cavern* Chthonic deities were thought of as dwelling underground, and Aeschylus' audience would have known the grotto between the Areopagus and the Acropolis where Athens honored the Erinyes under the cult name *Semnai* (see on 1158/992).

961 / 826 *why even bring it up?* Athena can answer threat with threat, but she prefers to use persuasion. Violent struggles like those of the past are always possible, but now not inevitable. The threat is dispelled immediately, and Zeus's lightning bolt is depicted as being kept under lock and key, in contrast to its unrestrained use at *Agamemnon*, 534–35/469–70 and 741/651 (with note).

965 / 829 *let me persuade you* Peithô (persuasion), which appeared in its negative incarnations as temptation and deception in the earlier plays, now

finally emerges as a constructive force, the power to convince by reason rather than subdue by force—the power needed to govern a democratic polis.

972–73 / 835 *children / . . . the marriage rite* The earlier opposition between blood ties and bonds of marriage disappears in Athena's promise of offerings made to ensure the success of both childbirth and marriage vows. The Greek phrase translated "for the fulfillment of the marriage rite" (*pro . . . gameliou telous*) alludes to the *proteleia* (sacrifice made before a marriage) that had appeared in distorted contexts of bloodshed in *Agamemnon* (see on **79–80/65, 260/226, 821/720**) and is now shorn of any sinister connotations and restored at last to its normal signification.

976–77 / 871 *Force me . . . / under this earth* The Erinyes associate Athena's offer of a new home underground with the dishonor and imprisonment of Cronus and the Titans, with which they reproached Zeus at **750/641**.

991–92 / 852 *you'll long just like a lover / for this country* Although the Erinyes are invited to remain in Athens as resident aliens, Athena predicts that they will feel what the city ideally meant to Athenian citizens. The language is reminiscent of the exhortation that Thucydides will later put into the mouth of Pericles in the famous Funeral Oration to "see the city's power in practice day by day and become its passionate lovers" (*History of the Peloponnesian War*, 2, 43.1).

999–1009 / 858–66 Although the desire to avert civil strife does not require special circumstances to motivate it (there is a similar prayer in Aeschylus, *Suppliants*, 678–83), the probability that Athenian political tensions were high in 458 (see the Introduction, footnote 12) may have made this theme more than usually urgent. The injunction to fight only foreign wars may reflect the ongoing Athenian expedition in Egypt (see on **337/292**).

1008–9 / 866 *a cock who fights / inside the nest* In addition to the pugnaciousness of fighting cocks in general (cf. **1002–4/861–63**), there is a suggestion here of the Greek belief that cocks were unusually prone to fight their kin. Cf. the image of Aegisthus, who has eliminated his rival and "brags on bravely, like a cock beside his hen" (*Agamemnon* **1932/1671**). And since Athena's concern is for reckless young men, she may also be glancing at the idea that young birds consider it "a fine thing to bite and throttle their fathers" (Aristophanes, *Birds*, 1337–38).

1032 / 886 *the power of my tongue to soothe and enchant* Persuasion in its positive form has the same power of enchantment that in early Greek thought was held (perhaps paradoxically from our point of view) to guarantee the truth of great poetry. See Walsh, *Varieties of Enchantment.*

1042 / 895 No *house will ever grow without your blessing* A complete reversal of the Erinyes' earlier description of their "calling" as "the destruction of houses" (416–17/354–55).

1081–82 / 928–29 *these powerful, / demanding goddesses* In the midst of the Erinyes' blessings on Athens, Athena does not let the audience forget that they have power to curse as well (1085–94/932–37, 1116/954–55), and that they must be propitiated with due honors (1156–60/992–95). The Erinyes are transformed in the course of the play, but that does not mean that their old functions or danger have been completely forgotten.

1135–36 / 973 *Zeus who guides / men's speech* This is Zeus *agoraios*, the god who presides over the *agora*, the public meeting place where he had an altar, but also over *agora* in its broader sense of public meetings and the persuasive speech with which decisions are reached in the legislative and judicial assemblies of the polis.

1150–51 / 985–86 *loving the common good, / hating a common foe* This is the fundamental principle of Greek popular ethics, "helping friends and harming enemies," expressed in communal terms as the antithesis of destructive civil strife.

1158 / 992 *these kindly ones* Athena calls the Erinyes *euphrones*, in effect conferring upon them a new and auspicious name. They are actually nowhere called Eumenides in the play as we have it, but since both words mean "well-minded" or "well-disposed," it is possible that the title of the play (which need not stem from Aeschylus) came from a mis-citation of this line by the author of the "hypothesis" (synopsis) found in our manuscript tradition. The synopsis says that Athena "having soothed the Erinyes, addressed them as 'Eumenides.'" Alternatively, it has been argued that a passage in which Athena gave them the actual title Eumenides has been lost. The title by which the Erinyes were worshipped at Athens, *Semnai Theai* (August or Awesome Goddesses), is used at 1218/1041 ("venerable ones" in our version).

1169 / 1002 The most remarkable of the passages in *Eumenides* that suggest the gods can feel respect and responsibility for mortals (cf. on 262–63, 882–84/

760–61. The verb used here, *azetai*, is usually used of the feelings of awe that mortals have for the gods.

1174 / 1006 *holy offerings Sphagiôn semnôn* refers literally to sacrificial victims that are august or awesome (the same word as the Erinyes' Athenian cult title *Semnai*; see on 1158/992). The animal(s) to be sacrificed would presumably be a black cow and/or ewe, the animals of choice for sacrifice to chthonic goddesses. Athena's pointing out of "these . . . offerings" appears to require that one or two be present on stage.

1182–83 / 1011 *our new / inhabitants Metoikoi* are literally "resident aliens." At *Libation Bearers*, 1096/971, the Erinyes are described as *metoikoi* who will be evicted from the house of Atreus; now, as Eumenides, they are offered a home in Athens (see further on 1203/1028).

1196 / 1022 *by the dancing light of torches* The torches present a visual conclusion and resolution for the trilogy's persistent imagery of light and dark. Light has been a symbol of hope from the beginning, when the Watchman saw the beacon fire he had been awaiting for so long, but just as persistently light yielded to darkness. Now the "dark" Erinyes move to their new home bathed in the light of Athenian torches to show that they are fully incorporated in the new civic order.

1198 / 1024 *my attendants* This group presumably includes the "escorts" referred to at 1172–73/1005 as holding the sacred light and perhaps Athena's priestess and one or more of the *arrêphoroi*, maidens who carried the symbols of Athena's cult in procession.

1203 / 1028 *in purple robes* These robes—the final transformation of the seductive embroideries and blood-stained nets of the earlier plays are what the *metoikoi*, Athens' resident aliens, wore in the great procession of the Panathenaea, the main Athenian festival in honor of Athena.

1208–9 / 1034 *aged children, / childless children* This translates the compact phrase *paides apaides*, literally, "children not children." This form of expression is particularly dear to the tragic poets (e.g., "city . . . no city" [*polin . . . apolin*], 543/457). Here it implies both that the goddesses are children and yet not children, because they are old; and that they are children who have no children, because they are virgins.

1211–12 / 1035 *and* 1215–16 / 1038 *Hush . . . speak well, / only auspicious words* This translates a single Greek word, *euphameite*, which literally means "speak well," but is used before religious rites as a ritual injunction to say nothing except the words prescribed by ritual. Since an inauspicious word could spoil the rite, silence was the safest course.

1221 / 1043 *and* **1225** / 1047 a joyous cry See on *Agamemnon* **33–34**/28.

GLOSSARY

ACHAEANS: Strictly speaking, designates the inhabitants of the north coast of the Peloponnese and southeastern Thessaly, but it is used by Homer and later poets to refer to Greeks in general.

ACHERON: River of the underworld.

AEGEAN (SEA): Sea that divides mainland Greece from Asia Minor, named for Aegeus.

AEGEUS: An early king of Athens and father of Theseus.

AEGISTHUS: Son of Atreus' brother Thyestes and thus cousin of Agamemnon; paramour of Clytemnestra in Agamemnon's absence. Thyestes was the only survivor of Atreus' slaughter of the children of Thyestes (see ATREUS).

AGAMEMNON: Son of Atreus, brother of Menelaus, and ruler of Argos; led the great expedition against Troy.

ALEXANDER: Another name for Paris.

ALTHAEA: Mother of Meleager, at whose birth the Fates prophesied that he would live no longer than a brand that was burning in the fire. Althaea hid the brand, but when the now adult Meleager quarreled with and killed her brothers, Althaea avenged them by burning the brand, thus causing Meleager's death.

AMAZONS: Tribe of warrior women from the region of the Black Sea, who invaded Attica after Theseus, the Athenian king, had stolen off their queen. They besieged the Acropolis, but were defeated in a great battle by the Athenians under Theseus' command. Aeschylus explains the name "Areopagus" with the story that the Amazons made their camp on the hill subsequently given that name, and sacrifice there to Ares.

APHRODITE: Goddess of love, personifies the power of sexual attraction.

APIAN LAND: Alternate name for the region of Argos.

APOLLO: God of prophecy, purification, and healing among other powers, and the son of Zeus and Leto. In the *Oresteia*, he is invoked as king of Pytho (through his association with the prophetic shrine of Delphi), Phoebus (meaning "bright one"), Loxias ("crooked" or "oblique," an epithet explained in antiquity by reference either to the oblique orbit of the sun, with which he is often identified, or to the ambiguity of his oracles), and Wolf-god (a possible meaning of the Greek word *lykaios*, which might refer to the god as a killer of wolves or suggest an origin in the region of Lycia in Asia Minor).

ARACHNE'S PEAK: Mountain in the Peloponnese; see note on *Agamemnon*, 320–59/281–316.

AREOPAGUS: "Hill of Ares," the seat of an aristocratic Athenian council, and the eponymous council, thought to have been founded as a court to try murder cases and restricted to that function by the reforms of Cleisthenes in 462. Aeschylus' account of the court's founding by Athena is apparently his own invention. For Aeschylus' etymology of the name, see amazons.

ARES: God of war, often treated in poetry as a figure for violence and destruction.

ARGIVES: Inhabitants of Argos.

ARGOS: Major city of the Argive plain in the Peloponnese, site of the palace of Agamemnon. For the treaty concluded with Argos by Athens in 462/61, see the note to *Eumenides*, 885–98/762–74.

ARTEMIS: Sister of Apollo, virgin goddess imaged both as hunter and protector of wild animals.

ASCLEPIUS: Healer, hero (in early sources), and god (in the later tradition). Aeschylus treats him as a mortal of extraordinary powers (see the note to *Agamemnon*, 1163–65/1022–24.

ASOPUS: River of Boeotia; see note on *Agamemnon*, 320–59/281–316.

ATHENA: Virgin goddess born full-grown and armed from the head of Zeus; a warrior goddess who supported the Greeks at Troy, but also the patron of women's crafts and of wisdom; patron goddess of Athens. She is often known by her cult name Pallas, whose origin and meaning are uncertain.

ATHOS: Mountain in northern Greece; see note on *Agamemnon*, 320–59/ 281–316.

ATREIDAE: Agamemnon and Menelaus, the sons of Atreus.

ATREUS: Son of Pelops, avenged his brother Thyestes' seduction of his wife by killing all of Thyestes' children (except Atreus) and serving them to their father at a banquet; father of Agamemnon and Menelaus.

AULIS: Port on the coast of Boeotia, from which the Greeks sailed to Troy after the sacrifice of Iphigenia.

BACCHANTS: Women devotees of Dionysus, the god of ecstatic possession (and thus, for example, of wine and theater), from his cult name "Bacchus."

BROMIUS: Cult name for Dionysus, meaning "roarer" or the like.

CALCHAS: Seer who accompanied the Greek expedition against Troy.

CASSANDRA: Daughter of Priam and Hecuba allotted to Agamemnon after the fall of Troy. Apollo gave her the gift of prophecy in return for the promise of a sexual liaison. When she broke her promise, Apollo could not take back her prophetic power, but punished her by seeing to it that no one would believe her.

CHALCIS: Town on the coast of Euboea opposite Attica.

CHRYSEIS: Daughter of Chryses, a priest of Apollo, she was awarded as a war prize to Agamemnon after the sacking of a city near Troy. Her father came to ransom her, and when Agamemnon refuses to give her back, Apollo sends a plague on the Greeks army. In Book 1 of Homer's *Iliad*, Agamemnon's quarrels with Achilles begins because he has to give her up; he tells the army meeting in assembly that he prefers her to Clytemnestra.

CILISSA: A slave in the palace at Argos who had been Orestes' nurse.

CITHAERON: Mountain to the south of Thebes; see note on *Agamemnon*, 320–59/281–316.

CLYTEMNESTRA: Daughter of Tyndareus and Leda; sister of Helen; wife of Agamemnon and paramour of Aegisthus; mother of Orestes, Electra, and Iphigenia.

COCYTUS: River of the underworld, whose name means lamentation.

CORYCIAN ROCK: Cave high on Mount Parnassus above Delphi, sacred to the Nymphs.

CRANAUS: Early and obscure king of Athens; Athenians are sometimes called children of Cranaus.

CRONUS: God of the Titan generation, son of Uranus, whom he castrated and dethroned; father of Zeus, who overthrew him and chained him and the other Titans in the bowels of the earth.

DANAANS: Another name for the Argives, after Danaus, an early king; used, like Achaeans, to describe the Greeks in general.

DAULIS: Town in Phocis.

DELOS: Island in the Aegean Sea where Apollo and Artemis were born.

DELPHI: Town on the slopes of Mount Parnassus; site of Apollo's great oracular shrine.

DELPHUS: Hero who gave his name to Delphi; said to have been reigning as king when Apollo arrived there.

EARTH: As a deity, mother of all life. Aeschylus makes her the first giver of oracles at Delphi.

ELECTRA: Daughter of Agamemnon and Clytemnestra; sister of Orestes and Iphigenia.

ERECHTHEUS: Among the most revered of the early Athenian kings.

ERINYES: Furies, female spirits of the underworld who spring from the blood spilt by victims of homicide and pursue vengeance on their behalf. The singular *Erinys* can refer to what we might call a hereditary curse.

EUMENIDES: "Kindly Ones," a cult name of the Erinyes, and the traditional name of the third play of the trilogy. The epithet actually given to the Erinyes by Athena after she has persuaded them to become a force for good in Athens is *euphrones*, which has a very similar meaning. See the note on *Eumenides*, 1158/992.

EURIPUS: Strait dividing Euboea from mainland Attica.

GERYON: Three-bodied giant killed by Heracles.

GORGONS: Three female monsters, with golden wings, huge tusks, bronze claws, and serpents for hair. One of them, Medusa, was mortal, but her face turned to stone anyone who looked at it. She was killed by Perseus, using a mirror given to him by Athena. For Gorgon Face, see note on *Agamemnon*, 320–59/281–316.

HADES: Ruler of the underworld; brother of Zeus and Poseidon; husband of Persephone.

HELEN: Daughter of Zeus and Leda; sister of Clytemnestra; married to Menelaus, she followed Paris to Troy and thus was held to be the cause of the Trojan War.

HEPHAESTUS: God of fire and the forge; said by the Athenians to be father of Erichthonius, one of their early kings (see note on *Eumenides*, 14/13).

HERA: Daughter of Cronus and Rhea; sister and wife of Zeus; patron goddess of marriage.

HERACLES: Son of Zeus and Alcmene and the greatest of Greek heroes, he was forced to serve Eurystheus of Argos and to undertake twelve labors at his command.

HERMES: Son of Zeus and Maia; messenger of the gods; escorter of souls between the worlds of the living and the dead; god of travel, commerce, and trickery. For the Rock of Hermes, see note on *Agamemnon*, 320–59/281–316.

IDA: Mountain near Troy; see note on *Agamemnon*, 320–59/281–316.

ILIUM: Another name for Troy.

INACHUS: Most important river of the Argive plain.

IPHIGENIA: Daughter of Agamemnon and Clytemnestra, sacrificed at Aulis.

ITYS: Son of Procne and Tereus, killed by his mother, who later was changed to a nightingale lamenting her lost son unceasingly. For the story, see the note on *Agamemnon*, 1305/1142.

IXION: King of the Lapiths in Thessaly, he murdered his father-in-law to avoid paying promised bridal gifts and became the first suppliant for purification of blood-guilt. Zeus purified him, but Ixion then attempted to seduce Hera, and Zeus punished him with eternal torment, attached to a burning, constantly rotating wheel.

LEDA: Mother of Clytemnestra (by her husband Tyndareus) and Helen (by Zeus).

LEMNOS: Aegean island. Its women, angered because their husbands took Thracian concubines, murdered all its men.

LETO: Mother of Apollo and Artemis.

LIBYA: Greek name for northern Africa in general; in the *Oresteia*, refers to the region where Athena is said to have been born.

LOXIAS: See APOLLO.

LYCIA: Country on the south coast of Asia Minor that was the principle ally of Troy; thus, "Lycian spear" at *Libation Bearers*, 396, stands for the enemy force in general.

MACISTUS: Mountain on the island of Euboea; see note on *Agamemnon*, 320–59/281–316.

MEDES: People of the mountainous country southwest of the Caspian Sea.

MENELAUS: Son of Atreus; husband of Helen and joint commander with his brother Agamemnon of the expedition against Troy to recapture her.

MESSAPION: Mountain on the coast of Boeotia; see note on *Agamemnon*, 320–59/281–316.

MINOS: King of Crete, said to have lived three generations before the Trojan War; see SCYLLA.

NISUS: King of Megara; see SCYLLA.

ODYSSEUS: King of Ithaca, his homecoming from the war at Troy is the subject of Homer's *Odyssey*.

OLYMPIANS: Collective name of the gods whose home was imagined to be atop Mount Olympus on the borders of Thessaly and Macedonia. These gods—most prominently Zeus and his wife Hera; his brothers Poseidon and Hades; and in the next generation Apollo, Artemis, and Athena—are regarded as the "younger gods" in relation to the Titans whom they overthrew and the chthonian (earth-dwelling) deities, such as the Erinyes, whose powers and honors their rule circumscribes.

ORESTES: Only son of Agamemnon and Clytemnestra.

ORPHEUS: Musician of Thrace; his singing had the power to charm even wild animals and trees.

PALLAS: See ATHENA.

PAN: A woodland deity connected to fertility, animals, and nature in general.

PARIS: Son of Priam and Hecuba, whose abduction of Helen while a guest at the house of Menelaus caused the Trojan War.

PARNASSUS: Mountain in Phocis that towers above Apollo's shrine at Delphi. Hence a "Parnassian accent" would be an inflection characteristic of Phocis.

PELOPS: King of Argos; father of Atreus and Thyestes; grandfather of Agamemnon, Menelaus, and Aegisthus.

PENTHEUS: King of Thebes, grandson of its founder Cadmus; he denied the divinity of Dionysus and opposed his return to Thebes, for which he was torn apart by bacchants, led by his own mother Agave.

PERSEPHONE: Daughter of Demeter, abducted by Hades and forced to live in the underworld for half of each year.

PERSEUS: Son of Zeus and Danaë who killed Medusa. See GORGONS.

PHERES: King of Thessaly; father of Admetus, whose life Apollo wrested from the Fates.

PHINEUS: King of Thrace who was persecuted by Harpies, winged female monsters who snatched away his food; the Argonauts killed them or drove them away.

PHLEGREAN PLAIN: Located on the peninsula of Pallene in Thrace; the site of a great battle of the gods and giants in which Athena played a decisive part.

PHOCIS: Region of central Greece around Mount Parnassus.

PHOEBE: Titan goddess, mother of Leto and grandmother of Apollo and Artemis.

PHOEBUS: See APOLLO.

PLEISTUS: River running through a deep gorge below Delphi.

POSEIDON: Lord of the sea, brother of Zeus and Hades.

PRIAM: King of Troy, father of Hector, Paris, Cassandra, and many others.

PYLADES: Son of Strophius of Phocis; friend and companion of Orestes.

PYTHIA: The priestess of Apollo who served at Delphi as the mouth-piece for prophecies she received from him in a trance-like state. She is named for Pytho. At *Libation Bearers*, 1069/940, the Chorus can even refer to Orestes as "the Pythian-guided exile" since he has consulted the oracle and acted on its authority.

PYTHO: A chthonian monster that held sway in Delphi until Apollo killed it with his arrows, according to the standard story that Aeschylus chooses to ignore. Although the monster Pytho is not mentioned in the *Oresteia*, the association of its name with Apollo and the Delphic oracle makes it natural to refer to Delphi as Pytho, and to the god as king of Pytho.

SARON, GULF OF: Separates the island of Aegina from the Peloponnese; see note on *Agamemnon*, 320–59/281–316.

SCAMANDER: Most important river of the Trojan plain.

SCYLLA: (1) The female monster, known from Homer's *Odyssey*, who preyed on ships in a strait opposite the whirlpool Charybdis.

(2) Daughter of Nisus of Megara, who made it possible for Minos of Crete to conquer Megara by accepting his bribe and cutting her father's hair, which gave him life.

SIMOIS: River on the Trojan plain.

SPARTA: Major city of the southern Peloponnese, royal seat of Menelaus and his Spartan wife, Helen.

STROPHIUS: King of Phocis; father of Pylades; host and guardian of the young Orestes.

STRYMON: River that divides Macedonia and Thrace in northern Greece.

SUSA: Capital city of Elam (in what is now Iran); in Aeschylus' day, it was an important city of the Persian Empire.

TANTALUS: Son of Zeus and, as father of Pelops and grandfather of Atreus, founder of the Argive royal line. He is said to have killed Pelops and served him to the gods at a banquet. When they discovered this transgression, the gods restored Pelops to life. Only Demeter had eaten from his flesh, but Hephaestus made him an ivory shoulder to replace what she consumed. The gods punished Tantalus in the underworld by placing him in a pool of water that recedes when he tries to drink it, and beneath branches laden with fruits that, whenever he tries to reach them, are blown beyond his grasp by a breeze.

THEMIS: Titan goddess, daughter of Earth; her name means "right" or "customary law," and her main function is to punish transgressors of that law; Aeschylus makes her the second giver of oracles at Delphi.

THESEUS: Greatest of Athens' early kings, who was believed to have lived in the generation before the Trojan War.

THESTIUS: King of Pleuron in Aetolia, father of Althaea and Leda.

THRACE: The most northeasterly region of Greece, whose natives the Greeks considered primitive and ferocious. The "Thracian winds" of *Agamemnon*, 746/654, would be fierce northerly blasts.

THYESTES: Son of Pelops, brother of Atreus; in the *Oresteia*, his seduction of Atreus' wife is the starting point of the chain of crimes that beset the house.

TRITON: River in Libya, traditional birthplace of Athena.

TROY: City of Phrygia, on the northwest coast of Asia Minor; sacked by the Greeks after a ten-year siege.

TYNDAREUS: King of Sparta; husband of Leda and father of Clytemnestra.

ZEPHYRUS: The West Wind, son of Eos (Dawn).

ZEUS: Most powerful of the gods, once having chained his father Cronus and the other Titans beneath the earth; chief of the Olympian gods and ruler of the realm of land (as Poseidon is of the sea and Hades of the underworld). Zeus is traditionally associated with the sanctity of oaths, of the relations of guest and host, and of suppliants and beggars. Although he is not regarded in the Greek tradition as omniscient or omnipotent, Aeschylus makes him something close to a supreme being and guarantor of cosmic order.

SELECTED BIBLIOGRAPHY

This is a highly selective list of books and articles in English of interest to students of Aeschylus and the *Oresteia*, including some reference works related to questions raised in the Introduction and Notes and all the studies referred to there by author and short title.

Bamberger, Joan. "The Myth of Matriarchy: Why Men Rule in Primitive Society." In *Women, Culture and Society*, ed. M. Rosaldo and L. Lamphere, 263–80. Stanford, Calif., 1974.

Burian, Peter. "*Zeus Sotêr Tritos* and Some Triads in Aeschylus' *Oresteia*," *American Journal of Philology* 107 (1986): 332–42.

Clay, Diskin. "Aeschylus' Trigeron Mythos." *Hermes* 97 (1969): 1–9.

Conacher, D. J. *Aeschylus Oresteia: A Literary Commentary*. Toronto, 1987.

Denniston, John, and Denys Page, eds. *Aeschylus: Agamemnon*. Oxford, 1957 (Greek text with commentary).

Dodds, E. R. "Morals and Politics in the *Oresteia*." *Proceedings of the Cambridge Philological Society* 6 (1960): 19–31; reprinted in *The Ancient Concept of Progress and Other Essays*, 45–63. Oxford, 1973.

Dover, K. J. "The Political Aspects of Aeschylus' *Eumenides*." *Journal of Hellenic Studies* 77 (1974): 230–37.

duBois, Page. *Centaurs and Amazons*. Ann Arbor, Mich., 1982.

Easterling, P. E., ed. *The Cambridge Companion to Greek Tragedy.* Cambridge, Eng., 1997.

———. "Presentation of Character in Aeschylus." *Greece and Rome* 20 (1973): 3–19.

Edwards, Mark W. "Agamemnon's Decision: Freedom and Folly in Aeschylus." *California Studies in Classical Antiquity* 10 (1977): 17–38.

Ewans, Michael. "Agamemnon at Aulis: A Study in the *Oresteia*." *Ramus* 4 (1975): 17–32.

Faraone, Christopher A. "Aeschylus' *Hymnos Desmios* (*Eum.* 306) and Attic Judicial Curse Tablets." *Journal of Hellenic Studies* 105 (1985): 150–54.

Gagarin, Michael. *Aescylean Drama.* Berkeley, 1976.

Gantz, Timothy. *Early Greek Myth.* Baltimore, 1993.

———. "The Fires of the *Oresteia*." *Journal of Hellenic Studies* 97 (1977): 28–38.

Garvie, A. F., ed. Aeschylus, *Choephori* [*Libation Bearers*]. Oxford, 1986 [Greek text with commentry].

Goldhill, Simon. *Aeschylus:The Oresteia.* Cambridge, Eng., 1992.

———. *Language, Sexuality, Narrative: The Oresteia.* Cambridge, Eng., 1984.

———. *Reading Greek Tragedy.* Cambridge, Eng., 1986.

Gould, John. "Dramatic Character and Human Intelligibility in Greek Tragedy," *Proceedings of the Cambridge Philological Society* 24 (1978): 19–31.

———. "Law, Custom and Myth: Aspects of the Social Position of Women in Classical Athens." *Journal of Hellenic Studies* 100 (1980): 38–59.

Griffith, Mark. "Brilliant Dynasts: Power and Politics in the *Oresteia*." *Classical Antiquity* 14 (1995): 63–129.

Hammond, N.G.L. "The Conditions of Dramatic Production to the Death of Aeschylus." *Greek, Roman and Byzantine Studies* 13 (1972): 387–450.

Herington, John. *Aeschylus*. New Haven, 1986.

Hester, D. A. "The Casting Vote." *American Journal of Philology* 102 (1981): 265–74.

Kirk, G. S., J. E. Raven, and M. Schofield. *The Presocratic Philosophers*, 2nd ed. Cambridge, Eng., 1983.

Kitto, H.D.F. *Form and Meaning in Greek Tragedy*. London, 1956.

Knox, Bernard. "The Lion in the House." *Classical Philology* 47 (1952): 17–25; reprinted in Knox, *Word and Action: Essays on the Ancient Theater*, 27–38. Baltimore, 1979.

———. "Aeschylus and the Third Actor." *American Journal of Philology* 93 (1972): 104–24; reprinted in *Word and Action*, 39–55.

Kuhns, Richard. *The House, the City and the Judge*. Indianapolis, 1962.

Lebeck, Anne. *The Oresteia: A Study in Language and Structure*. Washington, D.C., 1971.

Lloyd, G.E.R. *Science, Folklore and Ideology: Studies in the Life Sciences in Ancient Greece*. Cambridge, Eng., 1983.

MacDowell, Douglas M. *The Law in Classical Athens*. Ithaca, N.Y., 1978.

Macleod, Colin. "Politics and the *Oresteia*." *Journal of Hellenic Studies* 104 (1982): 124–44; reprinted in Macleod, *Collected Essays*, 20–40. Oxford, 1983.

McClure, Laura. "*Logos Gunaikos*: Speech, Gender, and Spectatorship in the *Oresteia*." *Helios* 24 (1997): 112–35.

Parker, Robert. *Miasma: Pollution and Purification in Early Greek Religion* Oxford, 1983.

Peradotto, John J. "Some Patterns of Nature Imagery in the *Oresteia.*" *American Journal of Philology* 85 (1964): 379–93.

Pickard-Cambridge, A. W. *The Dramatic Festivals of Athens,* 2nd ed. revised by J. Gould and D. M. Lewis. Oxford 1968.

Podlecki, A. J. Aeschylus, *Eumenides.* Warminster, 1989 [Greek text with literal translation and commentary keyed to the translation].

Poliakoff, Michael. "The Third Fall in the *Oresteia.*" *American Journal of Philology* 101 (1980): 251–59.

Rabinowitz, Nancy. "From Force to Persuasion: Aeschylus' *Oresteia* as Cosmogonic Myth." *Ramus* 10 (1981): 159–91.

Rose, Peter W. *Sons of the Gods, Children of Earth.* Ithaca, N.Y., 1992.

Rosenbloom, David. "Myth, History, and Hegemony in Aeschylus." In ed. *History, Tragedy, Theory,* B. Goff, 91–130. Austin, Tex., 1995.

Rosenmeyer, Thomas. *The Art of Aeschylus.* Berkeley, 1982.

Scott, William C. *Musical Design in Aeschylean Theater.* Hanover, N.H., 1984.

Seaford, Richard. "Historicizing Tragic Ambivalence: The Vote of Athena." In *History, Tragedy, Theory,* ed. B. Goff, 202–21. Austin, Tex., 1995.

Sommerstein, Alan H. ed. Aeschylus, *Eumenides.* Cambridge, Eng., 1989 [Greek text with commentary].

Sorvinou-Inwood, C. "Myth as History: The Previous Owners of the Delphic Oracle." In *Interpretations of Greek Mythology,* ed. J. Bremmer, 220–35. London, 1987.

Taplin, Oliver. *The Stagecraft of Aeschylus: The Dramatic Use of Exits and Entrances in Greek Tragedy*. Oxford, 1977.

Thomson, George, ed. *The Oresteia of Aeschylus*, 2nd ed. Amsterdam/ Prague, 1966 [text with commentary].

Tyrell, Wm. Blake *Amazons: A Study in Athenian Mythmaking*. Baltimore, 1984.

Vidal-Naquet, Pierre. "Hunting and Sacrifice in Aeschylus' *Oresteia*." In *Myth and Tragedy in Ancient Greece*, translated by J. Lloyd, ed. J.-P. Vernant and P. Vidal-Naquet, 141–60. (New York, 1988.

Wallace, Robert W. *The Areopagos Council, to 307 B.C..* Baltimore, 1989.

Walsh, George B. *The Varieties of Enchantment: Early Greek Views of the Nature and Function of Poetry*. Chapel Hill, N.C., 1984.

Whallon, William. *Problem and Spectacle: Studies in the Oresteia*. Heidelberg, 1980.

Wiles, David. *Greek Theatre Performance: An Introduction*. Cambridge, Eng., 2000.

———. *Tragedy in Athens: Performance Space and Theatrical Meaning* Cambridge, Eng., 1997.

Winnington-Ingram, R. P. *Studies in Aeschylus*. Cambridge, Eng., 1983.

Zeitlin, Froma. "The Motif of the Corrupted Sacrifice in Aeschylus' *Oresteia*." *Transactions and Proceedings of the American Philological Association* 96 (1965): 463–508.

———. "The Dynamics of Misogyny: Myth and Mythmaking in Aeschylus' *Oresteia*," *Arethusa* 11 (1978): 149–84; revised in Zeitlin, *Playing the Other*, 87–119. Chicago, 1996.